IDEOLOGY AND THE LABOUR MOVEMENT

John Saville

Ideology and the Labour Movement

ESSAYS PRESENTED TO JOHN SAVILLE

Edited by
DAVID E. MARTIN and DAVID RUBINSTEIN

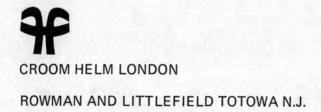

CROOM HELM LONDON

ROWMAN AND LITTLEFIELD TOTOWA N.J.

© 1979 This edition. Introduction, selection, editorial matter
David E. Martin and David Rubinstein. ©Ralph Miliband Ch. 2.
©Victor Kiernan Ch. 3. © Asa Briggs Ch. 4. © Alan J. Lee Ch. 5.
©Iris Minor Ch. 6. ©David E. Martin Ch. 7. ©Frank Matthews
Ch. 8. ©Sidney Pollard Ch. 9. ©Margaret Cole Ch. 10.
©David Rubinstein Ch. 11. ©Joyce M. Bellamy Ch. 12.

Croom Helm Ltd, 2-10 St. John's Road, London SW11

British Library Cataloguing in Publication Data

Ideology and the labour movement.
    1. Labor and laboring classes – Great Britain – History
    – Addresses – essays, lectures.
    I. Saville, John   II. Martin, David, b.1944   III. Rubinstein, David
    335'.1'0941   HD8388
ISBN 0-85664-437-4

First published in the United States 1979 by
Rowman and Littlefield
81 Adams Drive, Totowa, New Jersey

ISBN 0-8476-6123-7

CONTENTS

Preface

PREFACE

The pleasure of the editors in assembling this volume has been tempered only by the knowledge that space could not be found for contributions from a wider range of John Saville's colleagues, friends and students. Once the decision had been taken that the essays should relate to a central theme, we could not invite contributions from those whom John Saville had supervised or encouraged in a greater range of historical fields. Nevertheless, we are sure that they will wish to be associated with this tribute to an enthusiastic and inspiring scholar.

We should like to acknowledge the assistance we have received in the preparation of this book. A grant from the Nuffield Foundation helped to defray the expenses of a number of contributors. In these times of financial inclemency we are particularly grateful for this generous assistance. Our publisher David Croom faced delays in the completion of our manuscript with patient good-humour and for this and his general encouragement we thank him. Our colleague Joyce Bellamy took a lively interest in our progress and advised us on a number of problems. We are grateful also to Beverley Eaton and Eileen Lee for typing assistance.

DM

DR

August 1978

1 INTRODUCTION

'We English don't bother about theory much, for good or ill.' Thus Sir Charles Trevelyan, a minister in the first and second Labour governments, wrote to one of us in 1955, and a great deal of ink has been spilled to make the same point at greater length, both before and after he wrote. It is not the aim of this introduction, or of this book, to disprove Trevelyan's assertion, though we hope that our attempts to discuss 'theory' and to relate it to practice are based on more secure foundations than mere assertions about national character. Nor is it our aim here to explain at length the role of ideology in the history of the British labour movement. The essays which follow, and which deal with varied aspects of the history of labour and the working class, indicate the role of ideology far better than we can hope to do in a brief introduction. But it is fitting that we should try to draw together some of the threads of the subject.

By 'ideology' we understand, with the Oxford dictionary, a scheme of ideas which support a particular political or economic theory or system. It is evident that in Britain the working class as a whole has never professed adherence to such a scheme of ideas. We view with some scepticism the claims often made about other countries for ideological consistency and fidelity insofar as the majority of working men and women are concerned, but their history lies outside our present scope.

In understanding the British experience three principal points are worthy of special consideration. The first is that, until well after 1945, the majority of working people, in Britain as elsewhere, were concerned above all with the struggle for existence. For the whole of the working class life was hazardous, since illness and unemployment threatened to reduce them to the poverty which was the permanent lot of many of them. Day-to-day experience at the place of work and in the home provided most people with pragmatic attitudes to life, and the restricted and classbound nature of the formal system of education did little to stimulate the growth of a wider-ranging and longer-term ideology. Self-education, always a vigorous tradition among the working class, affected only a minority. Getting and spending have always been the normal human preoccupations, and it was seldom that affairs of state could be regarded as sufficiently immediate to have much meaning for most people of any social class. This was above all true of the class closest (from above or below) to the means of subsistence.

The lack of a systematic ideology helps to explain why practical mid-Victorian trade unionists like Robert Applegarth could be friendly with and influenced by Karl Marx. It also helps to explain how and why working people could enthusiastically support the kind of generalised statements in praise of liberty so strikingly pronounced by W.E. Gladstone, while at the same time largely limiting their political concern to particular, localised issues related to their own experience. It was the latter which made up the stuff of daily life and the former which acted as a kind of golden, semi-mythical hope of a better future. The organisation of political parties, the hard slog for either reform or revolution, fell between both stools and consequently lacked permanent, reliable support.

Secondly, Britain *was* different from elsewhere in the formative years of the nineteenth century, when an industrial society took shape. The roots of trade and industry were deeper; the peasantry had disappeared much earlier; and restrictions on commerce were fewer. Alone of the major European peoples Britain was a single nation (unlike Germany and Italy), with a system of government flexible enough to absorb political movements and demonstrations (unlike Russia and Austria-Hungary), and with a basic agreement about fundamental issues of state on the part of most politically conscious people (unlike France). In such circumstances it was natural for working-class people to work within the political and social system rather than outside it. Even in the United States, as Margaret Cole points out here, violence was far more common than in Britain, though the American labour movement as a whole was no more militant.

Margaret Cole also notes that the justification for labour gradualism was the unwillingness of the British ruling classes to engage in severe measures of repression. Robert Applegarth may again serve as an example. *The Times* of 15 September 1869 reported his speech to the delegates at the Congress of the International Working Men's Association in Basle: 'In England we have no need of creeping into holes and corners lest a policeman should see us . . . We have now household suffrage . . . Having got this political power, we shall soon find out how to use it.' Such a statement was hardly more than the truth, and the kind of attitude it represented passed into the inheritance of British socialism. Thus Ramsay MacDonald pointed out in his book *The Socialist Movement* in 1911 that the difference of methods between British and German socialists did not 'depend upon some fixed differences in national characteristics, but upon political systems'. Britain had democratic institutions, and 'what cannot be done at a ballot box in a democracy cannot be done at a barricade'. In so writing MacDonald echoed the words of Keir Hardie, whose *From Serfdom to Socialism* was published in 1907: 'With the enfranchisement of the masses it is recognised that the ballot is much more effective than the barricade.'

Thirdly and paradoxically, Britain was deeply divided on grounds of social class. The working class, divided among itself, was cut off from other classes and hostile to ideologies which seemed to reek of middle-class patronage. If accepted at all, middle-class reformers who tried to identify themselves with working-class interests tended to be regarded sceptically. In 1933, Lord Citrine later wrote in his memoirs, a group of leading left-wing intellectuals met Arthur Pugh and himself to discuss socialist politics. It was the wealthiest of the former, Sir Stafford Cripps, who said that at death all property worth over £1,000 should be taken by the state. Such statements and such men, Citrine thought, were remote from political reality and from trade unionists like Pugh and himself, and he suggested without contradiction that they were the only two people present who held life assurance policies for under £1,000. A similar gulf between the middle-class left and the majority of trade unionists was revealed in a conversation in the late 1930s between Sir Charles Trevelyan, then Lord Lieutenant of Northumberland, and Ernest Bevin, leader of the Transport and General Workers' Union. To Trevelyan's suggestion that workers should strike in protest against Neville Chamberlain's foreign policy Bevin, according to Kingsley Martin's recollection, replied: 'You want a strike? O.K. I am to call out 600,000 dockers; will you call out the Lord Lieutenants?'

Such attitudes were not invented in the 1930s. Indeed they were already well established by the middle of the nineteenth century, as Victor Kiernan shows in his essay. The working class was hostile to class war but suspicious of collaborating with middle-class radicals or socialists in either political or industrial struggles. Without a militant or revolutionary ideology, the working class and its institutions were bound to be defensive. Thus evolved the tenacious institution of labourism which, in one of his most perceptive essays, John Saville defines in its later nineteenth-century context as 'a theory and practice which accepted the possibility of social change within the existing framework of society'. The strength of its grasp is one part of the answer to the challenging query posed here by Ralph Miliband — why more young men and women did not join the Communist Party in the 1930s.

It is this theme of the continuous growth of working-class power within a strictly limited ideological framework with which the articles in this book are concerned, in part or in whole. David Martin shows in detail that the first Labour Members of Parliament were products of that gradualist movement which, at a time of growing working-class power and growing class antagonism, felt the need for its own political party, although the political attitudes of many of its leaders differed little from those of advanced Liberals. The very fact of social class was itself the most powerful ideological factor. Writing of the same period Iris Minor suggests that when middle-class social workers or even organisations based on the upper echelons of the working class attempted to influence social policy, they acted without and sometimes against the wishes and apparent interests of the poorer working class.

Asa Briggs comments on the anxiety of the socialist journals *Justice* and *Commonweal* in the 1880s to provide education and leadership for 'the masses', and refers to a letter written by William Morris in 1886: 'If you had only suffered as I have from the apathy of the English lower classes . . .' Victor Kiernan shows that it was largely the radical middle class from whom social reformers came and that most of the working class consistently disappointed the aspirations of middle-class socialists like Morris. As Kiernan concludes: 'It would seem that socialist consciousness has always been restricted to a very few, and that the bulk of the working class (as of every other, it may be) is inert except when activated by some direct material stimulus.' Frank Matthews examines the ideology of the largely middle-class guild socialist movement in its formative period centred round the weekly journal, *New Age*. Acute as were its criticisms of bourgeois values, the anti-parliamentary perspective of guild socialism failed to draw much working-class support except in limited and temporary circumstances during and after the 1914-18 War.

Absence of ideological commitment meant that working-class attitudes were fragmented and sometimes contradictory. Thus, as Alan Lee points out, working-class Conservatism was (as it remains) not a deviation from the 'correct' Liberal-Labour tradition, but an integral part of the working-class experience and outlook. Even within the Labour Party itself the gradualist tradition and ideological vagueness meant that the party could adopt fundamentally contradictory and ambiguous policies towards so central a political issue as the nationalisation of the banks, as Sidney Pollard shows here. David Rubinstein's concluding essay suggests that, while a relatively small number of mainly middle-class ideologues was urging the case for 'more socialism' between 1945 and 1950, the working class as a whole was more concerned with its pay packet and decent housing, regardless of wider political considerations. As for leisure interests, an article in *New Statesman and Nation* commented on 6 September 1947: 'Speculations as to the future activities of Stan Matthews and Bruce Woodcock are much more attractive to the mind of the average factory worker than speculations as to the future activities of Marshal Tito and Ho Chi Minh.' (An interesting anthology might be compiled of complaints by reformers about the workers' preference for sport to politics.)

Our essays are in large part concerned with the gap between the ostensible aspirations and actual performance of the labour movement. But what should be stressed heavily here is the assumption made explicitly or implicitly in every essay, that it is the working class and its industrial and political institutions which have been the motive force of modern history. 'The history of all hitherto existing society', Marx and Engels wrote in *The Communist Manifesto*, 'is the history of class struggles . . . Now and then the workers are victorious, but only for a time. The real fruit of their battles lies, not in the immediate result, but in the ever-expanding union of the workers . . . Of all the classes that stand face to face with the bourgeoisie today, the proletariat alone is a really revolutionary class.' It is our view that the history of the 130 years since these sentences were written, as of the decades which preceded them, has totally borne out their central assertion, even if in a different and more subtle way than that intended or expected by their authors.

For the history of British society and politics in the past 200 years is that of *reaction* by other social classes to movements of the working class, the only class whose actions, as Marx and Engels saw, irrespective of its intentions, must be seen as objectively revolutionary. Politics between the late eighteenth and the middle of the nineteenth centuries were profoundly affected by tempestuous working-class movements; the Reform Act of 1832 was only the most obvious fruit of working-class agitation. The influence of Chartism, while less productive of immediate reforms, helped to formulate that ruling class apprehension of severe repression to which Margaret Cole refers. Demonstrations in 1867 brought the parliamentary vote. Riots in 1886 brought an amelioration of the Poor Law and a somewhat less inhuman view of unemployment. The election of 30 Labour MPs in 1906 was followed by the beginnings of a welfare state. The rise of the Labour Party between the wars to a position of central importance was accompanied by the rise of social questions to central importance in domestic political life. The established order, in short, has been flexible and shrewd enough to accept and modify changes which it could not prevent, but the impetus has always been that of the working class.

During most of the period there has never been more than a small minority bent upon bursting the bonds of existing society, by whatever means. This minority has included sections of the Chartists in the 1840s; Marxists in the Social Democratic Federation late in the nineteenth century; syndicalist workers whose self-education reached an unprecedented and perhaps unique level before 1914; advocates of workers' control during and after the First World War; Communists between the wars; and various political and industrial groups, usually Communist- or Trotskyist-influenced, since 1945. But if the revolutionaries have never been numerous, and if mass political consciousness has always been sporadic, the threat of revolution has always been treated with the respect and fear which its looming potential has deserved.

Ideology is a difficult and many-headed concept. We contend that the absence of overt ideology amongst the bulk of the working class has itself been a kind of ideology, and that, despite this absence, it has been working-class demands which have influenced and shaped the British political and social system. In a variety of ways these and related themes are explored in the essays which follow.

David Martin

David Rubinstein

2 JOHN SAVILLE: A PRESENTATION

Ralph Miliband

John Saville was born in 1916 in Morton, a little village near Gainsborough in Lincolnshire.[1] His father, Orestes Stamatopoulos, was Greek, from a middle- to upper-class family, and had come to England after studying engineering at the University of Heidelberg. His mother, Edith Vessey, came from a working-class family from Morton. The father was recalled to Greece to fight in the war and was killed within a year of the birth of his son. His mother moved to London and eventually became housekeeper to Alfred James Saville, twice-widowed and the father of a young daughter. John's mother later married Mr Saville and this gave her and her son what he describes as a 'lower middle-class existence', which appears to have been marked by a very reasonable degree of security and comfort — Mr Saville was a master tailor employed as a senior executive in a tailoring firm. The grammar school to which John Saville went on a scholarship led him, also with scholarships, to the London School of Economics, where he arrived in the autumn of 1934. He joined the Communist Party two months after he got there.

There was nothing in his life until then which pointed to that destination. His home was quite conventional. His stepfather, with whom he got on well, was a dedicated Freemason and the family took the *Daily Mail* (which was in 1934 strongly supporting Sir Oswald Mosley). His mother, whom he remembers as a woman of great force and determination, was very fond of reading and she read Dickens to him as a boy, but she was not 'political'. The family belonged to the local Anglican church and Saville was a choirboy for two years before his voice broke. He was confirmed and became a server. His great interest from about the age of thirteen was sport. In his last year at school, when he was eighteen, he was head boy of the school, captain of association football, swimming and athletics. He represented Essex in all three sports in national competitions; he also played tennis well. It was after he had gone into the sixth form at the age of sixteen that he became 'passionately' interested in academic work, and he did outstandingly well in examinations. He recalls reading such books as R.H. Tawney's *Equality*, Arthur Salter's *Recovery* and Beverley Nichols's *Cry Havoc*, a study of war, armaments and pacifism, which was

15

published in 1933 and was part of the anti-war literature of the period. The book impressed him greatly 'and undoubtedly confirmed the shift towards radical attitudes that was beginning within me'. But nothing in all this, or in the English and French literature and poetry which he had read extensively provided an obvious point of entry to the Communist Party.

It is true that for a grammar school boy in his circumstances, Saville had unusually close connections with industrial working-class life. This came about because when his mother moved to London to get work after her husband had been killed, she left her son in the care of a woman whose husband was a boilermaker's labourer, and who was unemployed for almost all of the inter-war years. In the depth of the slump, something like 70 per cent of Gainsborough's workforce was unemployed. As a schoolboy, Saville went back every year and usually more than once a year to stay with this family, in whose home he had spent a few years as a small child. 'They were', he writes, 'respectable working class of the labouring stratum; their house was two up and two down except that they had an attic; the lavatory was across the yard and only in the middle 1920s did they get rid of the earth closets; there was no water in the house; an outside tap served two houses; and everything was cooked on a coal fire and in the attached oven.' His closeness to the family meant, he also says, that 'by the time I went to LSE, I knew what working-class life in a small northern industrial town was like'.

No doubt this was important to him, then and later. But it would be rash and simplistic to infer that this was what caused Saville to join the Communist Party. Nor does he himself make that inference. He recalls that 'almost the same day that I arrived in Houghton Street I began attending meetings of the left', but that 'I really cannot explain this'.

Of course, what made *this* particular young man attend meetings of the left and join the Communist Party is an immensely complicated business, as is any large choice which anybody makes. But what made a good many young men and women, of similar or even more unlikely background, move to the left in the early 1930s and join the Communist Party is much less complicated, and is in some ways not complicated at all. The pull has by now been thoroughly documented, and a recent essay by Saville himself[2] provides an illuminating account of its nature and strength. Unemployment and the Depression; the blandly reactionary face of Conservatism and the tarnished reality of British imperialism; the blatant inadequacies of Labourism; the rise of Fascism; Spain appeasement; the attractive certitudes of 'Marxism-Leninism'; the promise of a new world to be gained by striving and strife; the immensely strong will to believe that the new world was already being built in the Soviet Union and that it must be defended from the permanent threat of the old world — all this will surely do to be getting on with, even if it does not answer some very large and difficult questions. What is remarkable is not that many young men and women felt the pull to the left, but that there were not more of them.

As Saville also notes, LSE in the 1930s was one of the three centres of Communist influence in universities, the other two being Oxford and Cambridge; and LSE was concentrated and compact where Oxford and Cambridge were dispersed. 'LSE' must here be taken to mean its students, or at least some of its students, enough to provide a strong pole of attraction for an alert, energetic, vaguely radical new student.

It was certainly not LSE as an institution which pulled Saville to the left. Then as before and after, and contrary to a very stubborn legend, LSE was a quite conservative institution, graced with a numerically strong economics department that was then fighting, under the leadership of Lionel (now Lord) Robbins, the dangerously radical follies of Keynesianism and state interventionism. One of the things that gave LSE an unwarranted radical reputation, apart from its radical students, was the fact that other universities were even more conservative, and lacked one ingredient which LSE had, namely a number of teachers who were very closely associated with the leadership of the Labour Party. In the England of the 1920s and 1930s, this was enough to make it a 'radical' institution, indelibly stamped by its Fabian origins. Another ingredient which LSE had, and which greatly helped to foster its radical reputation, was Harold Laski, who was then by far the most prominent radical academic in the country.

However, Laski's relationship to left-wing students, and particularly to Communist students, was rather more complex than might be thought. On the one hand, he was sympathetic, encouraging, interested; and he shared and indeed voiced many of the anxieties, hopes and wishes of left-wing students. He also knew what they were talking about when they referred to Marx and Marxism, which was no small thing.

On the other hand, Laski, even in his most *marxisant* phase, of which the thirties was the peak, remained firmly rooted in a social democratic tradition which Marxist and Communist students spurned and denounced. He was always very firmly committed to the Labour Party, to whose National Executive Committee he was elected in 1937, while Communist students, even after the Popular Front strategy was adopted by the Comintern, viewed the Labour Party and particularly the Labour leaders with strong dislike and contempt. Laski might appear to the world at large and to many if not most of his respectable colleagues as a dangerous subversive; but this is not how he appeared to his revolutionary students.

Nor indeed did he indulge them. On the contrary, he could be relied on to challenge hard-line dogmatism and sectarianism, to deflate revolutionary shallowness and rhetoric, and to ask pointed questions about the USSR when he was in the company of students who uncritically worshipped all things Soviet, as Communist students then did. His lectures, particularly a general course he gave on the history of political thought, were in effect the vivid presentation of a great drama, consisting in the permanent and necessary struggle between reason and prejudice, knowledge and ignorance, freedom and tyranny, democracy and authoritarianism, equality and privilege, the arbitrary state and liberty-affirming dissent. It was not a Stalinist education; and there were a good many Communist students who considered Laski as an unreliable and suspect petty-bourgeois ally and influence, all the more suspect for his unique attraction as a captivating and compelling lecturer and teacher.

However, Laski was the only teacher whose lectures Saville attended regularly, even though Laski taught politics and Saville's degree was in economic geography. He recalls that from the time he joined the Communist Party in his first term until the end of his second year,

> I devoted the greater part of my time during term to student politics. I read widely but I had no time or little time for lectures and classes. I did not write a single essay during my first two years and did not attend a single course of lectures through to the end: save the general course that Harold Laski gave, and his I went to every week and repeated the following two years. It was Laski and Laski alone who stirred me to read. No one has ever communicated in the way that he did the passion for learning and the excitement of intellectual history . . . Laski, plus the political excitement of the CP and Marxism, combined to push me into the library, and to pull me out of it into practical political activity.

To join the Communist Party in 1934 was much less politically constricting than it would have been in the previous years. The grim 'Third Period' which the Comintern had imposed upon the world Communist movement in 1929 was drawing to a close. In that period, Stalinised

Communist Parties had worked according to the maxim 'anybody who is not with us is against us'; and since being 'with us' required total and unquestioning acceptance of every twist and turn of Soviet internal and external policy and action, this had led to extreme Communist isolation from the rest of the labour movement. Things were now changing. The USSR had joined the League of Nations in 1934 under the banner of collective security, and Communist Parties were soon reaching out, again in accordance with Comintern policy, for alliances with social democrats and others on the left whom they had so recently denounced as 'social fascists'. The period of the Popular Front was dawning and brought in a style of Communist politics that had fewer sectarian strands than had been the case in the 'Third Period'. Saville was lucky to have escaped the worst rigours of those years.

Membership of the CP introduced him to disciplined political work, and this marked him very deeply:

> There were two things expected of members of the CP: one was that they would engage in serious political work — and it was of a very organised nature. One was inculcated into disciplined habits — you never spoke in discussion without having made notes, for example; and you weren't expected, in the political discussion which preceded all our meetings, to speak more than once. Serious political work involved work outside the academic world although our main attention was always directed towards our fellow students.

Saville was working more or less full-time as a party organiser in his second year at LSE; and the accent was for him very much on effectiveness, seriousness, professionalism. However, he also continued with sports. Until his third year, he played football for LSE on Wednesdays and Saturdays, and he continued to play on Saturdays in his final year ('I reckon I was the first Marxist to play soccer for LSE first XI and for London University team').

The second thing which student members of the Communist Party were expected to do was to apply themselves to their studies as well as doing political work. 'Every Communist a First' was the somewhat heartless slogan which epitomised this attitude. Accordingly, Saville dropped all political activity at the beginning of the first term of his Finals year and concentrated on academic work. As he says, he 'started working twelve to fourteen hours a day in the library and at home. I went to a few tutorials, wrote a couple of essays but for most of the time just worked on my own.' Even so, he appears to have had a fairly busy social life, and it was in that Finals year that he met a first-year student, Constance Saunders, whom he later married. He took his final examinations in May/June 1937 and got a 'good' First.

He ought to have got a research scholarship but did not. In that summer of 1937, as in the summer of 1936, he worked abroad for a travel agency as a courier, and managed to be involved in a shipwreck in the Channel, landing in a small boat at Dunkirk. On two occasions, he carried letters for the Communist Party into Nazi Germany. He then worked as a volunteer for the Union of Democratic Control and the China Campaign Committee, on whose behalf he gave talks to Left Book Clubs and Labour and Communist Party branches. He was a schoolteacher for five weeks and did not like it; and he then got a job as assistant to the secretary of the Dictaphone Company at three pounds ten shillings a week. He was also very busy with Communist politics and agitation, was made London organiser of the student CP, and began to attend district committee meetings of the London Young Communist League. He was living with his family in Romford and also took on the job of party secretary for his local CP branch. All this political work was however cut short because he got a job as a research economist for British Home Stores in the spring of 1939. This involved a nine-month period of training in every grade of work in Home Stores shops in different parts of the country. He was called up in April 1940, and it was not until he had been in the Army for some time that he became again politically active.

His job with British Home Stores and his subsequent call-up into the Army saved Saville from much of the turmoil in which the Communist Party found itself as a result of the switch in policy in regard to the war which occurred in September-October 1939, when the Party, having first declared the war to be an anti-fascist struggle, discovered that it was an imperialist venture, and stayed with that discovery until June 1941, when the Soviet Union was attacked by Germany. Saville notes:

> When the war came, I was still reading party literature regularly and assiduously but I was moving around the country, working very hard in generally disorganised conditions, with the black-out and so on and I had little opportunity for serious discussion. I accepted the change of party line without much qualm — Constance never did — but the war was a very phoney one — the old gang were still in power and we could never believe that Chamberlain could be anything but anti-Soviet and an appeaser.

It was in the course of the war, he recalls, that he came to think and argue that the CP had been 'very wrong' not to support the war from the start. Even if he had taken that view earlier, it is unlikely that he would have done much about it. By 1940, he had been in the CP for six years as a very active and committed member, and he had sunk deep roots in the world of the Party. For him, there was nowhere else to go.

Saville was in the Army for six years, first as a member of an anti-aircraft battery in the docks of Liverpool as the first German raids were beginning. 'For the whole of the winter of 1940-41 we were firing pretty well every night', he recalls. He had become a sergeant in charge of a gun detachment within nine months of joining the Army, was 'forcibly' promoted to sergeant-major after eighteen months, and became a gunnery sergeant instructor after two and a half years. He was opposed to the Communist Party's policy that anyone who could should take officer rank. His reason for this is characteristic: he thought that if or when a crisis came, the place for a Communist like himself would be not among the officers, who would be on the wrong side, but with the rank and file, which could be influenced. He repeatedly refused to go to an Officer Training Unit and was sent to India in 1943. He did not return to England until April 1946. 'My most intensive political work was in India', he writes. 'I made contact with the CPI everywhere I went — I spent leaves in Bombay at the Party's central commune where there must have been three hundred full-time workers.' At the end of the war, he obtained study leave from the Army and spent every day at the Party's commune, 'where I did editorial work, wrote a couple of pamphlets and gave various lectures to selected party cadres who understood English'. When he returned to his own base in Karachi, 'I soon made contact with like minds and we had a party group of about twenty-five who used to meet under my chairmanship'. In the Transit Camp in Bombay to which he was sent on his way back to England, he took part in the 'Forces Parliament', and helped to put forward a motion of censure over the shooting of civilians by British troops in Bombay. The motion was duly passed, whereupon the 'Parliament' was duly closed down. On arrival in England, he learnt that one of the leaders of protests over the slowness of demobilisation in Karachi, Arthur Attwood, had been arrested, and he spent three months organising a 'Release Attwood' campaign, with the help of the CP. He was also much involved in the following fifteen months in political work associated with India, while holding a job in Whitehall as a member of the Economic Section of the Chief Scientific Adviser's Division in the Ministry of Works. In the autumn of 1947, he was appointed to an assistant lectureship in economic history at the University College of Hull, and thus became the only teacher of the subject there at that time.

I

Saville believes that the six years he spent in the Army were

> a very formative or strengthening period in the development of my own personality and especially my political personality. I came out very tough physically and mentally. I had had several large-scale quarrels with authority, although I was a good and efficient soldier; I had maintained my commitment to the CP throughout and nothing that I experienced or read about did anything but stiffen my political and intellectual position.

It is clear that by the time he went to Hull, at the age of thirty-one, he was indeed 'very tough, physically and mentally', an experienced and dedicated Communist, whose political commitment was the activating principle of his life.

Toughness and resilience were necessary qualities for Communists in the following years. After the Soviet Union had been brought into the war by German aggression, Communists had found their path to the 'outside world' greatly eased by the fact that Russia was now an ally, and also by their own attunement to the Coalition Government's broad purpose. But all was now changed. The Cold War had begun as soon as the Second World War had ended, though it did not yet have that name; and Communists again had a hard time by association — harder as time went on and the Cold War grew fiercer. Nor was it only the question of Russia which brought about renewed Communist isolation. Given the rapid degeneration of the Labour Government's purpose, such as it had in any case been at the start, Communists found themselves driven to adopt an ever more critical stance towards the government's policies at home as well as abroad.

The sense of isolation should not however be exaggerated. Given a certain degree of political resilience, which Communists usually had, it was not an impossibly difficult situation. On the contrary, it held a fair element of acceptable challenge. There was a perfectly cogent case to be mounted against the Labour Government's policies at home and abroad; and to the denunciations of the 'bankruptcy of Social Democracy', there could be juxtaposed the argument that the only socialist alternative to it was the Communist Party. As for Russia, it continued to be seen in the rosiest colours. To be a socialist, in the sense in which people like Saville understood the term, then included wholehearted support for 'the socialist sixth of the world', the more so since it now once again appeared threatened by the forces of reaction and imperialism. Such unease as there might have been about the purges of the 1930s, or the Nazi-Soviet Pact, or anything else, was put to rest by the sharp awareness of the decisive contribution which the Russians had made to the defeat of Fascism, and of the price in death and·destruction which they had paid for it.

To be in the Communist Party required acceptance of all things Russian; but the acceptance of all things Russian was made easy — or easier — by the belief that the Soviet Union and socialism were more or less synonymous, by the recollection of the anti-fascist struggle, and by the fact that all the wrong people were anti-Soviet. All this, and much else of the same sort, formed a structure of belief which held some of the best and most acute minds on the left in thrall until Khrushchev's 'secret speech' to the Twentieth Soviet Party Congress in 1956.

Saville was for some years chairman of the Hull branch of the British-Soviet Friendship Society. He delivered copies of the *Daily Worker* on his bicycle round a housing estate every weekend for at least five years; and much of the time that he had to spare from teaching and intellectual work he devoted to Party work. The two intersected particularly well at one point, in the Communist Party's Historians' Group, of which he was an active member, and which included an extraordinary number of talented people. 'It was a tough period', he recalls; 'I don't think I ever met more hostility than in the years of the Korean War.' But he was one of those people who found in that hostility cause to persist rather than desist.

Though Saville himself makes no claim to this effect, there may well have been doubts and uncertainties in his mind, not least because Constance Saville had long been gently but firmly sceptical about many Party orthodoxies. Also, he was by the early 1950s deep in an area of work, namely labour history, that was much less plagued by the catechismal rigidities which prevailed in such areas as philosophy and economics. The major figure in labour history was then G.D.H. Cole, who was not a Communist or a Marxist, but whose work commanded respect. Saville had published in 1952 a collection of Ernest Jones's writings, *Ernest Jones: Chartist*, with a long, scholarly and sensitive Introduction.[3] Two years later, he edited an important volume of essays, *Democracy and the Labour Movement: Essays in Honour of Dona Torr*, which also included a major essay by him, 'The Christian

Socialists of 1848'.[4] These essays by Saville are notable for their unsectarian fluency of style and content; and it would seem unlikely that the author of such essays could accept as gospel truth so much coming out of the Soviet Union and Eastern Europe that was absurd or monstrous or both. But I would not want to push this too hard; and there is in any case no question that Saville remained a loyal and devoted Party member, who gave no trouble to the leadership of the Party until 1956.

The publication of Khrushchev's 'secret speech' occurred in the United States and Britain at the beginning of June 1956. But various garbled accounts of it had begun to spread well before then. Party members began to ask questions, which remained unanswered. Saville was one such Party member, and a long letter from him, asking for answers from the leaders of the Party as to what had been said in Moscow and what it betokened, appeared in the Party's *World News* on 19 May 1956. The Communist Party's Historians' Group was also critical of the leadership's responses, with Saville as one of the most determined critics. He has recently written an account of how he and E.P. Thompson decided at the time that, since the leadership of the Party was obviously trying to limit and indeed stifle discussion inside the Party, they must start an independent discussion journal for the purpose.[5] But it is clear that they did not come to that decision easily.

In his account, Saville has recalled that

> we were highly committed Party members who had come through the tough and difficult years of the Cold War — more difficult than is often appreciated — and we had personal experiences of those who had left the Party to cultivate their own gardens, or of those who had left to become, in our eyes, renegades. One of the original sins for Communist Party members was to publish criticisms of the Party outside the Party press, and in this context journals such as *Tribune* and the *New Statesman* were no different from any other periodical. We therefore conceived our own independent journal as in no way disruptive of the Party to which we belonged, or, to be more accurate, to which we had dedicated ourselves.[6]

This was not at all how the Party leadership saw matters. Great pressure was brought to bear upon Saville and Thompson to discontinue publication of *The Reasoner*, the first issue of which had appeared in mid-July. They just managed to issue a second number before the Executive Committee of the Party formally proceeded to 'instruct Comrades Thompson and Saville to cease publication of *The Reasoner*'.[7] The instruction meant that continued publication must be followed by suspension or expulsion. How difficult they found the dilemma is well shown by their decision to publish a third issue *and* to announce that they were ceasing publication 'in what we conceived to be the best interests of the Party'.[8] But the Russian intervention in Hungary occurred while this third issue was being produced, and wrought further changes in attitude. Before the Russian intervention, Saville and Thompson wanted to fight from within for changes in the Party and in the Party's policies; and they still hoped to avoid a head-on clash with the leadership. After the Russian action in Hungary and the British Communist leadership's endorsement of it, they urged their Communist readers, in the third issue of *The Reasoner*, to dissociate themselves from their leaders. They were suspended from membership of the Party, and resigned. Saville had been a member for twenty-two years.

For many Communists everywhere, resignation from the Party is or at least used to be something of a traumatic wrench and a deeply un-hinging experience, commensurate with the depth of the commitment that membership implied and the sense of having been part of a very special world and of being so no longer. Nor would matters be made easier by the denunciations and accusations which dissent and exit or expulsion provoked from former comrades and leaders. Saville recalls that, by September 1956 (that is, before Hungary), 'we were having to spend some time with our correspondents denying allegations about our personal ambitions, our publication of material without the consent of authors, and the dark source of our finances'.[9] The hostility became much more pronounced after Budapest, and Saville also notes that '*The Reasoner* group' was then denounced at an aggregate meeting of his own Party branch as 'running dogs of imperialism'.[10]

Disagreeable though this must have been, and however great the wrench of leaving the Party after so many years, it appears to have left Saville remarkably unscathed. He had not joined the Party in a great fit of rebellion; and he did not leave it in a great fit of rejection. His atti-tude throughout seems to have been matter-of-fact, well-tempered and hard-headed, measured and reasonable. It was a very characteristic attitude. On the other hand, it left whole the question which giving up the Communist Party posed, or ought to have posed, namely in what other existing or to-be-created organisation it would be possible for Marxists to further the socialist cause. It was a question which con-fronted two different generations in 1956: the generation to which Saville belonged, and which had come to political life in the thirties and

in the Second World War; and also a new generation which came to
political life in 1956, with Suez and Hungary. As I see it, at a distance
of twenty years and more, neither generation was able to return a
satisfactory answer to that question; and it still remains unanswered.

II

The third issue of *The Reasoner* had also been the last one. But Saville
and Thompson then began to prepare the publication of a new journal,
the *New Reasoner*, whose first issue came out in the spring of 1957. It
was about that time that I first met Saville. I had written something for
the new *Universities and Left Review*, which had also published its first
number in the spring of 1957, and the editors of the *New Reasoner*
asked me if I would write for the journal. It was not long after that I
joined the editorial board — its only member, I think, who had not
been in the Communist Party. In the course of time, joint meetings of
the editorial boards of the two journals came to be held fairly regularly.
As I recall, Saville, who was a little older than most of us, and a good
deal older than some, very often tended to find himself chairing these
meetings, acting as a moderating and unifying influence, and trying to
get things *settled*, particularly when the issue was one of getting things
done.

The idea soon came up that the two journals should merge. On the
surface, this seemed a very reasonable and natural development. In fact,
it was not. However amicable and close the relations between the two
boards might be, its members did belong to two different political and
cultural traditions; and while there was some overlapping between
them, there was also a core of difference constituted by the fact that
the *New Reasoner* board was mostly made up of Marxists who had in
one way or another been deeply involved in the labour movement,
personally and directly, and who also had a strong sense of political
agencies as, coming out of the Communist Party, they could not help
but have. *Universities and Left Review*, on the other hand, was a venture that had originated among students at Oxford. Their own responses to the promptings of the times were fresh, innovative and unen-
cumbered by the weight and wounds of a battered tradition. But while
the *New Reasoner* people were intellectuals *of* the labour movement,
the *ULR* people were intellectuals *for* the labour movement, naturally
so, given their youth and background; and they were also part of a
more or less anti-organisation current, which was then flowing very
strongly.

As I see it now, and as I only dimly perceived it then, the *New*

Reasoner 'rebellion' should have been followed by a sustained and systematic attempt to regroup whoever was willing into a socialist association, league or party, of which the journal might have been the voice. But this is no more than hindsight; and there was then no steam behind any such idea. The reason for this goes well beyond the difficulties of the moment, the weariness with organisation of people who had gone through a searing experience at the hands of the Communist Party as had Saville and Thompson and many others who had left the Party. The main reason why the *New Reasoner* was not kept going is that there was no adequate perception that a new socialist organisation *was* needed, and where there was some kind of perception of it, there was no clear view as to what it should specifically stand for, in programmatic and organisational as well as in theoretical terms.

The merger of the two journals could not remedy this, and was not intended to do so; and the absence of any such intention produced near unanimity about the merger which resulted in the foundation of *New Left Review*. When the final vote was taken at the joint meeting of the two editorial boards which decided upon the merger, I was, as I recall, alone in opposing it. I thought that each journal had a distinctive role to perform; and I also thought that the demise of the *New Reasoner* was an opportunity forsaken to develop something important in and for the labour movement. I also recall Saville arguing with me that I was wrong, simply on the grounds of practicality: the journal, he believed, could not have been kept going. He was probably right; and if there *had* been the will to carve out an independent socialist position, in theoretical, programmatic and organisational terms, the merger, it is fair to argue, would not have prevented that will from being expressed in *New Left Review*.

The new journal duly appeared in January 1960 and led a rather difficult existence for some two years. It suffered from a considerable uncertainty of purpose and direction, or perhaps from an over-abundance of purposes and directions, which comes to the same thing. In 1962, what was then a seriously ailing venture was taken in hand by Perry Anderson and others, who themselves were part of a later and different generation from the one which had started *ULR*.

I think that Saville never identified closely with *New Left Review*: the end of the *New Reasoner* meant for him the end of a whole period of a certain kind of engagement. He remained deeply involved politically, supported causes, spoke at meetings, took part in demonstrations, ran for years a 'speakers' class' for trade unionists in Hull. But he did not join any particular grouping or party and did not find it uncomfortable to be politically homeless. For all his enduring political interests and activities, he was no longer as *absorbed* by politics of an immediate kind as he had been previously.

Nor even, in all probability, would he have wanted to be involved with me in the co-editorship of the *Socialist Register* if this had been conceived as anything more frequent than an annual volume of essays, from different authors, and bearing on different aspects of socialist theory and practice. The fourteen volumes of the *Register* which have been published so far could never have seen the light of day without his contribution to their production; and their production proved to be a demanding business. But it was not so unremittingly demanding as to interfere drastically with his paramount concerns of the years after the Communist Party, namely his engagement with historical research, writing and teaching.

Even at the time when he had been most fully involved in immediate politics of a sustained kind, he had also faithfully pursued work in economic and social history; and the book which he published in 1957 on *Rural Depopulation in England and Wales 1851-1951* has ever since been a standard text on the alterations produced by migration and other factors on rural social and occupational structures. But it is note-worthy that, while he continued to publish major articles, he chose to devote most of his energies as a scholar to what might be called the organisation of intellectual work. He seems to have decided very early on — in my view much too modestly — that his best contribution lay mainly in this direction; and he made that contribution in different ways, and most notably by way of editorial work, with the volumes of *Essays in Labour History*, which he edited with Asa Briggs, with the *Occasional Papers in Economic and Social History* for the University of Hull, and above all with the volumes of the *Dictionary of Labour Biography*, which he has edited with Joyce Bellamy.

Good editorial work is a particular kind of skill. It requires a combi-nation of firmness and tact, of decisiveness and patience, of tolerance and self-confidence, and a considerable capacity and willingness to devote time and energy to other people's work. These are qualities which Saville has brought in full measure to the editorial work which he has done over the years.

Nowhere have these qualities been more needed and displayed than in his editorship of the *Dictionary of Labour Biography*, which is well on the way to being, if it is not already, one of the major historiographi-cal achievements in Britain in this century. Four volumes of the work have so far appeared, in 1972, 1974, 1976 and 1977; and a fifth one is on the way, with an indefinite number of further volumes planned and in various stages of preparation. The intention behind the enterprise is simple: to produce biographical profiles of varying length of people who have played a part, great or small, in the British labour movement in the last 200 years. Some of the entries consist of only a few hundred words, others are much longer. Most of them are naturally concerned with men and women whose contribution to the life of the labour movement has been mostly local and, in terms of what is usually understood by 'history', quite limited. But one of the purposes of the *Dictionary* is precisely to show how dense and varied and woven in the tissue of 'civil society' has been the life of the movement, and how dependent it has been on the 'molecular' activism of the people at the grassroots and in the lower reaches of labour's many different institutions.

Labour history has now become academically respectable, much more so than when Saville embarked upon it in the late 1940s. But the subject easily lends itself to sentimentalism, idealisation and folklorism. The *Dictionary* altogether avoids these pitfalls. Saville is deeply interested in the past, and in the individuals who help to make up its history. But his involvement is dispassionate and his judgement cool. Above all, he works on the *Dictionary* with a profound sense of a *movement*, which has a past, a present and a future; which has mobilised countless energies, hopes, ambitions and expectations; which meanders onwards in ways much more complex than are susceptible to encapsulation in a single formula; and of which he himself feels strongly but unsentimentally that he is a part.

The *Dictionary* is the work of many hands. Dozens of people all over Britain have contributed entries to it, drawing upon national and local archives, newspapers, histories, memoirs and other records. Saville himself has been responsible for more of the text than any other collaborator. It is remarkable that two editors should have been able to do so much in so short a space of time; and it is a pleasing thought that historians of the labour movement will, a hundred years from now, be using the *Dictionary* as an absolutely essential resource.

On Saville's side, the work involved has been part of a load which would have been crushing had he not had what he once described as 'the physique and the psychological armour plating of a sergeant-major'. The description fits, except that sergeant-majors are not usually renowned for patience, tolerance and good humour. But sergeant-majors do have a sense of organisation, of being part of a purpose larger than themselves, of professional work that needs to be done efficiently, properly and without fuss. In these respects, sergeant-major Saville will do as a label. In others, chairman Saville will do better — chairman of the Department of Economic and Social History at Hull; chairman of the Oral History Society, in whose formation he played a notable part, as he had played a part, in the late 1950s, in the foundation of the Society for the Study of Labour History; chairman of the Economic and Social History Committee of the Social Science Research Council.

Finally, but certainly not least, there is teaching and the supervision of research. From being the only person teaching economic and social history at Hull, Saville has become the head of a substantial department, which he has also built up as a centre of graduate work in social and economic history. The supervision of graduate research is the most arduous, time-consuming and unglamorous part of academic life; and I have seen Saville devote an extraordinary amount of time, energy and care to it.

The springs of action of every single man and woman are endlessly varied and deeply buried. Everything that is said in this realm is by definition simplistic. Given these provisos, there remains in Saville's case a clear motivation for effort spent and work done, namely a commitment to the Good Old Cause, which was made, once and for all, some forty-five years ago. There are not many entries in the *Dictionary of Labour Biography* which record lives of greater dedication and integrity.

Notes

1. The biographical data for this essay was provided to me by John Saville in a personal memoir, for which I am grateful.

2. J. Saville, 'May Day 1937', in A. Briggs and J. Saville (eds.), *Essays in Labour History 1918-1939* (1977).

3. This was when I first came across his name. The occasion is suggestive of a certain political climate. I was then doing some occasional reviewing for *The Economist*, and rang up the paper to ask if I could have the book for review. It was readily agreed that I should, but weeks passed and the book did not arrive. I asked again, the book finally came, and the review was duly written and published. I was told later that the question whether a book published by Lawrence and Wishart should be reviewed in *The Economist* had to be decided at an editorial board meeting.

4. The other contributors to the volume were Henry Collins, Christopher Hill, Eric Hobsbawm, Victor Kiernan, S.F. Mason, R.L. Meek and Daphne Simon. The book has long been unavailable and ought to be reprinted.

5. J. Saville, 'The Twentieth Congress and the British Communist Party', in *The Socialist Register 1976*.

6. Ibid., p. 7.

7. Ibid., p. 11.

8. Ibid., p. 14.
9. Ibid., p. 20.
10. Ibid., p. 20.

3 LABOUR AND THE LITERATE IN NINETEENTH-CENTURY BRITAIN

Victor Kiernan

Nineteenth-century Britain, drifting into a new and strange epoch, and uneasily aware of a widening gulf between the classes, has left a voluminous record of the impressions of the better-off about the mass of their fellow-countrymen. They were for the most part gloomy, whether concerned with material or with moral conditions. A distinct part of the record is made up of the experiences of individuals who tried to surmount barriers and prejudices and to work actively with labour movements, hoping to provide these with ideas and guidance. As a rule they wanted to guide mass discontent into channels of gradual reform. A few saw it as a positive force which could transform society and put mankind on a new road. Of the two sorts, the gradualists sometimes met with disappointment; the revolutionisers, Chartist or socialist, far more frequently. Their frustration might be due to their own lack of clear practical ideas, or inability to win working-class confidence. But the same failure has befallen latter-day socialists with definite programmes. It has equally been the fate of individuals drawn from the working class itself. The uncrossable gap it seems has not been between class and class nearly so much as between idealistic groups and the bulk of any classes. Cobden and Bright, those middle-class revolutionisers, came to feel as deeply disillusioned with their own class as any worker socialist has been with his.

No review either of the impressions of the literate public, or of the experiences of literate individuals of whatever origin collaborating with the working class, can be more than fragmentary. The latter especially were often contradictory, and many opposite ones can be cited; the same men or women went through shifting moods, less or more hopeful, and no doubt age and fatigue brought despondency. Nevertheless, here too on the whole the gloomier note seems to prevail. There is moreover the objective fact that British society has not, after all, undergone a revolutionary change, though it has altered very greatly in very many ways; and today the mass of labour appears as little interested in any such transformation as it has ever been. It may almost seem as if a statistical law, the product of human existence from the beginning, forbids the great majority of human beings to respond to any but limited, short-term, tangible aims, and condemns the rest to be a perpetual small minority.

To the literate the ancient adage that there is as much difference between lettered and unlettered as between living and dead has often seemed a self-evident truth. Their efforts to guide and improve their fellows have often left them convinced that they were casting pearls before a swinish multitude. In the opening words of the *Essay on Satire* of Dryden's patron Lord Mulgrave:

> How dull, and how insensible a beast
> Is man, who yet would lord it o'er the rest?
> Philosophers and poets vainly strove
> In every age the lumpish mass to move.

Over Christendom there has always lain its archetypal image of the people's Friend murdered by the people. A legion of the disappointed must have recalled it, as Macaulay was transparently doing when he consoled himself for the loss of his Edinburgh seat in 1847 by writing high-falutin' verses about his destiny from the cradle as a superior man, far above worldly success or the breath of popularity, one born to defy

> A sullen priesthood and a raving crowd
> Amidst the din of all things fell and vile,
> Hate's yell, and envy's hiss, and folly's bray.

He had in fact been a very unsatisfactory MP.[1]

In Wordsworth's youth all his love was 'given to the people', as he recalled in *The Prelude*. It was a mystic marriage gone through by many others, analogous with the Romantic proclivity for falling in love with women, and equally a leap in the dark. All the Romantic poets withdrew before long into seclusion or exile, whether they turned conservative or remained progressive; from an obscure conviction perhaps that the bustle of the streets and the writing of poetry could not go together, but also perhaps from an uneasy sense of failure to reach a meeting of minds with the people. Byron and Shelley did all the same find a popular audience; Chartist writings are full of echoes of them, and their influence, along with that of the theatre, may be felt in the high-flown rhetoric which labour agitators seem to have indulged in.

Hazlitt, always a staunch radical as well as the greatest of English journalists, was not without an appreciation of the common man. Writing 'On the Ignorance of the Learned' he declared that 'more *home*

truths are to be learnt from listening to a noisy debate in an alehouse
than from attending to a formal one in the House of Commons . . . the
mass of society have common sense, which the learned in all ages want'.
But he was too much a pessimist, early youth once gone by, to put his
faith in any popular movement (he died two years before the first
Reform Act). He concluded that men are only brought together by
interest and prejudice, and to be kept together must be approached on
their worse side; he saw reformers drifting apart into opinionated,
quarrelling cliques.[2] For his own moral reinforcement he turned abroad,
giving a dogged loyalty to revolutionary France and then, much less
wholesomely, to Napoleon, as champion of the people and apotheosis
of the career open to talent.

Industrialism was marking off the working classes from the rest
more rigidly, and making 'People' a far less attractive word: it was
Beauty turning into Beast, instead of the other way round. England like
China in those days was a country increasingly urbanised yet still
governed by landlords and the habits of mind their sway had formed.
Trollope contrasted docile farm-labourers with rowdy brickfield workers,[3] and it was men like these, or the semi-nomad navvies, on the
fringes of orderly life, that the better-off were likely to encounter at
times and shy away from. But it was the remote, unknown mass of
labour in the industrial towns of the north that bulked largest and most
frighteningly in the upper-class imagination; the distance between the
classes was geographical as well as social. The southern yokel might be
boorish, Gissing wrote, but at least he belonged to an old pattern,
represented 'an immemorial subordination', unlike the northern workman 'just emerged from barbarism', with a 'frank brutality' of mind
and manner native to his 'primitive state'.[4] Gissing was not exceptional
as a literary man, one of the aristocracy of mental labour, in suffering
from a general distaste for humanity, which the airs and graces of
'refinement' could divert like the perfumes of Versailles and its unwashed courtiers, leaving it to concentrate itself on the workers.

Mutterings or tumults in the factory districts were the more alarming
because of an uneasy sensation that industrialism had made the country
unbalanced, unstable, vulnerable as Lord Melbourne wrote to Queen
Victoria on 17 August 1842 to all 'the wild and extravagant opinions
which are naturally generated in an advanced and speculative state of
society'. That the rich ought to be less rich and the poor less poor was
clearly one such opinion. Half a century later it was remarked that
most of those who talked about the proletariat without first-hand
knowledge of it were apt to suppose, mistakenly, that 'working men

must be men of extreme and revolutionary opinions'.[5] Their jumping
to this conclusion suggests guilty consciences; at an earlier date it may
not have been so wide of the mark. Another symptom of ignorance
was that pictures of the working class were strongly coloured by impressions of foreign lands. It was a long time before the shadow of the
French Revolution, above all, ceased to fall darkly across the English
mind. With Melbourne that 'extraordinary shock . . . loomed ever at
the back of his consciousness'.[6] When the revolutions of 1848 broke
out the dismayed reformer Brougham quoted lurid reports of drunken
Paris mobs fighting over their loot, and added that at Messina things
had been worse still: 'there is no doubt whatever that sixty Neapolitans
were roasted and devoured by those infernal furies, those worse than
barbarous cannibals'.[7] A more sober commentator, James Mill, was
horrified by a socialistic speech of Attwood during the 1831 agitation,
as opening up prospects 'worse than the overwhelming deluge of Huns
and Tartars'. His son, John Stuart, endorsed a foreign observer's view of
British workers as skilled at their tasks, but 'in conduct the most dis-
orderly, debauched, and unruly, and least respectable and trustworthy
of any nation', only kept in hand by 'iron discipline'.[8]

It was a fact moreover that a large proportion of the new working
class was of alien origin and speech, Irish in Lancashire and Highland in
Glasgow. Engels's well-known description of the 'Milesians' is not much
less horrific than Carlyle's. There must have seemed a further risk of
Irishmen in England picking up subversive ideas which might filter back
to their already troublesome homeland. It was partly in order to strike
awe into Ireland that the Queen wrote to her ministers on 23 June
1843, when there were riots in South Wales, calling for 'measures of the
greatest severity . . . to suppress the revolutionary spirit'.

There was an ominous likeness to 1789 in the fact that religion
seemed to have lost its virtue as the time-honoured harmoniser of
classes and bridle of discontent. Side by side with Methodism there was
a plebeian rationalism which rejected the doctrine preached, for instance, at Edinburgh on the General Thanksgiving day in 1798, that the
Christian is to study Scripture 'with a child-like, with an humble and
teachable disposition', and learn from it 'that the powers that be are
ordained of God'.[9] Here too rural and industrial labour stood in contrast. The worthy pastor in John Galt's *Annals of the Parish* (1821) was
happy to find the bumpkins in his flock in 1795 'uncontaminated by
that seditious infection which fevered the minds of the sedentary
weavers, and working like flatulence in the stomachs of the cotton-
spinners, sent up into their heads a vain and diseased fume of infidel

philosophy' (ch. 36). In the industrial slums of Lancashire it was rather indifference that prevailed. Religious ignorance among 'these degraded beings', wrote P. Gaskell, 'is truly astonishing . . . often there is no belief in the superintending care of a Beneficent Creator'.[10] Even the pious minority were mostly Dissenters, and all dissent implied a degree of frowardness, while some sectaries were positively disaffected. Browning's long poem 'Christmas Eve and Easter Day' vividly expresses the educated man's inability, in spite of Christian duty, to feel any fellowship with the botched, the sickly, the stupid, of a working-class chapel in 1849.

Religion in danger, family in danger. Gaskell's survey of the working class, some years before Engels's, might rather be termed an indictment of a class 'filled with immorality . . . ingratitude, ignorance, and vice, in every conceivable form in which it can develop itself' (p. 106). At bottom these miscreants were suffering, he argued, not from shortage of money but from break-up of family life. Cottage industry had 'fostered the establishment of parental authority and domestic discipline' (p. 19), whereas now the family was 'a body of distinct individuals', all earning 'and considering themselves as lodgers merely' (p. 93). This disintegration was 'the most powerfully demoralizing' consequence of the factory system (p. 99), and he clearly saw in it a menace to order as well as to morals: 'Politically speaking, the common people may be a dead letter, whilst their homes exhibit private independence and social enjoyment.' Conversely they may carry political weight 'whilst their homes exhibit social disorganization and moral worthlessness' (pp. 105-6). There may well be some truth in this; the disruption of old social and familial patterns may have been liberating and stimulating for the labour movement, whereas later on, as industrial life settled down to more normal standards, the patriarchal family could rebuild itself, and fit better with cautious reformism than with the daring hopes of earlier years.

Any inclination of the workers to meddle with politics, the preserve of their superiors, Gaskell like most others reckoned among their bad proclivities – 'the pursuit of debasing pleasures, if they can be so called; viz. in the beer-shop, the gin-vault, or the political club' (p. 275). Drunkenness was a very frequent charge – though high society was at least as alcoholic – and was thought to go with inflammatory politics. One of Harriet Martineau's edifying stories, *Cousin Marshall* (1832), opens on a Sunday morning scene of workmen sprawling in the street where they have sunk down at the end of the previous night's debauch. Some shrewd heads must have seen in this kind of thing an insurance against any proletarian uprising worth the name.

Even a man like the economist T.R. Edmonds, whose ideal was a sort of socialist society, felt that any changes brought about by the working class itself must be impractical and self-defeating: 'The establishment of the social system should be the work of the thinking and richer classes, for only to them would the bulk of the population pay attention'.[11] It is indeed remarkable that out of a mass so 'degraded' and 'demoralised' a labour movement of such dimensions and vitality should have arisen. On the economic side, Galt noted how skilled were 'weavers and cotton-mill folk', as early as 1803, 'in the way of committees and associating together' (ch. 44). Ideas of political reform or socialism came from outside. Between the two appeals there was an oscillation of interest. They converged most closely in the hopeful early years of Chartism, inaugurated in 1837-8 and accompanied by campaigning for more factory legislation and shorter hours. Mill could speak of Chartism in 1845 as 'the revolt of nearly all the active talent, and a great part of the physical force, of the working classes, against their whole relation to society'.[12]

During these stormy years some national as well as many local leaders arose from the ranks. To rise like this required a fair equipment of education, often self-education, which was bound to alter them and make them in some measure strangers to their own class. Discords among them partly reflected a diversity of social elements within the working class, and the superior mental mobility of the craftsman compared with the mill-hand. William Lovett was a skilled artisan who helped to organise the London Working Men's Association and launch the Charter, but after a painful spell in prison during 1839-40 he was regarded as a traitor to the cause when he argued that the first requirement was self-education and self-improvement by the workers. Another of this type who came to grief was Thomas Cooper, son of a dyer and wretchedly poor in boyhood, but a prodigy at picking up learning. He came out of prison in 1845 more inclined than before to rely on peaceful methods, quarrelled with O'Connor over this and other issues, and in 1846 was denounced at the Chartist Convention and expelled. In later years he was a Baptist preacher. Chartism's history and epitaph were written by another active member, Gammage, originally a cartwright from Northampton, then a shoemaker, in later days a doctor. His book is often gloomy in tone: 'It is by no means a pleasant task to wade through the mass of treachery, falsehood, and folly, that engrafted itself on one of the noblest movements that ever engaged the energies of a people'.[13]

It went with the heterogeneity of the working classes, and their un-
even development, that a number of the most prominent figures were
drawn from far outside their ranks. They too had their share of dissen-
sions and disappointments. Robert Owen was a Welshman from
Scotland. Like most others who have come forward to save the people,
he wanted also to save them from themselves, to transform them. He
offered them his assistance on condition of their agreeing to 'renounce
all violence and hatred against the possessing and ruling classes' (Beer,
vol. 1, p. 173). Gandhi was to offer the same pledge on the same terms
a hundred years later. On his deathbed in 1858 Owen was still convinced that he had been right, not the public: 'I gave important truths
to the world, and it was only for want of understanding that they were
disregarded' (Beer, vol. 2, p. 174). J.F. Bray, author of 'the last and
most powerful manifesto of Owenism', was born in America and
returned there in 1842, convinced that the working class was on the
wrong road with its trade unionism and politics (Beer, vol. 1, p. 236).
Bronterre O'Brien, known as 'the schoolmaster' or chief theorist of
Chartism, was an Irishman, son of a once prosperous merchant, and a
brilliant student drawn away from the bar into left-wing journalism.
In 1833 his emphasis on the necessity of political action exposed him
to a charge of hostility to trade unionism. Later on he fell foul of
'O'Connorism', a blend according to his loyal disciple Gammage of
'ignorance and fanaticism' (p. 204).

Feargus O'Connor was another Irishman, with a career at Trinity
College, Dublin, and the Irish bar, and as MP for County Cork, before
he threw in his lot with the English labour movement. He soon stood
out as its foremost man of action in the eyes of the northern mill-
workers, whose massed numbers gave them preponderance, and made a
contribution to the movement which, whatever his failings, commands
admiration. His critics accused him of domineering, and a man of his
flamboyant temper, descending from a higher social level, might well
be bent on asserting himself, and claim the first place as his due. They
found fault too with his habit of indulging in insurrectionary talk. This
may have had its uses in rousing hearers who wanted a simpler, plainer
message than O'Brien or Lovett could offer them; but it served to keep
O'Connor in the forefront as well. Prison may have undermined him, as
it did others, more than he realised, and the final Chartist flare-up in
1848 found him unequal to it. Suddenly placed between excited multitude and embattled government, he looked 'pale and frightened', Lord
John Russell the Prime Minister reported to his sovereign on 10 April,
ate humble pie, rebuked the crowd for its 'folly'. From that moment

his reputation was wilting, and between failure and mortification his mind gave way. His private resources had been swallowed up in his abortive land settlement scheme. When he died in 1855 the people remembered their former hero well enough to turn out in thousands for his funeral.

Ernest Jones, the son of an army officer with very distinguished connections, was an even more surprising recruit to Chartism. He joined late, not long before its collapse, and was soon one of O'Connor's lieutenants. His writings make an impression of sincerity as well as of brilliant talent, an impression confirmed by John Saville's well-known study of him. Gammage, with some rancour of class it may be, a self-educated man's envy of the silver spoon, judged him 'ambitious and mercenary', one who must 'command the movement, or he would reduce it to nothing', and full of disguised cunning (p. 400). On his side Jones was far from uncritical of his party. His military parentage may have done something to make him a realist about organisation. Other movements, from Christianity to Free Trade, he was writing in 1848, had been spread by missionary effort, 'whereas Chartism has proselytised less than any other great principle or dogma in the world. We have not of late years taken much pains to make converts; lectures have been given – but mostly in obscure places and to the same audiences.'[14] Innumerable later movements have been open to the same reproach. Jones stood firm in that year, was imprisoned, and subsequently made desperate but unavailing efforts to revive the Charter.

A Chartist of fiction admired O'Connor as 'a glorious man . . . the descendant of the ancient kings, throwing away his rank, his name . . . for the cause of the suffering millions!'[15] 'An Aristocrat is always most acceptable to the working class, even to Democrats', Gammage commented sourly on the speedy elevation of Jones (p. 282). There may really have been some legacy to the industrial age from an older world where poor folk rebelling did like to have men of position – priests, squires, even lords – in the van, and might even compel them to take the lead. John Frost, the Radical transported to Tasmania after the 'Newport rising' of 1839, is said to have declared in jail that he was forced by extremists to put himself at their head. But much in the Chartist record has a bearing on problems of the psychology of leadership, or of the relation, peculiar and complex as some of these men saw it to be, between leader and led.

There was the impulse of all mass movements to believe and expect too much of their chiefs, strongest again among the northern factory workers with their vigorous but crude political consciousness. They were to be seen streaming in long processions to their open-air meetings, says Gammage, 'making the heavens echo with the thunder of their cheers on recognizing the idols of their worship in the men who were to address them' (p. 94). But to these idols it might feel as though they were in the grip of an irresistible force:

> I was the people's instrument [Cooper wrote] rather than their
> director . . . And it is thus, in all ages and in every country, whether
> on a large or small scale, that a popular leader keeps the lead: his
> temperament, nature, and powers fit him . . . to become the people's
> mouthpiece, hand, and arm, either for good or evil.[16]

'I don't lead; I am driven by the people', O'Connor declared. He was blaming the workers' rough ways and readiness to resort to force on 'those who have kept the workmen in ignorance and who degraded them' (Beer, vol. 2, p. 129). Awareness of these defects may have helped to unnerve him in 1848. Other leaders as well were more apt to recognise deficiencies in the masses than the latter in them. O'Brien came to believe that there could be no quick transition 'from our present iniquitous and corrupt state of society into Owen's social paradise': much must first be done 'to rescue the people from their present brutalised condition of ignorance and vassalage' (Beer, vol. 2, p. 20). Jones warned his hearers in a speech of 1846 that 'while we desire to reform others, we must not be blind to the fact that we want reforming ourselves. That it might elevate the mind, and strengthen the frame of men, if they went less to the gin-palace.'[17] In a narrative of the Peasants' Revolt of 1381, one of several historical sketches he wrote during 1847-8, he depicted a band of mutineers getting hopelessly drunk; he must have feared that the same might happen over again. In the end his rebels tamely submit, paralysed by 'hereditary fear' of those above them, and surrender their leaders to the king.[18]

Close to the people by virtue of his yeoman birth, and blessed with a sanguine temperament, Cobbett could sometimes at any rate feel more confidence in his public than most of the popular leaders. Englishmen he declared only wanted 'to live like men, and not like hogs and dogs . . . There never was a working people in the whole world, so reasonable, so just, and so easily satisfied.'[19] On a Rural Ride in 1826 he 'found the working people at Frome very intelligent; very well informed as to the cause of their misery; not at all humbugged by the canters, whether about religion or loyalty'; while talking to ordinary folk at Ely in 1830 satisfied him afresh that 'there are very few, even amongst the labourers, who do not clearly understand the cause of their ruin'.[20] He was addressing farmers as well as labourers, and his tours and meetings convinced him that both were very ready to agree with him, and to act together against the old gang of landlords and stock-jobbers. But he too had his misgivings, and was not always so hopeful.

All this time urban, middle-class Radicalism was waging its campaign against the old gang, for parliamentary and economic reform, a struggle separate from that of the workers but impinging on it at many points. Labour support was often sought, but most often by demagogue politicians in search of catspaws. The scene in *Felix Holt* (ch. 11) where the Radical agent cajoles a set of bemused coalminers into promising strong-arm assistance on election day is a good epitome of how the masses were encouraged to demonstrate, even riot, during 1831-2 for a Reform Bill which would do them no good. As Borrow was to write of 'Pseudo-Radicals' in *The Romany Rye* (1857): 'They egged on poor ignorant mechanics and rustics, and got them hanged for pulling down and burning', while they looked on from a safe distance (App., ch. 10). Later on there were genuine proposals of alliance from a left wing of the middle classes, men like Joseph Sturge at Birmingham. At a joint conference there in 1842 O'Brien argued that denunciation of the middle classes might be abated, because they had grown less hostile to labour since 1834: 'now vast numbers of them not only recognise us as an integral part of the body politic, but they have actually paid court to us'. Opponents condemned all this as 'an act of treachery directed against the working class, and as an attempt to weaken or obliterate the class war' (Beer, vol. 2, p. 125). Disillusion had sunk deep since 1832; and manufacturers were not prepared to pay for labour's political backing with concessions in terms of wages and hours. Cobden inveighed against trade unions as 'founded upon principles of brutal tyranny and monopoly. I would rather live under a Dey of Algiers than a Trades' Committee.' Much to his disgust the bulk of labour held aloof from his campaign against the Corn Laws; he believed that intriguers were deluding the workers, and accused the latter of 'allowing a parcel of lads, with hired knaves for leaders, to interrupt their meetings'.[21] He was failing to understand what Mill saw very clearly – the total alienation of the working class: 'the *sourde* animosity which is universal in this country towards the whole class of employers in the whole class of the employed'.[22]

Reluctance on the part of the industrialists or their spokesmen to make any better offer to the workers left the way open for thoughts, or fancies, of intervention on their behalf by aristocracy, as *deus ex machina.* A Scots peasant, Carlyle, was the odd standard-bearer of this paternalism. His feeling about the workers comes out in his praise of Plato — 'With what disdain he speaks of the great unwashed and their blatant democracies!'[23] One of the seer's pipe-dreams, in the first of his *Latter-day Pamphlets* of 1850, was of an heroic premier presenting the unemployed with a scheme for enrolling them into labour battalions: 'Disobey the rules, — I will admonish and endeavour to incite you; if in vain, I will flog you; if still in vain, I will at last shoot you.' A notion that the workers were famishing for leadership from above — not simply to welcome an individual who left his own sphere to join them — had a long lease of life in other minds too. Disraeli concocted a model factory, ventilated on a new plan, employing 2,000 workers, with model housing attached; all the work of a Mr Trafford, younger son of an old landed family, who was guided by 'the baronial principle, reviving in a new form . . . a correct conception of the relations which should subsist between the employer and the employed'.[24]

Ruskin might have been recalling this fable when he satirised the upper-class dream of an ideal existence in a lovely mansion and park supported by a mill whose workers 'never drink, never strike, always go to church on Sunday, and always express themselves in respectful language'. Yet Ruskin himself could succumb to the same kind of fantasy, as when he assured a genteel audience: 'The people are crying to you for command . . . You think they don't want to be commanded; try them . . . "Govern us", they cry with one heart, though many minds. They *can* be governed still, these English . . . They love their old ways yet, and their old masters, and their old land'.[25] This rigmarole was addressed not to the Horse Marines but to the Royal Artillery Institute at Woolwich. A generation later Gissing would be furbishing the old legend afresh: 'Profoundly aristocratic in his sympathies, the Englishman has always seen in the patrician class not merely a social, but a moral, superiority . . . Very significant is the cordial alliance from old time between nobles and people.'[26]

On a more practical level paternalism manifested itself chiefly through the Christian Socialists. These men were prepared to collaborate with labour on humanitarian grounds, in opposition to the Poor Law of 1834, or for factory legislation and restriction of working hours. Kingsley and others even gave active support to a strike of Manchester ironworkers over piecework and overtime. On this plane too those who took the lead had their tribulations, if seldom as severe as Oastler's when philanthropy landed him in jail for debt. They were depressingly few, for one thing, though it is true that upstairs as well as downstairs in society an energetic group may have disproportionate influence. When Ashley (later Lord Shaftesbury) took up advocacy of the ten-hour day he hoped that many of his class would join him, but scarcely any did.

In Parliament he 'regarded himself as the choice of the workers', but in his eyes socialism and Chartism were 'the two great demons in morals and politics',[27] and a good half of the purpose of all leadership like his was to guide labour away from its own path. Between such a man and the rank and file, relations could only be precarious. They broke down in 1850 when he decided to accept a modification of the Ten Hour Act. He had what he considered valid reasons, but he wrote in his diary: 'Expect from manufacturing districts a storm of violence and hatred. I might have taken a more popular and belauded course, but I should have ruined the question; one more easy to myself, but far from *true* to the people.' Indignation did run high, all the more because he had made the decision without consulting the workers, and a Lancashire committee passed a resolution deploring 'the infatuation which led to the cause of the factory workers being intrusted to Lord Ashley'.[28] By this time, also, Chartism was on the wane, and with it the atmosphere of crisis which had gained Christian Socialism a hearing among the well-off. 'When this boisterous pressure was withdrawn, nobody troubled about *Parson Lot* [Kingsley], or the scruples of Maurice and his friends.'[29]

'We say to the great minds of the day, come among the people, write for the people, and your fame will live for ever.'[30] Ernest Jones was anticipating Mao's call to the writers. Chartism had many of its own, but not of a calibre to be heard outside the movement. Of the others, a few novelists did try to write about the working classes, though scarcely *for* them, and as sympathetic critics rather than allies. What stands out in their thinking is a contradiction none of them could resolve between the harshness of daily life for labour and the futility or worse, to their minds, of its more impatient efforts to emancipate itself. Instead public opinion, that slumbering giant, was somehow to be aroused, and somehow to find a way of solving the insoluble. Strife between capital and labour was regularly deplored: each ought to recognise its obligations to the other. To Elizabeth Gaskell, writing *Mary Barton*, 'The most deplorable and enduring evil' from the depression and strife of 1839-41 was the 'feeling of alienation between the different classes of society' (ch. 8). In Harriet Martineau's story *A Manchester Strike* the men's leader Allen and the employer Mr Wentworth are both meritorious human beings, and she ends with the words: 'When will masters and men work cheerfully together for their common good?'

Allen has been pushed by his fellows into taking the lead, reluctantly because he has a family and fears to be victimised, and after its failure cannot get his job back and has to spend the rest of his life as a street-cleaner. A far more lurid picture of a strike occurs in Mrs Gaskell's *North and South*, with a riot against an employer who is importing Irish blacklegs: 'As soon as they saw Mr. Thornton they set up a yell – to call it not human is nothing – it was as the demoniac desire of some terrible wild beast for the food that is withheld from his ravening' (ch. 17). Trade unions still had a secret-society flavour which lost nothing in middle-class imagination. Mary Barton's father and friends took 'one of those fierce terrible oaths which bind members of Trade Unions to any given purpose', and drew lots for the duty of committing a murder (ch. 16). Disraeli conjured up in *Sybil* (bk. 4, ch. 4) a ritual of robes and masks for the initiation of a new devotee vowed to carry out all union behests, including 'the chastisement of Nobs, the assassination of oppressive and tyrannical masters'.

In 1848 Kingsley issued a manifesto to the 'Workmen of England', asking them: 'Will the Charter make you free? Will it free you from the slavery to ten-pound bribes? Slavery to beer and gin? Slavery to every spouter who flatters your self-conceit?'[31] The contrast between bitter wrongs and the folly of trying to set them right by force came out most strongly of all in his *Alton Locke*, in 1850. A farm-labourers' riot – 'the old crust of sullen, dogged patience' exploding into 'reckless fury and brutal revenge' – is easily routed by a few armed men (ch. 28). The half-reluctant hero, an artisan whose education has the familiar double effect of deepening his sympathy for his class while putting a distance between him and it, finds himself to his dismay in a London garret 'full of pikes and daggers, brandished by some dozen miserable, ragged, half-starved artisans . . . the untaught, the despairing, the insane; "the dangerous classes", which society creates, and then shrinks in horror, like Frankenstein' (ch. 33).

In *Barnaby Rudge*, in 1841, Dickens drew a melodramatic picture of the Gordon Riots; in *Hard Times*, in 1854, he wrote with more discretion. By now the danger of a violent upheaval was receding, and he had made a sally from his London to see things in the industrial north for himself. In his description of a workers' meeting, the men are misled in their purpose of sending a workmate to Coventry for refusing to come into their plans; but there is a chairman to see fair play, the culprit is given his chance to speak, and the men are 'gravely, deeply, faithfully in earnest . . . these men, through their very delusions, showed great qualities, susceptible of being turned to the happiest and best account' (ch. 4). There is a Carlylean inflexion in Dickens's language here, as if he were at a loss for words to express something novel to him. But in his essay on 'The Working Man', in *The Uncommercial Traveller*, he was to declaim against one of Carlyle's sins — 'that great impertinence, Patronage', and to praise the workman for 'the instinctive revolt of his spirit' against the floods of patronising talk bestowed on him.

The honest toilers of *Hard Times* contrast forcibly with the agitator, Slackbridge, who is egging them on in pseudo-heroic accents — 'Oh my friends and fellow-countrymen, the slaves of an iron-handed and a grinding despotism!' Slackbridge is cunning, vindictive, inferior in every way to his untutored hearers. He belongs to a gallery of such portraits: the figure of the agitator was a bogy to the better-off classes, because it jarred with their creed that the poor ought to wait for public opinion to do its work instead of trying to work out their own redemption. There ought to be no representatives coming between workers and masters, wrote P. Gaskell; such men were picked in hours of excitement, likely to throw up 'the brawler, the factious man, the specious scoundrel' (p. 304). Mrs Gaskell could feel with Mary Barton's embittered father, and the 'hoards of vengeance in his heart against the employers', but she could not help adding a censure on ringleaders who inflame such passions (ch. 3). Her London delegate coming to organise the Manchester workers 'might have been a disgraced medical student of the Bob Sawyer class, or an unsuccessful actor, or a flashy shopman', and began with bombast 'in which he blended the deeds of the elder and the younger Brutus' — though he was businesslike enough when he came to the matter in hand (ch. 16). In later, less perilous times the sinister agitator could turn into a mere soapbox spouter like Anstey's bellowing republican: 'Hour turn'll come some day! We sha'n't *halways* be 'eld down, and muzzled, and silenced, and prevented uttering the hindignation we've a right to feel!'[32]

George Eliot, an impressionable young observer during the 1840s, could welcome the February revolution of 1848 in Paris, but had no desire to see it emulated on her side of the Channel. 'Our working classes are eminently inferior to the mass of the French people', with little 'perception or desire of justice', only selfish greed: 'a revolutionary movement would be simply destructive'.[33] *Felix Holt* came out in 1866, when political emotions could be recollected in relative tranquillity. Its moral is that labour ought to have leaders of its own, who will remain faithful to their class while rising above its weaknesses, as Felix (a skilled craftsman, not a mill-hand) is resolved to do:

Why should I want to get into the middle class because I have some
learning . . . That's how the working men are left to foolish devices
and keep worsening themselves: the best heads among them forsake
their born comrades, and go in for a house with a high door-step and
a brass knocker (ch. 5).

He is clear-sighted about the drunken habits of the neighbouring
colliers, and he tells a workers' meeting that they are not yet fit for
voting rights; he wants them to have power, but only for good and
constructive purposes (as usual, left undefined) — 'and I can see plainly
enough that our all having votes will do little towards it at present'
(ch. 30). His gospel, like his creator's, is public opinion. It is a symbolic
part of this idealist's fate to be injured in a senseless mob riot he tried
to restrain, and to be accused of provoking it (ch. 33). In 1867 George
Eliot distilled his and her philosophy into an 'Address to Working Men,
by Felix Holt', inculcating the lesson of every class's 'responsibility to
the nation at large'.

Mark Rutherford's *Revolution in Tanner's Lane*, equally remarkable
in its way, came another twenty years later. It might be called an
elegy for obscure and unavailing martyrs:

Who remembers the poor creatures who met in the early mornings
on the Lancashire moors or were shot by the yeomanry? They sleep
in graves over which stands no tombstone, or probably their bodies
have been carted away to make room for a railway which has been
driven through their resting-place (ch. 8).

At this date the uproar of past days could appear meaningless incoherence; what stood out was

the undisciplined wildness and feebleness of the attempts made by
the people to better themselves . . . the spectacle of a huge mass of
humanity goaded, writhing, starving, and yet so ignorant that it cannot choose capable leaders, cannot obey them if perchance it gets
them (ch. 11).

The two characters we admire are both out of tune with the movement
they have joined, one set apart from it by self-education and Calvinist
fervour, the other by birth. Zachariah is disgusted by the imbecile
applause of the streets for a Bourbon prince about to return to France
on the fall of Napoleon — 'the mob crying out, "God bless your

Majesty!" as if they owed him all they had' — and ruminates: 'As for the people so-called . . . I doubt whether they are worth saving' (ch. 1). When heated demands for action arise among the Friends of the People, Major Maitland warns them 'that not only were the middle classes all against them, but their own class was hostile. This was perfectly true, though it was a truth so unpleasant that he had to endure some very strong language, and even hints of treason' (ch. 8). Zachariah gets into prison, Maitland loses his life when an ill-planned Blanketeers' march is attacked by the Yeomanry. Rioters break into an inn cellar, and are then quickly mastered (ch. 25); a stock episode in the political novel. 'I ain't a Radical, I ain't', says a thirsty plebeian in another Rutherford novel: 'Wy, I've seed in my time an election last a week, and beer a-runnin' down the gutters. It was the only chance a poor man 'ad. Wot sort of chance 'as he got now?'[34]

Whatever their weaknesses, it appears that the first generations of the proletariat were capable of some vision of a world cleansed and renovated, and of the mighty put down from their seats. As their descendants became habituated to the mill, the slum, the industrial existence, shades of the prison-house seem to have closed on them. There used to be a Russian adage that the peasant must be boiled in the factory pot before he becomes a revolutionary; but it may be equally true that if he is kept in it too long the revolutionary juices are boiled out of him. After mid-century the labour movement was stiffening into 'labourism', content with what improvements could be got by trade unions, and relinquishing any design of transforming society. Part of the cause must be looked for in the abandonment of its own 'mission' by the industrial bourgeoisie, which it signalised by throwing its hat in the air for the Crimean War and ditching Cobden and Bright in the election of 1857. Henceforth each class was satisfied to find a place in the existing order, and to tail politically behind the one in front of it.

Many old Chartists were now, as one of them at Halifax wrote in 1859, 'so thoroughly disgusted at the indifference and utter inattention of the multitude to their best interests that they too are resolved to make no more sacrifices in a public cause' (Saville, p. 74). A legion of such former stalwarts shook their country's dust off their feet and emigrated. Jones remonstrated, and called on 'the tyrant-scourged pallid workers' to stay in England and make further sacrifices for their class (ibid., p. 196). Yet he often showed remarkable insight into the springs of mass action, the urge of material benefit required to fire the train, to attach a multitude of men and women to progressive causes. Between this and the call to heroic abnegation there was a deep-seated incongruity which has haunted socialism from the cradle. Emigration had an evident affinity with retreat into merely economic struggle, and Jones was indignant at this too, all the more because it meant that the better-placed workers — 'that worst of all aristocracies, the aristocracy of labour' — were practising a self-help which ignored the interests of the less fortunate. '*All Trades-unions are lamentable fallacies*', he declared. (ibid., pp. 194-5). On 12 May 1865 Engels reported to Marx: 'It seems to me that he has no longer any real faith in the proletarian movement as a whole.' O'Brien had lately died in poverty and neglect. In 1869-70 Thomas Cooper found the northern mill-workers better off, but 'noticed with pain that their moral and intellectual condition had deteriorated' (Beer, vol. 2, p. 221). No doubt there was some nostalgic mirage in his memories of ragged toilers enthralled by debates on justice and socialism; but times really had changed.

In this climate Positivism had a part to play with the working class like Christian Socialism in the Chartist epoch. Its highly elitist thinking could infuriate an old working-class Chartist and secularist like Holyoake, converted though he might be in his later years to collaboration with Liberalism. He derided the heaven offered to the workers by Comtists as a model pigsty, 'where the straw should be clean, the trough copious, the wash abundant, and where the Comtist priests would oft come and graciously pat their sleek backs, provided they did not squeal to get out'.[35] This was too sweeping a criticism, at least of men like Frederic Harrison, whom George Eliot, an admirer of Comte, consulted about the political side of *Felix Holt*, and Professor Beesly. Their object was 'the creation of an organised and all-powerful public opinion' guided by men of wisdom, but they looked to the workers as the class 'best prepared to receive large principles', because least corrupted by property. In this spirit, these two could be during the 1860s 'quite the closest and most influential advisers of the trade-union movement'.[36] They furnished also some of the scanty knowledge of the working classes gained by a new and somewhat anaemic generation of progressive intellectuals.[37] Beesly would have liked the unions to widen their horizons and be readier to take political action; in later years his influence on the labour movement faded.

When Samuel Plimsoll went into Parliament in 1868 to press for protection for seamen against the owners of 'coffin ships', and failed to carry his bill or to get a Royal Commission, he turned to the trade union movement for support. 'For years I was in very close contact with him', George Howell records.[38] No such contact had been sought by Captain Marryat when he wanted to get life in the navy made less evil for seamen, and appealed to middle-class opinion in 1836 with his *Mr Midshipman Easy*. One of his aims, doubtless, was to ensure naval loyalty at a time when Order was under threat, and the novel was also a satire on the democratic notions swallowed by Jack Easy's foolish parent. Old Mr Easy is a figure of fun, though his patent machine for altering the shape of men's skulls, and with it their characters, might serve as a warning against all mechanical or bureaucratic reformism.

When labour grievances broke out menacingly again, union leaders found an unexpected patron in Cardinal Manning. As head of a minority church, he wanted to enlarge its numbers; as scion of a wealthy family he wanted to shepherd labour away from socialism. In his biography of Cobden in 1881 Morley could credit the advent of a more civilised, less brutish trade unionism 'in no small degree to an active fraternization, to use Cobden's own word, with the leaders of the workmen by members of the middle class, who represented the best moral and social elements in the public opinion of their time' (vol. 2, p. 299). Well before this date Bright had been arguing that it was time for the working class to be given the vote, and maintaining, as he did in a speech at Birmingham on 29 January 1864, that there was now a more peaceful atmosphere, a wider acceptance of law and order: 'are not magistrates and all men in authority held in better regard than they were thirty or forty years ago?' There was enough agreement with this for him to carry the Reform Bill of 1867, against the rearguard headed by Robert Lowe with his alarmist talk of the ignorant and inebriated masses and his doctrine of élite rule – very close to Dr Johnson's definition of good government in 1773 as one where 'the wise see for the simple, and the regular act for the capricious'. Over this issue labour came back into politics, but with far more limited aspirations than in Chartist days. A vote now meant the right to ask for more porridge, not a new world.

One sequel was the Education Act of 1870. Bright pointed out in his speech at Edinburgh on 5 November 1868 that, though Britain led in so many fields, 'in the education of the people, of the working classes, we are much behind very many of the civilized and Christian nations of the world'. Teaching and learning had always been a debatable land between the classes, and on both sides there were contradictory attitudes. In *Mary Barton* we hear of hand-weavers round Oldham working away while 'Newton's *Principia* lies open on the loom, to be snatched at in work hours, but revelled over in meal times, or at night' (ch. 5). Factory life was only too likely to wipe out such thirst for knowledge: the new existence might lead towards better material rewards, but the old dying crafts could do more at times to stimulate mental alertness. Manchester workmen might be splendid at their duties, Brougham told the Mechanics' Institute, but they were deficient in 'love of scientific knowledge and useful learning'. This was in 1835, when Radical spokesmen were brimming with confidence, and he could proclaim that 'whatever improves men's minds tends to give them sober and virtuous habits'.[39] Conservatives had their doubts, like the Reverend Dr Folliott in Peacock's novel *Crotchet Castle* in 1831, indignant about the way his haystacks had been set on fire and his house broken into 'on the most scientific principles. All this comes of education' (ch. 17). E.P. Thompson quotes an old grumble that 'charity schools are nurses of Rebellion'. As time went on employers were in a quandary. Technical advances required literate workers: 'On the other hand, as the far-seeing ones clearly saw, an educated working class sooner or later made for radical changes . . . Education meant bigger immediate profits, but it was gambling with "revolution".'[40]

On the other hand again, education from above could be the means of instilling into working-class children ideas proper to their station. Cobbett felt misgivings about this when he visited New Lanark: his comment would apply still more obviously to any state-run primary education — 'it fashions the rising generation to habits of *implicit submission*, which is only another term for civil and political slavery'.[41] Teaching ragged boys and girls from mining villages to sing 'Happy English children!' was evidently meant to convince them that the working class had nothing to complain of.[42] Education as it emerged was of very poor quality, likely to perpetuate mental inertia and hinder any rising above the level of 'labourism'. Reciprocally, labourism damped any desire for more knowledge. As one self-taught and highly literate workman came to realise, late in the century: 'There was very little enthusiasm for education among the working classes themselves, though popular shibboleths and party catchwords were shouted loudly from their platforms.'[43] He was conscious that his own attainments made him a stranger in the eyes of his fellows. ' "I can't stick him: you never see him without a book", was a remark made about myself at a Congress' (p. 239). Such experiments as the founding of Toynbee Hall in 1884, which he helped to bring about, had little or no leavening effect on the lump. Working-class withdrawal from the political arena and from the national culture went together. One more feature of the retreat was a fading of the militant anti-religious or anti-clerical spirit of earlier days. Workmen might not be religious, but it was easy to prejudice them against anything that could be called atheistic.[44]

Cobden had endeavoured to convince businessmen that votes for workers would not bring socialism, but would turn them into 'conservatives', willing to 'elect their chiefs from a higher class than their own'.[45] His prediction was to be verified, as Gladstone, a late convert to extension of the franchise, saw. In his philosophy, expounded in an article of 1878 in the *Nineteenth Century*, however many might vote the few must rule: 'It is written in legible characters, and with a pen of iron, on the rock of human destiny, that within the domain of practical politics the people must in the main be passive.' Realistic enough about capitalist democracy, the People's William observed how acquiescence on the part of the working masses might turn into 'subserviency': 'We cannot be surprised if the mere desire to please the employer or the landlord, as such, steps into the vacant or lethargic mind.'

'Deference voting' did indeed come naturally to many sections of the working class as well as of the lower middle class; labourism could lend a morbid degree of truth to the legend of the masses pining for upper-class 'leadership'. Lancashire mill-hands, as the Webbs described them in *Industrial Democracy* (1897) were well organised, but politically naive compared with, for instance, the miners; engrossed with their chapels and co-operatives, they were ready to take their opinions on other things from mill-owners and land-owners (p. 259). There was of course India with its markets to provide a bond of interest between cottonworkers and their employers.

It was a paradox of these decades that while labour was drifting away from any socialist ideal, a number of intellectuals, especially among men of letters, were moving towards it. They were disillusioned with their society, deprived of forward momentum by the inertia of the bourgeoisie, and turned with more or less hopefulness towards the working class, if only as an unknown quantity. Mill, if very tentatively, pointed the way, under the tuition of Harriet Taylor, whom he married in 1851. She softened his animus against socialism, and persuaded him to write that 'The poor have come out of leading-strings, and cannot any longer be governed or treated like children' (*Life*, p. 307; cf. p. 312).

But a bridge to span the wide chasm was not soon built. Ruskin was typical of a good many intellectuals in being capable of much searching criticism of things as they were, but far less of seeing how they could be bettered, and what part the workers could play in the process. How, he asked in a lecture in the late 1860s at a Mechanics' Institute, was the manual worker to be 'comforted, redeemed, and rewarded? . . . Well, my good, laborious friends, these questions will take a little time to answer yet.'[46] It was for thinkers like himself to find the answers, he implied. He was one of several whom the Paris Commune, like the revolutions of 1848, pushed further left, making him more definitely a socialist if still a paternalistic one, while it horrified the bulk of respectable opinion. Another was George Meredith, who wrote that 'The people are the Power to come', and by the people meant the working class.[47]

In a more distinctly political and organised form the intellectuals of the Social Democratic Federation were trying to bring labour's mind back from bread-and-butter to higher things. Tom Mann, the pioneer working-class socialist, says that when he objected to the SDF's sweeping dismissal of trade unionism, its leader Hyndman exclaimed 'What were these precious unions? By whom were they led? By the most stodgy-brained, dull-witted, and slow-going time-servers in the country.'[48] There was a regrettable measure of truth in this dictum, but it is not one that a trade unionist could accept. Hyndman moreover was an 'aristocrat', and not of a sort to be congenial to labour. To a Scottish worker-socialist who encountered him at an Edinburgh meeting he seemed to belong to 'a world far removed from my humble environment and not at all like the disciple of Marx . . . He gave us a few words of advice how to behave and work for the social revolution and the party and we left quite unmoved.'[49] A brother Scot summed him up more bluntly as 'a vain, egotistical old peacock'.[50]

William Morris and his friends broke away from the SDF in 1884 to form the Socialist League. He too rejected trade unionism as irrelevant to socialism, and also rejected parliamentarism; which left the great task, 'the making of Socialists', too much abstracted from workaday life. In *Signs of Change* (1888) he paid tribute to Chartism as 'thoroughly a working-class movement', set going by 'the simplest and most powerful of all causes — hunger', but in its goals too one-sidedly political (pp. 102-4). In the utopian *News from Nowhere* in 1890, looking back on the revolution as something already got through, he ascribed it to idealism instead of hunger: 'the great motive-power of the change was a longing for freedom and equality', which touched the masses too, even though 'the slave-class could not conceive the happiness of a free life' (ch. 17). All this was remote enough from how labour in his Britain was really feeling, and in fact, after years of hopeful endeavour during the 1880s, Morris was deeply pessimistic at the end of the decade.

Young intellectuals in the 1880s fancied, as Shaw said, that 'Socialism had only to be put clearly before the working classes to concentrate the power of their immense numbers in one irresistible organisation.'[51]

This was proving an illusion on a par with that of the Narodnik students who tried to throw their arms round the Russian peasantry. Socialists, the Webbs objected in *Industrial Democracy*, lacked any intimate knowledge of trade union wants, while they brandished revolutionary programmes incomprehensible to the plain man (p. 539). Talented trade unionists, as in other countries, prized their sphere of work because it was their own, not shared like the management of political movements with men from outside whose superior training gave them the advantage. Snowden recalls in his autobiography that older trade union officials were undisguisedly hostile to the ILP in its early days, and the only insults Keir Hardie met with when he entered the House of Commons came from labour camp-followers of Liberalism (vol. 1, p. 75).

Mann convinced himself that 'the real educational work on labour questions is now going on mainly in the thousands of trade union branches and trades councils that exist in all centres of industry'.[52] Hence he called for decentralising of government. In fact England already had more of this than most countries, and it did make for labour participation in local business. But this might push bigger issues out of sight. Living among Lancashire workers in 1883 the future Beatrice Webb, not yet a socialist, found them diligent in matters of their own district, which they understood, but indifferent to anything further away: 'Parliament is such a far-off thing, that the more practical and industrious lot say that it is "gormless meddling with it" (useless), and they leave it to the "gabblers".' This she welcomed as 'one of the best preventives against the socialistic tendency of the coming democracy'.[53] They were prophetic words.

Fabian Socialism, starting in 1884, was as much a response to labour's political atrophy as a design to bring it about. Fabians had none of Marx's or Morris's 'faith in the people', but it is not clear that in the long run the presence or absence of such faith has made much difference either to the people or to the advance of socialism. And while labourism helped to mould a sober municipal-socialist mentality at one end of the scale, at the other it helped to produce by force of repulsion a bevy of highly individualistic socialists, among whom Shaw was only the most eccentric and perhaps the most talented. He was converted by *Das Kapital*, and set out with a desire to preach to the workers; his first open-air speech, to a couple of loafers on the grass of Hyde Park, may be said to have struck the keynote of his experience of them. Subsequently he came to the conclusion that 'proletarian agitation' only appealed to 'sects of idealists and cranks': solid trade unionists were interested in mundane things alone.[54]

Shaw's extraordinary medley of sense and nonsense may be put down to lack of the ballast that a strong popular movement (or belief in it, whether well-founded or illusory) could have given him. For want of this he often sank to being no more than an entertainer of the middle classes. His brigand band in Act III of *Man and Superman* (1903), with its comic anarchist and three wrangling social democrats, might almost be intended to reassure timorous capitalists that they had nothing to fear. His faith in socialism persisted, but it was a highly bureaucratic one. Nationalising industry would not affect the workers in any way, he held. 'To them the change will be only a change of masters.' Near the end of his biggest political work he wrote what may be taken as both his first and last word on his fellow-men. 'Capitalist mankind in the lump is detestable . . . Both rich and poor are really hateful in themselves. For my part I hate the poor.'[55]

H.G. Wells was never a devotee of Marx, and had no liking or respect for the working class to live down. His origin from a social level just above it left him with an ingrained repugnance, recognisable in his *Time Machine* nightmare of helots turned by ages of servitude into cannibal beasts. It was dawning on the upper classes, he wrote in his Fabian essay 'This Misery of Boots' in 1907, that they would be 'happier and more comfortable' under socialism:

> Much more likely to obstruct the way to Socialism is the ignorance, the want of courage, the stupid want of imagination of the very poor . . .! But, even with them, education is doing its work; and I do not fear but that in the next generation we shall find Socialists even in the slums (section 4).

Bizarre as this may sound, and deceptive as was Wells's notion of socialist enlightenment floating down like manna, not many working-class socialists have been produced by any other recipe. Easy optimism ended for him, as for so many others, with the Great War. Myriads of those caught up in it, he reflected, were doing no more thinking about it than a pet monkey in a house on fire. He like Shaw came to a conclusion gloomy but hard to dispute: 'The human mind is an instrument very easily fatigued. Only a few exceptions go on thinking restlessly — to the extreme exasperation of their neighbours.'[56]

Other socialists outside the labour ranks formed a variegated bevy. Some were only following a fashion, like G.K. Chesterton who joined, as he tells us in his autobiography, only because 'not being a Socialist

was a perfectly ghastly thing' (p. 111). Edward Carpenter was a Tol-
stoyan figure, 'a middle class man who wandered the streets in sandals
and broad hats copied from the American poet Walt Whitman, who
tried to live intimately with people of a lower social station and combine intellectual and manual work'.[57] Cunninghame Graham, injured
and arrested on Bloody Sunday in 1887, the year when he helped Keir
Hardie to found the Scottish Labour Party, was a laughing cavalier with
a strong dose of cynical humour, better fitted than graver men to survive in the left-wing wilderness: his wanderings carried him into many
other strange lands. Belfort Bax wandered into many corners of history,
and cherished a socialist 'religion' based, as he wrote in *The Ethics of
Socialism*, on an

> objective social morality, of which we see the germs even in the
> working classes of to-day when at their best — and when they are
> not, as they are to a large extent in this country, completely brutal-
> ised by the conditions of their life (p. 18).

One early middle-class Communist who got into Parliament adapted
himself to these conditions by going about

> unkempt and unshaven, wearing a dirty collar and clothes, trying to
> look 'proletarian'! He was an example of . . . the type that believes
> one has to use the most vulgar swear words when speaking; to be
> regardless of dress and a stranger to soap; and wear hobnailed boots
> and corduroys.[58]

Bax was hopeful enough to think that socialist ideas were penetrating
the trade unions, breaching 'the solid front of true British stupidity, of
which, unfortunately, hitherto they have been the embodiment' (Preface, 2nd ed.). In fact, what a critic had said long before of Lovett and
his friends, that they had no more influence over the workers of London
than of Constantinople,[59] might have been said now of these socialists.
Two works of fiction, by a socialist workman and anti-socialist with
working-class relatives, provide commentaries each as bleak as the
other. Robert Tressell the house-painter carries us into a frowsy world
where a few devoted socialists strive with faint success to lighten the
gloom of ignorance and nonsense, and toil-worn women skimping their
families on bread and margarine grow angry at the thought of 'the
wicked Socialists . . . trying to bring Ruin upon them'. He like so many
other novelists describes an election, when ragged workers throw them-

selves with senseless excitement into cheering for one or other of their rival exploiters[60] – an excitement sublimated since then, it often appears, into enthusiasm for football teams. In Gissing's *Demos, a Story of English Socialism* (1886), the working class is dangerous as well as ridiculous. An ardent young socialist workman, Mutimer, comes into money and drifts apart from his class, while striving to fulfil his ideals; he is denounced as a renegade. In the end Demos, tired of palaver, is ready for 'a good wild-beast roar, for a taste of bloodshed': Mutimer's house is besieged by a mob, and he is hit by a stone and killed while – a neatly ironical touch – a party of police is hurrying to the rescue.

Some could still believe in an unfolding alliance between elite and mass. J.A. Hobson saw the 1910 election as displaying an advance of rationality, Liberalism fortified by 'associated labour power'. In their confidence in mind's unfolding ascendancy over brute forces such men 'exalted their own role'.[61] It has been a chronic inclination of intellectuals to see a movement of the many in their own image. More frequent were misgivings, deepened by the exploration now spasmodically in progress into the lower social depths. Glimpses of lurking horrors caught the eye, like 'the crowded couch of incest in the warrens of the poor' in Tennyson's 'Locksley Hall Sixty Years After'. Against this background many doubts arose as to whether England's adulterated democracy could really bring the classes together, except at their worst points.

Trollope described a London election campaign in a novel of 1864-5 – *Can You Forgive Her?* – in a vein close to Carlyle's verdict on politics as 'beer and balderdash'. A few years later he tried one for himself, as Liberal candidate at Beverley, and his autobiography records it as just as disgusting. This was early in the new dispensation, but though bribery gave way as time went on to other modes of inducement these were often little more refined, and a long purse was as potent as ever. Watching voters at a London County Council polling station in a poor district, confused and tired, one of them drunk, Graham Wallas experienced 'an intense conviction that this could not be accepted as even a decently satisfactory method' of choosing a city government.[62] 'Thirty years ago', G.W.E. Russell wrote of democracy in 1909, 'it was an ideal which ardent and generous souls honestly worshipped . . . Beyond all question the result has been disappointment and disillusionment.'[63]

What was flourishing instead was Tory demagogy, an easier and cheaper substitute for Christian Socialism whose nostrum was turning social resentment into anti-foreign feeling. J.M. Barrie was to make fun in *The Admirable Crichton* of an amiable earl who held monthly tea parties where his family had to wait on the servants, a ceremony equally irksome to both sides. But in the form of Primrose League jollities this kind of hobnobbing had a large share in Tory strategy. 'The most dangerous demagogues', a Liberal commented wryly, 'are the clever Conservatives who despise the people.'[64] In the years before 1914 progressives from the working class or from outside it often suffered from the same despondency. 'At this moment the Roman decadent phase of *panem et circenses* is being inaugurated under our eyes', Shaw wrote in the preface to *Man and Superman*. Frederick Rogers was conventionally patriotic, but a meeting with leading Co-operators during the Boer War left him disgusted: 'I was hardly prepared for the solid unbending Toryism of the older men, and the meek acquiescence or flippant contempt of the younger ones, in relation to social affairs.'[65] By this time a high Anglican, Rogers turned to Conservatism towards the end of his life. In Galsworthy's novel of 1911, *The Patrician* (pt. 1, ch. 22), an old Chartist stands in a crowd waiting to hear an election result announced, and there are 'tears rolling down his cheeks into his beard' as the Radical candidate is beaten: 'You wouldn't remember forty-eight, I suppose. There was a feeling in the people then – we would ha' died for things in those days.'

Marx and Engels cast the horoscope of the working class at a time when to most it seemed no more than a useful or troublesome drudge. How precisely, under what impulses or compulsions, it was to perform its task of transforming society and abolishing class, is an intricate question which they never fully answered. But as time went on they grew impatient to see it setting about its task in good earnest. Engels could sound as disillusioned as he reproached Jones with becoming. Of the 1868 election he wrote to Marx on 18 November: 'Once again the proletariat has discredited itself terribly ... Everywhere the proletariat are the tag, rag and bobtail of the official parties.'[66] On a more humdrum level he was conscious of awkwardness in the way of co-operation with it. 'Woe be to the man', he warned his friend Florence Wischnewetzsky in a letter of 9 February 1887, 'who, being of bourgeois origin or superior education, goes into the movement and is rash enough to enter into money relations with the working-class element. There is sure to be a dispute', and suspicion that he is out to make a profit.

Marx's last years may have been overshadowed by a failing conviction of the proletariat being equal to its mission. He had called spirits from the vasty deep; perhaps there were moments when Hotspur's ironical rejoinder to Glendower struck on his ear — 'But will they come, when you do call for them?' Writing on 9 April 1870 to Meyer and Vogt he gave it as his mature opinion that the decisive blow at the British ruling class would have to be launched in Ireland, not at home. 'Every industrial and commercial centre in England now possesses a working-class population divided into two *hostile* camps, English proletarians and Irish proletarians. . . . This antagonism is artificially kept alive and intensified . . . by all the means at the disposal of the ruling classes.'[67] There had been political as well as economic gain to capitalism from bringing over Irish blacklegs. His disciple Kautsky, after several years in England, wrote scathingly of the working class there and its lack of any desire to revolutionise society, which alone, he argued, could give any working class an ethic and ideals of its own (or, he might have added, class consciousness in the fullest sense):

> The emancipation of their class appears to them as a foolish dream. Consequently, it is foot-ball, boxing, horse racing and opportunities for gambling which move them the deepest and to which their entire leisure time, their individual powers, and their material means are devoted.[68]

Years went by, and another voice was to be heard lamenting that the modern British workman, preoccupied with demarcation disputes, was as 'hopelessly Conservative' as the handicraftsman of old: 'The great fault of the mass of wage-labour is the failure to think scientifically at all. The most elementary questions are often beyond their understanding.' Above all, they were destitute of any knowledge of history, of great changes having taken place in the past and therefore being possible again in the future (Clunie, vol. 2, p. 111). Without memory of yesterday there can indeed be no vision of tomorrow, and in this light history is indispensable to progress. Not surprisingly against this background, elitist attitudes were tenacious among more or less progressive social thinkers. J.M. Keynes dismissed Communism on the ground that it 'exalts the boorish proletariat above the bourgeois and intelligentsia who, with whatever faults, are the quality of life and surely carry the seeds of all advancement'. Beatrice Webb found Beveridge alarmed by the shocks of 1940 into recognition of the need for social planning: 'But as of old, Beveridge is obstinately convinced that he and his class have to do the job, and the Trade Unionists have to be ignored and the wage-earner *ordered* to work.'[69]

A century before this the old Radical Bamford was looking back gloomily on what he could only see as a record of failure and folly: 'Groping in a mental and political twilight, we stumbled from error to error, the dim-eyed calling on the blind to follow.'[70] Socialist parties in our own day, if equally candid, would have not many fewer short-comings to confess. But whatever the defects of leadership or programme, it would seem that socialist consciousness has always been restricted to a very few, and that the bulk of the working class (as of every other, it may be) is inert except when activated by some direct material stimulus. This in turn would imply that most collective conduct is 'behaviouristic', and most of history mechanically determined, with little room for dialectical subtlety of combination and change except at corners and fringes, whence forces may on rare occasions emerge and intervene decisively. It must be added that in spite of long investigation the true nature of classes remains not much less mysterious than the cloudy figures of Blake's prophetic poems, masked actors of the drama of history.

Notes

1. Sir G.O. Trevelyan, *Life and Letters of Lord Macaulay* (1876), ch. 10.

2. *Collected Works*, vol. 3, ed. A.R. Waller and A. Glover (1902), pp. 37-8.

3. *The Last Chronicle of Barset* (1867), ch. 12.

4. *The Private Papers of Henry Ryecroft* (1903), part 4, no. 14.

5. St Loe Strachey, 'Infringing a Political Patent' (1895), in M. Goodwin (ed.), *Nineteenth Century Opinion* (Harmondsworth, 1951), p. 69.

6. D. Cecil, *Melbourne* (1954 ed.), p. 72.

7. Lord Brougham, *Letter to the Marquess of Lansdowne . . . on the Late Revolution in France* (3rd ed., 1848), p. 89.

8. M. St J. Packe, *The Life of John Stuart Mill* (1954), pp. 101, 298.

9. Rev. G. Ewing, *The Duty of Christians to Civil Government* (Edinburgh, 1799), pp. 12-13.

10. P. Gaskell, *The Manufacturing Population of England* (1833), p. 282.

11. M. Beer, *A History of British Socialism*, vol. 1 (1929 ed.), p. 235.

12. 'The Claims of Labour', in *Edinburgh Review*, vol. 81 (1845), p. 503.

13. R.G. Gammage, *History of the Chartist Movement 1837-1854* (1854; new ed., Newcastle, 1894), pp. 266-7.

14. John Saville, *Ernest Jones: Chartist* (1952), p. 106.

15. Charles Kingsley, *Alton Locke, Tailor and Poet* (1850), ch. 33.

16. Gammage, *History of the Chartist Movement*, p. 408.

17. Saville, *Ernest Jones*, p. 90.

18. Y.V. Kovaleva, *An Anthology of Chartist Literature* (Moscow, 1956), pp. 350, 353.

19. *Tour in Scotland and in the Four Northern Counties of England* (1833), p. 55.

20. *Rural Rides*, vol. 2 (Everyman ed., 1912), pp. 73, 231.

21. J. Morley, *The Life of Richard Cobden*, vol. 1 (1881), pp. 249, 299.

22. Extract in M. Palmer (ed.), *Writing and Action* (1938), p. 289.

23. D.A. Wilson, *Carlyle to Threescore-and-Ten* (1929), p. 248.

24. B. Disraeli, *Sybil, or the Two Nations* (1845), bk 3, ch. 8.

25. *The Crown of Wild Olive* (lectures of the 1860s) (1906) pp. 105-6, 181-2.

26. *Henry Ryecroft*, part 2, no. 22.

27. J.L. and B. Hammond, *Lord Shaftesbury* (1923; Harmondsworth, 1939 ed.), pp. 29, 55.

28. Ibid., pp. 135-6.

29. Ibid., p. 248.

30. Kovaleva, *Chartist Literature*, p. 312.

31. S.E. Baldwin, *Charles Kingsley* (Ithaca, 1934), pp. 43-4.

32. 'F. Anstey', *Voces Populi*, 2nd series (1892; 1912 ed.), p. 145.

33. J.W. Cross, *George Eliot's Life* (New York, 1885), vol. 1, p. 131.

34. 'Mark Rutherford', *Catharine Furze* (1893), ch. 16.

35. G.J. Holyoake, 'Impatience in Politics' (1877), in Goodwin, *Nineteenth Century Opinion*, p. 222.

36. R. Harrison, 'Professor Beesly and the Working-class Movement', in A. Briggs and J. Saville (eds), *Essays in Labour History* (1960), pp. 209, 213.

37. See C. Harvie, *The Lights of Liberalism: University Liberals and the Challenge of Democracy 1860-86* (1976), pp. 147 ff.

38. G. Howell, *Labour Legislation, Labour Movements and Labour Leaders* (1902; 2nd ed., 1905), p. 265.

39. *Speeches of Henry Lord Brougham*, vol. 3 (Edinburgh, 1838), pp. 161, 171.

40. T. Johnston, *The History of the Working Classes in Scotland* (Glasgow, [1929]), p. 288.

41. *Tour in Scotland . . .*, pp. 208 ff.

42. See R. Colls, ' "Oh Happy English Children!"': Coal, Class and Education in the North-East', in *Past and Present* no. 73 (1976).

43. Frederick Rogers, *Labour, Life and Literature. Some Memories of Sixty Years* (1913; ed. D. Rubinstein, Brighton, 1973), p. 52.

44. See O. Chadwick, *The Secularization of the European Mind in the Nineteenth Century* (Cambridge, 1975), ch. 4: 'The attitudes of the worker'.

45. Letter to *The Scotsman*, 25 January 1858, in Johnston, *Working Classes in Scotland*, p. 258.

46. *The Crown of Wild Olive*, pp. 50-1.

47. See Jack Lindsay, 'The Commune of Paris and English Literature', in *Marxist Quarterly*, July 1954.

48. Dona Torr, *Tom Mann and his Times* (1956), p. 207.

49. J. Clunie, *Labour is my Faith. The Autobiography of a House Painter*, vol. 1 (Dunfermline, 1954), p. 92.

50. T. Bell, *Pioneering Days* (1941), p. 38.

51. Torr, *Tom Mann*, p. 180.

52. T. Mann, 'The Development of the Labour Movement' (1890), in Goodwin, *Nineteenth Century Opinion*, p. 210.

53. Beatrice Webb, *My Apprenticeship* (1926; 1929 ed.), p. 139.

54. *The Intelligent Woman's Guide to Socialism, Capitalism, Sovietism and Fascism* (1928; 1929 ed.), p. 478.

55. Ibid., pp. 383, 489.

56. *War and the Future* (1917), pp. 182-3, 187.

57. Sheila Rowbotham, 'In Search of Carpenter', in *History Workshop*, no. 3 (1977), p. 126.

58. Bell, *Pioneering Days*, p. 263.

59. T. Rothstein, *From Chartism to Labourism* (1929), part 1, ch. 5.

60. Robert Tressell, *The Ragged Trousered Philanthropists* (1914; 1955 ed.), ch. 48.

61. P.F. Clarke, 'The Progressive Movement in England', in *Trans. Royal Hist.*

Soc., 5th Series, vol. 24 (1974), pp. 168-9.
  62. *Human Nature in Politics* (1908), pp. 229-30.
  63. *Collections and Recollections,* Series 2 (1909), p. 78.
  64. J.A. Spender, *The Comments of Bagshot* (1907), p. 23.
  65. Rogers, *Labour, Life and Literature,* p. xxii.
  66. Dona Torr, *The Correspondence of Marx and Engels* (1934), pp. 251-2.
  67. Ibid., pp. 288-90.
  68. *The Social Revolution* (1902; English ed., Chicago, 1916), p. 102.
  69. P. Addison, *The Road to 1945* (1975), pp. 37, 118.
  70. *Bamford's Passages in the Life of a Radical,* vol. 2 (ed. H. Dunckley, 1893), p. 184.

4 THE LANGUAGE OF 'MASS' AND 'MASSES' IN NINETEENTH-CENTURY ENGLAND

Asa Briggs

Out of the crucible of early industrialisation in England there emerged, along with much else, a new language of social 'class'.[1] Yet the new language neither completely supplanted the older language of 'ranks', 'orders' and 'degrees' nor excluded the use and development through use of other social concepts. Some of these concepts, indeed, were capable, like the concept of 'class' itself, both of expressing and of accelerating new ways of thinking and feeling about group consciousness and action. They could also serve, even if sometimes confusingly, as central concepts in general social analysis. Like the term 'class' or political terms like 'the People', they each have their own history.

The alternative social concepts include the words 'mass' and 'masses'. These were not completely new terms in 1800, but as late as 1837 Tom Moore could still refer not directly to 'the masses' but rather to ' "the masses" as they are called'.[2] The quotation marks around the word 'masses' (though they had never been thought necessary around the word 'mass') did not completely disappear until the last decades of the century.

One of the most remarkable early nineteenth-century references to the term 'masses' within quotation marks – a passage from the young Disraeli, written in 'Carlylese' – suggested that the term, which he disliked as much as the term 'the People', had only just been invented by 'Papineau' orators and writers. 'Who can resist the Masses? Mighty Masses, mighty mysterious!' Disraeli asked. 'Papineau writers out of Parliament concoct articles in reviews, specially in Sunday journals, about the Masses; would have no tax on pen, ink, or paper, or be supplied by the Government gratis, that Masses may read and believe their lucubrations, which all others do most heartily resist.' There were to be many glimpses across the Atlantic to the United States and some across the seas to Australia when later in the nineteenth century writers and politicians complained of the power of 'the masses', but Disraeli on this early occasion was referring to Canada where Papineau, the leader of the 'reform party', had been associated with the rebellion of 1837. Disraeli feared contagion:

What if said Papineau orators and writers by some mischance of a *lapsus linguae* . . . do but omit the initial letter of that name, wherewith they have defined, and in a manner baptised, their countrymen? And may not the next stage come even to this? —

First	Public
Second	People
Third	Masses
Fourth	Asses

'O Richard! *O Mon Roi!*' O England! O my country! Shall I live even to see this?[3]

By the end of the nineteenth century Englishmen had lived through many different 'stages' of political, economic and social evolution, and orators and writers were using the terms 'mass' and 'masses' more than they had done during the 1830s. They were backed, too, by changing market forces, expressed in the rise of disposable incomes, the production of 'branded' goods, the growth of advertising and the beginnings of 'mass entertainment'. The 'masses' had become a target, and it could be stated in 1897, however misleadingly — before the term 'mass advertising' came into use — that 'the hoardings . . . act as a pretty safe index to the taste of the masses'.[4] Although twentieth-century terms like 'mass entertainment' (or for that matter 'mass production' and 'mass distribution') were also not yet in use, men like William Lever or Alfred Harmsworth knew what they implied and built their growing enterprises on an appeal to 'the millions'.[5] There were occasional customers or readers, moreover, who knew exactly what was happening. Thus, a *Tit-Bits* reader in 1897 claimed that while 'the classes take in the daily newspapers . . . the masses prefer to take in the weekly supplements, where the week's news is served up with a liberal seasoning of anecdotes, extracts from books, with instalments of one or two serial stories thrown in'.[6]

Meanwhile, the political uses of the term 'masses' were pointing not to manipulation but to militancy. When Thomas Kirkup noted in 1887 'a growing spirit of righteous discontent with our social and economic arrangements' among 'the mass of serious and thinking men',[7] the term 'masses' was already in widespread use in socialist circles. Morris thought of himself and his comrades as 'instructors of the masses'[8], although he used the term rather sparingly, and a little later (albeit viewed in retrospect) Tom Mann discussed his determination 'to arouse the inert mass of workers with the old religious fervour'.[9]

It became possible by the early twentieth century to summarise history in 'mass' terms, relating it to biological evolution.[10] 'The conflicts and movements that make history', J.R. MacDonald wrote in 1911, 'have been the conflicts and movements of masses and organisations. The colossal historical figure has been the man endowed with the capacity to gather up in himself the life of his time.'[11]

To try to trace the changing way in which the words 'mass' and 'masses' were used in the nineteenth century is no more of an academic exercise than my earlier attempt to trace the language of 'class', for developments in social nomenclature and vocabulary usually reflect basic changes not only in men's ways of viewing society but in society itself. Aspects of nineteenth-century history can be illuminated in the process, not least developments in both the political and economic systems. There is an added interest, however, in such an attempt in that the language of 'mass' and 'masses', then rudimentary, was to become a major language in the distant future. Indeed, it has been only during the second half of the twentieth century — in a different, if at the same time derived, economic, social and cultural context from that of the early years of industrialisation — that composite terms involving 'mass' and 'masses' have proliferated.[12] There are now so many of them that they play an important part in almost every kind of contemporary social analysis, whether or not the analysis continues to rest on or cling to the language of 'class' also. 'Orders', 'ranks' and 'degrees' have long seemed to belong to the past. 'Mass' concepts, however, are felt to belong to the future, to 'post-industrial' as much as to 'industrial' societies.

Most contemporary analysts, with the exception of Raymond Williams,[13] have ignored the nineteenth-century history of the term or have dealt with it sketchily or misleadingly, often paraphrasing in the language of 'mass' and 'masses' the arguments of nineteenth-century writers who did not use this language themselves.[14] It is important to remember how recent much of the development of that 'mass' language has been. Thus, the *Supplement to the Oxford Dictionary* selects a sentence in Richard Hoggart's *The Uses of Literacy* as the first English source of the use of the term 'mass culture', and this book, interesting also in relation to the history of 'class', did not appear until 1957.[15] T.S. Eliot's *Notes Towards A Definition of Culture* (1948) is cited for the first English use noted of the even more basic term 'mass society'.[16]

The nineteenth-century historical background of the second of these concepts has been over-simplified even by the most interesting writers on the subject, who have almost always preferred attaching labels to exploring trails. When they give nineteenth-century references, they refer usually to non-English writers — sometimes Marx, but more often de Maistre, de Tocqueville, Durkheim, Tönnies, Tarde and Le Bon, not all of whom used the word 'masses'. Indeed it was only the last of these at the end of the century (1895), who stated categorically that 'the destinies of nations are elaborated at present in the heart of the masses, and no longer in the councils of princes'.[17] Le Bon was disturbed by the 'irrationality' of 'mass politics' and the 'determination' of the 'masses' utterly 'to destroy society as it now exists'.[18] He shifted his attention very quickly, however, from 'masses' to 'crowds' so that his (inadequately documented) observation and speculation have tended to be regarded as a contribution to the study of 'collective' or 'mass behaviour' rather than to intellectual or social history.[19] His pre-occupations, though not his values, have been shared by recent generations of social historians who have concerned themselves increasingly with 'crowds', defined by one of the most interesting and influential of them as 'direct face-to-face groups'.[20] The history of the term 'masses', a broader and a vaguer term, has remained unwritten, although it raises more complex social issues concerning organisation as well as protest and both apathy (or 'manipulation') and militancy.[21] The face-to-face restriction is removed too.

Two twentieth-century books, more mentioned than read — and neither within an 'English tradition' — have tended to block the way to detailed historical enquiry — Ortega y Gasset's *The Revolt of the Masses* (1930), which appeared in English two years later, and Karl Mannheim's *Man and Society in An Age of Reconstruction* (1940). Neither is of much help to historians, although the latter includes excellent bibliographical footnotes on the German approaches to 'mass' and 'masses', particularly relating to the twentieth century.[22] The contribution of the Frankfurt School to the study of the subject, based as it was on a reading both of Marx and of Freud, treated Le Bon's work, too, as 'the beginning of modern "mass psychology" ', and characteristically drew on no English sources.[23] It was strongly influenced, moreover, by twentieth-century experience of war and 'totalitarianism' which shaped later studies of 'mass society', like those of Hannah Arendt. The Second World War, indeed, influenced the language of 'mass' even more than the Napoleonic Wars had influenced the development of the language of 'class'.[24]

Ortega y Gasset, writing before the rise of Hitler, was more influenced by Spengler than by Marx or Freud. In his far from consistent argument he deliberately separated questions of 'mass' from questions of 'class' by defining the term 'masses' not as 'solely or mainly the working masses', but as 'the average man' multiplied. He began not with the past but with 'the visual experience' of 'the present moment':

> Towns are full of people, houses full of tenants, hotels full of guests, trains full of travellers, cafés full of customers, parks full of promenaders, consulting-rooms of famous doctors full of patients, theatres full of spectators, and beaches full of bathers. What previously was, in general, no problem, now begins to be an everyday one, namely to find a room.[25]

We start – not unengagingly – neither with society nor with history, but with population. But we go on to unsubstantiated assertion. 'In the presence of one individual we can decide whether he is "mass" or not. The mass is all that which sets no value on itself – good or ill – based on specific ground but which feels itself "just like everybody", and nevertheless is not concerned about it.'[26] Such equations can scarcely help social understanding, but to understand how it became possible to formulate them in the early twentieth century it is useful to look back to the nineteenth.

I

In the early nineteenth century the idea of 'the mass' was obviously related both to number and to scale and to 'massing', the bringing together of people in towns or in factories. 'The rapid progress of our manufactures and commerce', wrote a reviewer in 1833, 'has accumulated great masses of population, in which society has assumed new relations among its several classes.'[27] This review is interesting in that it registers the confluence of different streams of language. 'The various orders of society are mutually dependent', the reviewer began. 'Their interests are interwoven with a complexity which cannot be unravelled; and natural connexions tend to diffuse throughout the mass the happiness or misery suffered by any particular portion.'[28]

Already the words 'mass' and 'masses' were being treated as more than numerical aggregates.[29] Like the word 'multitude' which preceded them, they already had connotations of value. Just as the 'multitude' could be conceived of either as 'a many-headed monster' or as a source of popular strength,[30] so the terms 'mass' and 'multitude' and 'masses' could carry with them a sense either of fear (and mystery) or of power. Disraeli was not always thinking of Papineau when he used the term, and he could curdle the imagination of his readers when he wrote of 'the mighty mysterious masses of the swollen towns'.[31] Like Carlyle, who also expressed sympathy towards the 'miserable millions . . . fermenting into unmeasured masses of failure' and 'the dumb millions born to toil',[32] he appreciated that they could be stirred.[33] 'The way to move great masses of men is to show that you yourself are moved', Hazlitt had written in 1825.[34] But there was more than one way. 'Men who discern in the misery of the toiling complaining millions not misery, but only a raw-material which can be wrought upon and traded in, for one's own poor hide-bound theories and egoisms', Carlyle claimed, were 'men . . . of the questionable species'. They were demagogues 'to whom millions of living fellow-creatures, with beating hearts in their bosoms, beating, suffering, hoping' were 'masses' — and he used quotation marks — 'mere "explosive masses for blowing down Bastilles with", for voting at hustings for *us*'.[35]

For Carlyle, as for Disraeli, demagogues were manipulators. Parents, teachers, supervisors, leaders, deserved 'obedience': they were part of a hierarchy, and *they* did not think in terms of 'masses'. Demagogues did. This argument was related first to Carlyle's profound interest in the French Revolution and in the 'sans culottism' which he saw at the heart of it and second to his concern that the laissez-faire society in England, which as he conceived it had been created by a parallel English industrial revolution, should find proper 'governance'. 'How an Aristocracy, in these present times and circumstances, could, if never so well disposed, set about governing the Under Class? What they should do; endeavour or attempt to do? That is even the question of questions.'[36]

Carlyle did not know how to answer it. Others believed that the answer could only be found in 'the masses' themselves. 'The spark of patriotism runs with electric until the whole mass vibrates in unison swiftness from pulse to pulse', the *Black Dwarf* exclaimed in what reads like late nineteenth-century language in 1819. 'Then, despots, tremble for the hour of retribution is at hand.'[37] In 1831 during the struggle for the Reform Act the *Manchester Guardian* could pin its faith not in revolution, but in reform, with a new electorate consisting of 'the great mass of the property, the knowledge, the moral energy and the respectability of the country'. A writer in the same issue, however, was aware of the contrast between political hopes and economic facts and spoke of 'the great mass of the lower classes' being obliged 'by the necessity of earning a subsistence to submit to a daily and protracted toil'.[38] Such contrasts were further sharpened after the passing of the Reform Bill and during the political and economic crises of the late 1830s and 1840s, when the language of 'class' was sharpened.[39] Yet it

was W. Cooke Taylor, an apologist of the new industrial system, who
held that one day 'the masses' must 'like the slow rising and gradual
swelling of an ocean . . . bear all the elements of society aloft upon its
bosom'.[40]

One of the most interesting pieces of early writing on 'the masses'
— and one which exposes some of the difficulties in handling the concept — is a remarkable early essay by John Stuart Mill, first published
in 1836.[41] As 'civilization' advances, Mill argued, 'power passes more
and more from individuals, and small knots of individuals, to masses'.
Indeed, it is a 'law of human affairs' — and of 'progress' — that in the
process 'the importance of the masses becomes constantly greater, that
of individuals less'. Within the masses Mill included both 'a middle class'
and 'operative classes', each benefiting — through education and property — from the advance of 'civilization'. Like his father before him,
he did not suggest any possible conflict of interest between them, and
his conclusion — though he quoted de Tocqueville — was optimistic.[42]
'When the masses become powerful, an individual, or a small band of
individuals, can be nothing except by influencing the masses.' He
urged 'those who call themselves Conservatives' to consider carefully
'whether, when the whole power in society is passing into the hands of
the masses, they really think it possible to prevent the masses from
making that power predominant as well in the government as elsewhere'.

Mill's main doubts about the future concerned not politics but
culture, and he got near to anticipating not only most of the arguments which he was to advance twenty years later in *On Liberty* but
also to the arguments of David Riesman and even of Ortega y Gasset.[43]
With the rise of 'the masses', the individual got so 'lost in the crowd' —
he repeated this phrase after a page or two and he used it again in *On
Liberty*[44] — that he was in peril of losing his individuality. 'When the
opinions of masses of merely average men are everywhere become or
becoming the dominant power', he wrote in *On Liberty*, 'exceptional
individuals, instead of being deterred, should be encouraged in acting
differently from the mass.' The 'danger' which threatened 'human
nature' was not 'the excess but the deficiency of personal impulses
and preferences'.[45]

Accusations have been made against Mill that he generalised too
remotely and bookishly about social context,[46] and it is certainly
remarkable how close were Mill's judgements on the 1830s and 1850s
given the marked social, political and cultural differences between them.
Already, indeed, he was discerning in the 1830s 'mass' problems con-

cerning what came to be called in the twentieth century 'mass advertising' and 'public relations'. As people ceased to know everybody,
'quackery' and 'puffing' became more and more commonplace and
corrupting. Mill pointed too to what in the twentieth century became
thought of as problems of 'mass culture'. 'This is a reading age; and
precisely because it is so reading an age, any book which is the result
of profound meditation is, perhaps, less likely to be duly and profitably
read than at a former period.' Similar points were to be taken up by
Matthew Arnold in *Culture and Anarchy* in 1869, although the philosophical and cultural approach was different, as was the political context.[47] 'Our society is probably destined to become more democratic',
Arnold had written in 1861, 'Who or what will give a high tone to the
nation then?'[48] 'The question is not about individuals', he went on, as
Ortega y Gasset might have done. 'The question is about the common
bulk of mankind, persons without extraordinary gifts or exceptional
energy.'[49]

Mill ended his 1836 essay with a provocative but bracing appeal for
individualism. 'The main thing which social changes can do . . . — and
it is what the progress of democracy is insensibly but certainly accom-
plishing — is gradually to put an end to every kind of unearned distinction, and let the only road open to honour and ascendancy be that of
personal qualities.' This was a not dissimilar message to that of Samuel
Smiles, whose *Self-Help* appeared in the same years as *On Liberty*.
Smiles summarised the essence of his message most succinctly not in
1859 but in 1880, however, on the eve of a socialist upthrust:

> Men cannot be raised in masses as the mountains were in the early
> geological states of the world. They must be dealt with as units; for
> it is only by the elevation of individuals that the elevation of the
> masses can be effectively secured.[50]

By then Mill had been dead for seven years. His 'chapters on socialism',
however, written in 1869, had only just been published for the first
time. They recognised more explicitly than Mill had ever done before
that distinctive 'working-class' claims were being and would increasingly
be put forward — and resisted — in a way which would transform politics. Mill no longer used the word 'mass' or implied an identity of
interest. 'The classes, which the system of society makes subordinate,
have little reason to put faith in any of the maxims which the same
system of society may have established as principles.'[51]

II

Before turning to the development of a socialist vocabulary of 'mass' and 'masses', it is necessary to consider more fully the middle years of the nineteenth century, when the ideas of 'mass' and 'masses' were related not only to arguments about individualism and individuality but to arguments about 'brains and numbers', what we would now call the role of elites.[52] 'The extreme advanced party is likely for the future to have on its side a great portion of the most highly cultivated intellect in the nation', wrote John Morley in 1867, 'and the contest will lie between brains and numbers on the one side, and wealth, rank, vested interest, possession in short, on the other.'[53]

The issue of franchise reform stimulated intellectual discussion of such subjects between 1865 and 1874, but the discussion did not start or end there. It ranged widely over the long period of history since the 'dual revolutions', political and industrial, in France and in England in the late eighteenth century (with occasional references back to the ancient world) and over countries as different from each other and as widely separated as the United States, Australia and Germany as well. Thus, Morley related his speculations to those of Burke and de Maistre,[54] while in his notebooks for 1868 Arnold quoted a letter of Baron Bunsen, written in 1814, 'it is too true that our own class, the guild of the studious, does too little with the object of working upon the nation'.[55]

Both the 'nation' and 'humanity' had their disciples during the mid-Victorian years, with Matthew Arnold drawing attention to 'the fermenting mind of the Nation' and the Positivists, 'the party of Humanity', looking to the 'working classes', what Frederic Harrison, one of the most active English followers of Comte, called 'the horny-handed millions'.[56] On his first visit to the industrial north Harrison was awed rather than frightened by 'the enormous weight, mass and power of the manufacturing districts'.[57] 'The working class is the only class which (to use a paradox) is not a class', he generalised. 'It is the nation.'[58]

It was not only the Positivists who shared this conviction: it runs through many of the essays written for the remarkable volume of 1867, *Essays on Reform*,[59] many of them inspired by a deep distaste for the speeches and writings of Robert Lowe. And once reform had been accomplished — the second Reform Act of 1867 — John Morley could write with delight of the transfer of power 'from a class to the nation'.[60] For Morley, as for several of the essayists, 'class' and 'nation' (they did not use the term 'masses') were in opposition. 'Classes' were not conceived of in Marxist or proto-Marxist terms. 'What is a "class"?', G.C. Brodrick, the first of the essayists asked, 'but a purely artificial aggregate, which may consist of hundreds, thousands or millions, according to the fancy or design of its framer?'[61] The 'educated classes' might ally themselves with 'the masses' serving as vanguards or elites, but the 'privileged classes' would inevitably stand in the way.[62]

This was a way of viewing society which reached its classic climax in a famous Gladstone speech of 1886 when he told a Liverpool crowd that 'all the world over' he would 'back the masses against the classes'.[63] Already by 1870, however, Gladstone's future biographer, Morley, looked forward to a day 'when all this talk about classes shall be at an end, and when every citizen shall be able to rise to the conception of a national life'. Meanwhile, he insisted, 'in the multitude you have the only body whose real interests can never like those of special classes and minor orders [note the linking], become anti-social'.[64]

This view, strongly opposed by Lowe, lost some of its point for educated 'liberal' sympathisers with the 'masses' when the Conservative Party, not the Liberal Party, won the General Election of 1874. It seemed then, indeed, however justly, that the strongest 'mass' element in the 'masses' — what John Bright had called 'the residuum'[65] — was more willing to respond to bribes than to arguments. The demand for popular education, so eloquently advanced by John Morley, was as urgent for him as it was for Lowe. Disraeli, of course, saw things differently, believing that the attraction of his anti-egalitarian philosophy of life saved civilised society from being reduced 'to human flocks and herds'.[66] Meanwhile, Walter Bagehot, who had maintained in 1867 that 'the mass of uneducated men' could not be expected to 'choose' their rulers, put his trust not in philosophies of life but in working-men's continuing 'deference'. 'If you look at the mass of the constituencies, you will see that they are not very interesting people . . . The mass of the people yield obedience to a select few.'[67]

Such assessments were based partly on observation, partly on meditation. Both the observation and the meditation changed, as Lowe predicted that they would, by the end of the century.[68] The further extension of the franchise in 1884 guaranteed that the new electorate would be 'a great seething and swaying mass'.[69] It was at its noisiest during the last years of the century, when 'mass meetings' — and much 'mass entertainment' — turned jingoistic, provoking anti-imperialist Liberals to complain bitterly of a decline in political behaviour.[70] This was not surprisingly the decade of Le Bon — and of Harmsworth.

Already within two years of the passing of the 1884 Reform Act

Salisbury, who had been opposed to the 1867 Act, was writing to Lord
Randolph Churchill that while 'the "classes and the dependents of class"
are the strongest ingredients in our composition . . . we have so to conduct our legislation that we shall give some satisfaction to both classes
and masses'.[71] This was explicit if private. For the Liberals there was
nothing private in acknowledging the need to 'blend' the traditions of
'the older Liberalism' with 'the new aspirations of the labouring masses
out of which the party of the future must spring'.[72]

While statistically minded political economists were noting with
satisfaction a continued material improvement in the position of 'the
masses',[73] Liberal politicians were drawn inevitably into the politics of
poverty. An active minority of them held that they had a special duty
to deal with matters affecting the food, health, housing and amusement
of the working classes, 'the great mass of our fellow-citizens'[74] although
it was an exaggeration to say, as was said in the 1890s, that the whole
theory of modern liberals was that the State was to take in hand the control of the masses.[75] There were competing theories, not all of them
expressed in 'mass terms', as the long and rich legacy of 'liberal individualism' was re-examined.

A few progressive (and realistic) liberals, like J.A. Hobson, denied
that mass appeals to the working classes represented any transcendence
of class on the part of the Liberal Party. 'The labour movement',
Hobson insisted at the end of the century, 'even in its widest significance is still a class movement.' It had to be considered, he went on,
both as a sectional interest, the biggest of such interests, and as 'the
largest form of individualism'.[76] Hobson's views are always stimulating, whether he was writing about the psychology of mass meetings
during the Boer War or about the vested interests which he believed
inspired it.

III

The labour movement had certainly been transformed between 1880
and the end of the century. The socialist upthrust of the 1880s began
with the revolt of a few, the 'pioneers', against the presuppositions and
conventions, economic, political and otherwise, of mid-Victorian
England. As the decade went by, however, large numbers of trade
unionists and unemployed workers were drawn into what was soon
described as 'the movement'. There was a strong sense of threat in the
air and the language of politics was often the language of threat:

A million of starving people, with another million on the verge of starvation, represent a potential of destructive force to measure which no dynamometer has yet been made, but which will, if suddenly liberated, assuredly and absolutely destroy every vestige of nineteenth-century civilization so-called.[77]

Economic forces and a sequence of unprecedented political events, culminating in the Liberal split of 1886, were in the background. Yet once again the perspectives were large. Socialists and anti-socialists alike scanned the centuries. William Morris and Belfort Bax's *Socialism: its Growth and Outcome* (1893) began with 'ancient society' and ended with an appendix on the ancient city, Greek, Roman and Hebrew. It did not touch, however, on the language of social thought (of analysis or threat) in the ancient world which provided a starting point for many nineteenth-century thinkers.

A sense of identification of the 'mass' or 'masses' with the 'working class' had never been entirely absent at the grass roots level during the middle years of the century, when there was often a wide gap between social practice and social thought. Two of the most remarkable examples of the mid-century sense of identification have been noted by G.D.H. Cole and A.W. Filson. Faced with what it called 'the mass of factory tyranny', the *People's Paper* wrote in 1852 of the continuation of 'the social war'.[78] Two years later a 'Labour Parliament' in Manchester set out to organise what it called 'The Mass Movement'.[79] Yet, in general, throughout the 1850s and early 1860s 'the masses' proved singularly unwilling to move. As the *National Review* put it in 1863, 'the masses, if not contented, have at least arrived at the conviction that they are not wilfully injured'.[80]

The socialists of the 1880s started with a sense not only of injury but of what Hyndman called 'approaching trouble'. Both intimations, he argued, 'move vital masses of men to almost religious exasperation against their fellows'.[81] They believed, too, that they were already moving from an 'individualist' to a 'collectivist' society. What Sidney Webb called 'unconscious socialism' was the current of the age. Belfort Bax, avowedly 'metaphysical' as well as avowedly Marxist socialist, went further — and along a different path — when he traced stages in the development of 'new consciousness' which would culminate in the end of the 'subjective' and the triumph of 'social and objective virtues'.[82]

For socialists of every persuasion the 'masses' were the 'working classes', and economics determined the equation. As an early (and basic) exposition of socialism put it in 1888, 'the mass of the people, the working class, produce and distribute all commodities, while the minority of the people, the middle and upper classes, possess these commodities'.[83]

Such language was derived directly or indirectly from Marx and Engels, though there were few manifestations of it in the English translation of Engels's *The Condition of the Working Class in England* which appeared in 1892.[84] Even before he consolidated his economic theories, the young Marx had seized upon the revolutionary potential of numbers. The proletariat was the majority, and although most English socialists were to put their trust in the ballot box rather than in a revolution, revolutionaries and non-revolutionaries alike realised in the 1880s and 1890s that they would have to turn to the 'masses' in the social struggle. In the social context of the age not all of them found their own identification with the 'masses' easy,[85] but in the process of mobilisation enough working-class socialists emerged to speak not on behalf of but as members of 'the masses'.

It is interesting to trace the language of 'mass' and 'masses' in the two early socialist journals *Justice* (founded 1884) and *Commonweal* (founded 1885). The first issue of the latter – a monthly until April 1886 – referred to the 'mass of workers' (as did the fifteenth, eighteenth and twentieth) and the second to 'the great masses of working people' and 'the working masses of the town'.[86] The eighth mentioned 'the masses of people out of work'.[87] *Commonweal* recognised, like *Justice*, that 'the masses' had to be awakened or activated.[88] Otherwise, they might be 'deluded' as well as 'oppressed'.[89] Because they 'might not understand their position', they needed both to be 'educated' and 'inspired'.[90] There was always a danger it was argued, too, that they might split into 'factions' or 'sectional' interests.[91] Distinctions were often drawn – and they were relevant to the whole history of trade unionism – between the specific interests of a union and the general interests of 'the masses' as a whole.[92]

'A trades society', it had been noted long before, when trade unionism was restricted mainly to skilled workers, was 'necessarily confined to the interests of one special class, although it may heartily sympathise with the objects of all the industrial classes'.[93] As the unskilled began to become organised, they sometimes thought of themselves as 'masses' as opposed to 'trades'. This was a new distinction, and their perception of their own interest, economic and political, was to influence both the politics of the ballot box and the related development of industrial trade unionism in the late nineteenth and early twentieth centuries.

It was not only socialists who were interested in reaching 'the masses' during the 1880s and 1890s. When unemployed workers began to organise parades to the churches, including St Paul's Cathedral, in 1887, Thomas Hancock, a Christian Socialist, was delighted on two counts. 'The non-churchgoing "masses" have taken to churchgoing', he said in a famous sermon, subsequently printed. 'We have seen what journalists of Mammon and Caste call an "invasion of the Churches" by the poor socialists. We have seen nothing else like it in our generation.'[94]

If socialists often talked of socialism in terms of religion, religious leaders sometimes approached the task of reaching 'the masses' in very similar ways to the socialists. Even before the Religious Census of 1851 established facts, opinions were expressed that 'the masses' did not attend church.[95] Most of the 'neglecters', the Census showed, belonged to 'the masses of our working population . . . never or but seldom seen in our religious congregations'.[96] Social reasons were often given. Bishop Fraser of Manchester spoke in 1872 of a 'huge mass of ignorance, poverty, and wretchedness' in the 'manufacturing towns'[97] and there were many similar statements about 'the metropolis'.[98] F.D. Maurice welcomed the increasing signs of working-class organisation — including trade union organisation — as a way of getting rid of 'a wild floating mass of atoms'.[99]

The phrase 'the lapsed masses' was sometimes used.[100] It suggested that there had once been a social order more favourable to religious attendance than the social order of the nineteenth century. Occasionally the language of 'class' and 'masses' was employed. The clergy must 'take the side of the masses against the classes', Stewart Headlam urged.[101] 'The Church is mostly administered and officered by the classes', wrote a headmaster in 1898, 'her influential laity belong almost wholly to the class. She is doing a great and growing work among the masses, but the deep sympathies of the clergy with the poor are largely obscured to the eyes of the masses by the fact that social rank and social position secured by wealth and tradition, still count for so much in her service, both amongst clergy and laity.'[102] At least once it was suggested that socialists and Christians faced the same problems. 'The overwhelming majority of the masses of the people no more want the economic ideals of the "Labour Programme" than either the classes or the masses want the distinctive message of the Church.'[103]

IV

It has been the purpose of this article to explore the use of language, not to examine the validity of the arguments which it seeks to express.

'Men grope in a kind of linguistic bewilderment until the phrase-monger comes along, and gives them a proper form of expression', a late nineteenth-century journalist remarked. 'Then they are as if a great light had suddenly beamed upon them. The lucky words relieve a strain, and enthusiasm follows.'[104]

It is not only 'enthusiasm' which may follow, however. The language of 'masses' creates many difficulties, since it raises awkward separations – between 'them' and 'us'; 'above' and 'below'; 'brains and numbers'; 'individuals and crowds'. 'Mass is not only a very common but a very complex word in social description', Raymond Williams begins his article on Masses in *Keywords*, and he has explored some of the complexities himself in several places.[105] The use of such a generalised term could carry with it both condescension and confusion – even contempt – during the nineteenth century, as it has done since. Thus, *The Economist* in 1846 had 'no hesitation in pronouncing, because the masses are suffering, and have long been suffering, without much amending their condition, that they are greatly to blame . . . Nature makes them responsible for their conduct – why should not we?'[106] In the same decade, a Leeds minister, the Reverend R.W. Hamilton, properly complained that 'our judgments are distorted by the phrase [the masses]. We unconsciously glide into a prejudice. We have joined a total without thinking of the parts. It is a heap, but it has strangely become indivisible.'[107]

'Thinking of the parts', as Hamilton recognised, involves thinking about relations. So does all social history.[108] Use of the word 'class' necessarily involves an understanding of critical social relationships: use of the word 'mass' or 'masses' frequently involves a failure to understand and to communicate. Real people are turned into abstractions. A clarification of language is a necessary element, therefore, in the process of understanding. George Eliot should perhaps have the last word. She began a review written in 1856 with these words, 'It is an interesting branch of psychological observation to note the images that are habitually associated with abstract or collective terms – what may be called the picture-writing of the mind.' Her conclusion, however, was that those who use terms like 'the people', 'the masses', 'the proletariat' or 'the peasantry' reveal as much concrete knowledge of any actual social world as a mere passenger might have of the workings of a railway.[109]

Notes

1. See my article, 'The Language of "Class" in Early Nineteenth-Century

England' in A. Briggs and J. Saville (eds.), *Essays in Labour History* (1960), pp. 43-73.

2. Quoted by Raymond Williams in *Keywords* (1976), p. 160.

3. 'Nation-cries', one of a series of 'Old England' articles written for *The Times* in January 1838. Disraeli used the pseudonym 'Coeur-de-Lion'. The articles are reprinted in W. Hutcheon (ed.), *Whigs and Whiggism* (1913), pp. 416-17.

4. *Illustrated London News,* 10 July 1897.

5. For Harmsworth's interest both in the attitudes of 'the millions' and in the exact size of magazine and newspaper circulations – one of the first deliberate exercises in 'mass measuring' – see R. Pound and G. Harmsworth, *Northcliffe* (1959), esp. pp. 128, 130, 138, 165. For Lever, see C.H. Wilson, *The History of Unilever,* vol. 1 (1954). By 1892, four years before the founding of the *Daily Mail,* Harmsworth publications were claimed to have 'the largest circulation in the world'. The word 'masses' or 'mass circulation' does not seem to have been used by Northcliffe before 1900, nor did Lever (or Lipton) talk of 'mass distribution'. J.B. Jefferys, *Retail Trading in Britain, 1850-1950* (1954) is uninterested in the contemporary language of retailing. I was not able to note any use of the term myself in *Friends of the People* (1956), a study of Lewis's.

6. *Tit-Bits,* 10 April 1897.

7. T. Kirkup, *An Inquiry into Socialism* (1887), p. 20.

8. A statement of 1885, quoted in E.P. Thompson, *William Morris* (1977 ed.), p. 379. The title of the next chapter, 'The Socialists make contact with the Masses', suggests a more frequent use of the term 'the masses' than was the case. The word 'masses' does not appear in the anthology of contemporary extracts edited by E.J. Hobsbawm, *Labour's Turning Point* (1948).

9. T. Mann, *Memoirs* (1923). For religion and 'the masses', see below, p. 75.

10. See J.R. MacDonald, *Socialism and Society* (1905), and E. Ferri, *Socialism and Positive Science* (1905), the first volume in 'The Socialist Library'.

11. J.R. MacDonald, *The Socialist Movement* [1911], p. 15.

12. See volume 2 of *A Supplement to the Oxford Dictionary* (1976), p. 849, for more than forty examples, described as 'a selection', of nouns prefixed by 'mass', such as 'mass communications', 'mass culture' and 'mass society'. Some of these terms are what H.W. Fowler would have called 'vogue-words'. See *Modern English Usage* (1962 ed.), p. 697: 'Every now and then a word emerges from obscurity, or even from nothingness or a merely potential and not actual existence, into sudden popularity.'

13. See, in addition to *Keywords, Culture and Society* (1954) and *The Long Revolution* (1961), although the second of these rests more on generalised argument than on strict chronological dating.

14. The same has been true, of course, of many writers on 'class', who used the term in interpretation of societies to whom it would have been alien. This habit has declined in recent years largely as a result of more sophisticated approaches to social history, some of them influenced by anthropology. Anthropologists have always paid close attention to word patterns.

15. An earlier American use is cited – *Life* magazine in 1939: 'The State of Texas . . . has never been properly recognized for its contributions to US mass culture.'

16. For 'mass society', see inter alia Daniel Bell, 'America as a Mass Society' in *The End of Ideology* (Chicago, 1960): E. Shils, 'The Theory of Mass Society' in *Diogenes,* vol. 39 (1962), pp. 45-66; and W. Kornhauser, 'Mass Society' in the *International Encyclopedia of the Social Sciences,* vol. 10 (1968), pp. 58-64.

17. G. Le Bon, *The Crowd: A Study of the Popular Mind* (English ed., 1903), p. 15. 'Crowds had their own psychology', Sidney Webb explained in *Fabian News,* November 1896.

18. Le Bon, *The Crowd*, p. 16. Cf. Robert Southey's epic poem *Roderick* (1814), in which one of the characters, Prince Pelayo, states: 'Our portentous age, as with an earthquake's desolating force, hath loosen'd and disjointed the whole frame of social order'.

19. The collective behaviour tradition is well outlined in the *International Encyclopedia of the Social Sciences* article on 'Mass Phenomena' (vol. 10, pp. 54-8) and in the article on 'Collective Behaviour' (vol. 2, pp. 556-65). See also inter alia H. Toch, *The Social Psychology of Social Movements* (Indianapolis, 1965); E. Canetti, *Crowds and Power* (1960); and R.A. Nye, *The Origins of Crowd Psychology* (1975).

20. G. Rudé, *The Crowd in History, 1730-1848* (1964), p. 3. The pioneer was G. Lefebvre, whose article on 'Foules révolutionnaires' (1934) is reprinted in translation in J. Kaplow (ed.), *New Perspectives on the French Revolution* (New York, 1965), pp. 173-90. Lefebvre's definition was rather different.

21. Steven Lukes has attempted to relate crowd behaviour to Durkheimian theories of social integration in his article, 'Political Ritual and Social Integration' in *Sociology*, vol. 9 (1975), pp. 289-308. See also his *Emile Durkheim, His Life and Work* (1973), pp. 1-22.

22. K. Mannheim, *Man and Society in an Age of Reconstruction* (1940), esp. the footnote references on p. 60 and p. 107. Mannheim's own comments are always pertinent and interesting. He refers to 'the literature on crowds and masses, which began with the well known works of Sighele and Le Bon, and which since then has been raised to a much broader level of discussion in various countries' (p. 107). Note the choice of the word 'broader'.

23. The *American Journal of Sociology* was using the term 'mass psychology' by 1900. Four years earlier a popular English science magazine, *Science Siftings*, 1 August 1896, referred to 'the spontaneous phenomena which the Germans call *Massenpsychosen* − a word denoting a state of mind shared by a people at once'. For the approach of the Frankfurt School see *Soziologische Exkurse* (Frankfurt/Main, 1956), published in English as *Aspects of Sociology* (1972), ch. 5, 'Masses'. Freud's major contribution was his *Massenpsychologie und Ich-Analyse* (Leipzig, 1921).

24. See H. Arendt, *Origins of Totalitarianism* (New York, 1951). There is a useful chapter on 'the sociology of war' in P. Sorokin, *Contemporary Sociological Theories* (1928), ch. 6. See also ibid., pp. 752-5, which cites both Le Bon and E. Toller, *Masse Mensch* (Potsdam, 1921). For the effects of the Napoleonic Wars on the language of 'class', see Briggs, loc. cit., pp. 53-4.

25. *The Revolt of the Masses*, pp. 11-12.

26. Ibid., p. 15. Chapter 8 is entitled 'Why the Masses intervene in Everything and why their Intervention is solely by Violence'. This is a very inadequate link with the Arendt thesis.

27. *Westminster Review*, vol. 18 (1833), p. 382.

28. Ibid., p. 380. The author was reviewing J.P. Kay's *The Moral and Physical Condition of the Working Classes in Manchester* (1833). P. Gaskell in his parallel book on *The Manufacturing Population of England* (1833) observed in ch. 6 how 'the steam engine had drawn together the population into dense masses'.

29. For nineteenth-century argument about aggregates (and statistical approaches to measuring them), see A. Briggs, 'The Human Aggregate' in H.J. Dyos and M. Wolff (eds.), *The Victorian City* (1973), vol. 1, ch. 3.

30. For the word 'multitude' (with cross references, as in Rudé, to the word 'mob'), see Christopher Hill, 'The Multitude: The Many-Headed Monster' in *Change and Continuity in Seventeenth-Century England* (1974). For the possibility of standing anti-popular rhetoric on its head, note how Paine, Cobbett and others turned Burke's term 'the swinish multitude' into a battle cry. See for

example, pamphlets like *Rights of Swine* (1794) and *A Rod for the Burkites by one of the 'Swinish Multitude'* (1794) and the *Political Register*, 2 Nov. 1816: 'With [a] correct idea of your own worth in your minds, with what indignation must you have heard yourselves called the Populace, the Rabble, the Mob, the Swinish Multitude?

31. *Sybil* (1845), ch. 4. Disraeli was always anxious, none the less, to maintain and even to extend the concept of 'gradation of ranks' in an industrial society.

32. T. Carlyle, *On Heroes, Hero-Worship and the Heroic in History* (1841), lecture 6; *Past and Present* (1843), book 3, ch. 13.

33. He compared Thomas Attwood of Birmingham with Tamburlaine. See Hutcheon, *Whigs and Whiggism*, p. 248.

34. W. Hazlitt, essay on 'Mr Horne Tooke' in *The Spirit of the Age* (1825).

35. T. Carlyle, *Chartism* (1840), ch. 9.

36. Ibid., ch. 7. Cf. *Past and Present*, book 1, ch. 5, 'Aristocracy of Talent'.

37. *Black Dwarf*, vol. 3, p. 695.

38. *Manchester Guardian*, 5 March 1831.

39. See Briggs, 'The Language of Class', loc. cit., pp. 69-73.

40. W. Cooke Taylor, *Notes of a Tour in the Manufacturing Districts of Lancashire* (1842), p. 5; idem, *The Natural History of Society* (1840).

41. J.S. Mill, 'Civilization', originally published in the *London and Westminster Review*, vol. 3 and 25 (1836), pp. 1-28, and reprinted in *Dissertations and Discussions*, vol. 1 (1859), the year of the publication of his famous essay *On Liberty*.

42. For James Mill's belief in the identity of interests, a matter of passion to him as well as of logic, see his *Essay on Government* (1819), section 10. See also G. Duncan, *Marx and Mill: Two Views of Social Conflict and Social Harmony* (1973). De Tocqueville shared John Stuart Mill's belief that England was becoming a 'mass' society. He commented in his notes on his *Journey to England* (ed. by J.P. Mayer, 1958, pp. 59-61) on the strength of the aristocracy; but believed none the less that 'in due time' England, like other countries, would become 'democratic' (pp. 66-7). 'The masses' had not developed very radical ideas about property (p. 72), but there was a 'general movement common to humanity the world over' towards 'democracy'. 'The century is primarily democratic.' De Tocqueville's attitude towards 'class' but not towards 'mass' is explored in S. Drescher, *Tocqueville and England* (Cambridge, Mass., 1964). See also for the ambiguities of the word 'democracy', A. Naess et al., *Democracy, Ideology and Objectivity: Studies in the Semantics and Cognitive Analysis of Ideological Controversy* (Oslo and Oxford, 1956).

43. Although Riesman quoted Mill several times in his remarkable and widely read book *The Lonely Crowd* (New Haven, 1950), he did not quote any of the most relevant passages from Mill. The only nineteenth-century writers mentioned by Ortega y Gasset — and then cursorily — were Hegel, Comte and Nietzsche. R. Williams in *Culture and Society* limits the range of discussion of Mill in ch. 3 by restricting it to Mill's essays on Bentham and Coleridge.

44. *On Liberty*, ch. 3: 'individuals are lost in the crowd'.

45. Ibid., ch. 3, which he called 'Of Individuality, as one of the Elements of Well-Being'. By then de Tocqueville was less willing to generalise. In his *Ancien Régime* (Paris, 1856), vol. 1, p.146, he observed that in England 'common interests had closely knit together the various social classes . . . but liberty, which enjoys that admirable power of creating among all citizens necessary relations and mutual ties of dependence, does not always make them similar.'

46. J. Vincent, *The Formation of the Liberal Party 1857-1868* (1966), p. 152.

47. For Mill and Arnold compared, see E. Alexander, *Matthew Arnold and John Stuart Mill* (1965).

48. M. Arnold, 'Democracy', the introduction to *The Popular Education of France* (1861). Williams does not refer to this important essay which also draws on de Tocqueville. He does refer, however, to the other important contribution of Arnold to this subject, *Friendship's Garland* (1871). See also P.J. McCarthy, *Matthew Arnold and the Three Classes* (New York, 1964).

49. 'Democracy', p. 7. For the twentieth-century American development of the argument (with no debts acknowledged to Arnold), see inter alia, D. Macdonald, *Against the American Grain: Essays on the Effects of Mass Culture* (New York, 1962), the first essay a brilliant study of 'mass-cult and mid-cult', first published in 1960; B. Rosenberg and D.M. White (eds.), *Mass Culture* (Glencoe, Ill., 1957); N. Jacobs (ed.), *Culture for the Millions?* (Princeton, 1961); and H.J. Gans, *Popular Culture and High Culture* (New York, 1974).

50. S. Smiles, *Duty* (1880), p. 26. For the background see A. Briggs, 'Samuel Smiles and the Gospel of Work' in *Victorian People* (1954).

51. H. Taylor, 'Chapters on Socialism. By John Stuart Mill' in the *Fortnightly Review*, vol. 25 (1879). They are reprinted in J.S. Mill, *Essays on Economics and Society* (Toronto, 1967), vol. 5 of his *Collected Works*.

52. The study of political elites is relatively recent in this country, although it has become better known since the Open University began to work with this language. (see C.T. Harvie, 'Concepts of Elites' and 'Intellectuals and Society' in *British Elites, 1750-1870* (1974)). Elitism was not a nineteenth-century word, and the two classic Italian texts – those of Mosca, whose study of 'the ruling class' first appeared in 1896 in his *Elementi di scienza politica*, and Pareto, who wrote on the subject in many places – were little studied until the 1930s and not related to English practice until the 1950s and 1960s. See W.L. Guttsman, *The British Political Elite* (1963); T.B. Bottomore, *Elites and Society* (1964); J.H. Meisel, *The Myth of the Ruling Class: Gaetano Mosca and the 'Elite'* (Ann Arbor, 1958); P. Bachrach, *The Theory of Democratic Elitism: A Critique* (1967); and the article on 'Elites' in the *International Encyclopedia of the Social Sciences*, vol. 5 (1968), pp. 26-9.

53. J. Morley, review of *Essays on Reform* in the *Fortnightly Review*, vol. 7 (1867), pp. 491-2.

54. J. Morley, *Edmund Burke: A Historical Study* (1867) and an essay on de Maistre written in 1868, reprinted in *Miscellanies* (1886).

55. H.F. Lowry, K. Young and W.H. Dunn (eds.), *The Note-Books of Matthew Arnold* (1952), p. 83. Cf. p. 37 for an 1866 note, ' "the feeling between classes" but the distinction of classes should die away and we should be one people'. This followed a quotation from a speech by John Bright.

56. M. Arnold, *Culture and Anarchy:* an 1856 reference, quoted in C. Kent, *Brains and Numbers* (1978), p. 71.

57. Quoted in ibid., p. 73.

58. Quoted in ibid., p. 68. 'Reform' meant 'the placing of ultimate control of the State in the hands of the mass of the people' (A Scheme of Reform in *Commonwealth*, March 1866).

59. See, in particular, R.H. Hutton's essay 'The Political Character of the Working Classes'. For Lowe, see Briggs, *Victorian People*, ch. 9, 'Robert Lowe and the fear of Democracy' and J. Winter, *Robert Lowe* (Toronto, 1976). Lowe, who thought in terms of a 'top' and 'bottom' to society, related the struggle for 'democracy', which he deplored, to the struggle for trade union power and protectionist changes in economic policy which he equally strongly deplored. He feared that the working classes, once given the vote, would launch themselves in 'one compact mass' on all British institutions (*Speeches and Letters on Reform* (1867), p. 55). See also below, p. 71.

60. J. Morley, 'The Liberal Programme' in the *Fortnightly Review*, vol. 8 (1867), p. 359.

61. G. Brodrick 'The Utilitarian Argument against Reform' in *Essays on Reform*, p. 7.

62. For Comte's views on elites and mass, see H.B. Acton, 'Comte's Positivism and the Science of Society' in *Philosophy*, vol. 26 (1951); and G. Lenzer (ed.), *Auguste Comte and Positivism* (New York, 1975). For the Oxford and Cambridge background of the English 'educated classes', see C.T. Harvie, *The Lights of Liberalism* (1976).

63. Speech at Liverpool, 28 June 1886, quoted in *The Times,* 29 June 1886.

64. *Fortnightly Review*, vol. 14 (1870), p. 591. This was a few months before the Paris Commune, stoutly defended by the Positivists. See R. Harrison, *The English Defence of the Commune 1871* (1971). For a Tennysonian vision of the end of 'class', see his poem 'Freedom':

> Of Knowledge fusing class with class
> Of civic Hate no more to be,
> Of Love to leaven all the mass,
> Till every Soul be free.
> (Tennyson, *Tiresias and Other Poems* (1895), p. 199)

65. See Briggs, *Victorian People,* ch. 8, 'John Bright and the Creed of Reform' for the idea of a residuum unworthy of the right to vote.

66. A speech of November 1873 at the University of Glasgow, quoted in G. Watson, *The English Ideology* (1973), p. 166. See also Watson, ch. 10, on 'Class or Rank'. Ruskin, like Carlyle, believed that 'all forms of government are good just so far as they attain this one vital necessity of policy – *that the wise and kind, few or many, shall govern the unwise and unkind'* (E.T. Cook and A. Wedderburn (eds.), *The Works of John Ruskin,* vol. 17 (1905), p. 248).

67. W. Bagehot, *The English Constitution* (1867), reprinted in its second edition (1872) form in N. St John-Stevas (ed.), *The Collected Works of Walter Bagehot,* vol. 5 (1974), pp. 369, 378. The second passage follows a famous reference to public opinion as 'the opinion of the bald-headed man at the back of the omnibus'. Cf. *Reynolds News* which claimed to represent that opinion, 23 August 1885: 'Toryism is today what it always was – exclusiveness. It is a representation of privileges and vested interests.'

68. 'They [the working classes] will soon possess the secret of their own power, and then what is to prevent them from using it? What are the restraints that you propose? I know that very pretty metaphors have been given us; we were told, for instance, that society is divided into vertical instead of horizontal strata, but nevertheless, when men have power conferred upon them, infallibly they will employ it for their own purpose' (Lowe, *Speeches and Letters on Reform,* p. 53).

69. A phrase of Lord Randolph Churchill, quoted by W.S. Churchill, *Lord Randolph Churchill* (1906), vol. 1, p. 294.

70. See J.A. Hobson, *The War in South Africa* (1900) and *The Psychology of Jingoism* (1901). The theme is well handled in R. Price, *An Imperial War and the British Working Class: Working-Class Attitudes and Reactions to the Boer War 1899-1902* (1972), esp. ch. 4, 'The Jingo Crowd'.

71. W.S. Churchill, *Lord Randolph Churchill*, vol. 2, p. 224.

72. *Manchester Guardian,* 11 May 1894.

73. Sir Robert Giffen is the best source. See his collected papers, *Economic Inquiries and Studies* (1904).

74. G.W.E. Russell, 'The New Liberalism: A Response' in the *Nineteenth Century,* vol. 26 (1889), p. 496. See also R.B. Haldane, 'The New Liberalism' in the *Progressive Review,* vol. 1 (1896), pp. 133-43.

75. For a general view, see R.A. Woods, *English Social Movements* (New York, 1891).

76. J.A. Hobson, 'Of Labour' in J.E. Hand (ed.), *Good Citizenship* (1899), p. 105. See M. Freeden, *The New Liberalism: An Ideology of Social Reform* (1978), esp. ch. 4, 'The Nature of Liberal Social Reform', section 5, ' "The Masses versus the Classes" ' – the striving for Non-Sectionalism'.

77. H. Halliday Sparling, *Men versus Machinery* (1888), quoted in Thompson *William Morris*, p. 292.

78. *People's Paper*, 13 November 1852.

79. See G.D.H. Cole and A.W. Filson, *British Working Class Movements, Select Documents 1789-1875* (1951), pp. 418-21.

80. *National Review*, April 1863, quoted by H.M. Lynd, *England in the Eighteen-Eighties* (1945), p. 250.

81. H.M. Hyndman, 'The Dawn of a Revolutionary Epoch' in the *Nineteenth Century*, vol. 9 (1881), pp. 1-18.

82. See his *The Religion of Socialism* (1886) and *The Ethics of Socialism* (1889).

83. Quoted in Thompson, *William Morris*, pp. 331-2, from a privately printed pamphlet by Edward Aveling and Eleanor Marx-Aveling.

84. Although Engels devoted a paragraph in his introduction to social and political terms, the words 'mass' and 'masses' were not on his list. In his chapter on 'Labour Movements', however, he stated that the object of the trade unions was 'to deal, *en masse*, as a power, with the employers'.

85. George Gissing, whose *New Grub Street* (1891) has rightly been noted as a key novel in the history of 'mass culture' (which he perceptively described), said through one of his characters in *The Unclassed* (1880) that his 'zeal on behalf of the suffering masses was nothing more nor less than disguised zeal on behalf of my own starved passions'. This might be one difficulty. Another was the difficulty of communication. Gissing's *Demos* (1886) is a fascinating novel in this context.

86. *Commonweal*, February, March 1885. The March number included an article by Engels, 'England in 1845 and in 1885' which was later included as the preface to the first English edition of *The Condition of the Working Class in England in 1844*.

87. *Commonweal*, September 1885.

88. The word 'apathetic' was used in relation to 'the masses' in *Commonweal*, September 1886. Cf. a Morris letter of 1886 cited in Thompson, *William Morris*, p. 411. For 'apathy' as a concept, see S. Yeo, 'On the Uses of "Apathy" ', in *Archives Européennes de Sociologie*, vol. 15 (1974), pp. 279-311.

89. *Commonweal*, July 1885, September 1886.

90. Ibid., August 1886, December 1886.

91. For 'factions', see a note by J.L. Mahon in *Commonweal*, October 1887. Mahon often used the language of 'masses'. For 'sectional interests', represented particularly in the trade union structure, see ibid., September 1889.

92. See, for example, the Socialist League's *Strikes and the Labour Struggle*, cited in Thompson, *William Morris*, pp. 435-6, and a comment by Morris in *Commonweal*, September 1889, on 'class jealousy among the workers themselves'.

93. *Bee-Hive*, 2 June 1866.

94. T. Hancock, 'The Banner of Christ in the Hands of the Socialists', reprinted in *The Pulpit and the Press* (1904). See also M.B. Reckitt, *Maurice to Temple* (1946), ch. 5.

95. See, for example, Engels, *The Condition of the Working Class in England*, p. 125.

96. PP1852-3: vol. LXXXIX, [Command] 1690, p. clviii. Horace Mann, who conducted the Census, liked to talk of the 'myriads', and the phrase 'the thronging myriads' was also used by a Methodist minister in 1883. (E. Smith, *The Great Problem of the Times* (1883), p. 3).

97. J. Fraser, *Charge* (1872), pp. 76-7, quoted in K.S. Inglis, *Churches and the Working Classes in Victorian England* (1963), p. 25.

98. See ibid., p. 68.

99. F.D. Maurice, *On the Reformation of Society* (1851), p. 36.

100. Inglis, *Churches,* p. 83.

101. S. Headlam, *The Clergy as Public Leaders* (n.d.), p. 13.

102. T.C. Fry in C. Gore, *Essays in Aid of the Reform of the Church* (1898), p. 303. (quoted in ibid., p. 60).

103. Rev. Ambrose Shepherd, *The Gospel and Social Questions* (1902), quoted in S. Yeo, *Religion and Voluntary Organisations in Crisis* (1976), p. 291.

104. *Science Siftings,* 3 April 1897. This magazine often used the language of 'the masses'. Thus, it suggested (31 July 1897) that public opinion was 'not dictated by leaders and adopted by the masses, but evolved by the masses, and accepted by the leaders'. The problem was taken up more seriously by James Bryce, one of the essayists on reform of 1867, in his *The American Commonwealth,* vol. 2 (1888; New York, 1918 ed., pp. 257-8): 'Sometimes a leading statesman or journalist takes a line to which he finds that the mass of those who usually agree with him are not responsive. He perceives that they will not follow him, and that he must choose between isolation and a modification of his own views. A statesman may sometimes venture on the former course . . . a journalist, however, is obliged to hark back if he has inadvertently taken up a position disagreeable to his *clientèle,* because the proprietors of the paper have their circulation to consider . . . He tries to feel the pulse of average citizens; and as the mass, on the other hand, look to him for initiative, this is a delicate process . . . This mutual action and reaction of the makers or leaders of opinion upon the mass, and of the mass upon them, is the most curious part of the whole process by which opinion is produced.'

105. R. Williams, *Keywords,* p. 158. See also *Culture and Society,* esp. pp. 297-319; *The Long Revolution,* p. 95 (an interesting discussion of 'individualism' and 'individuality'), pp. 110-11 (which touches on the problem of elites) and p. 334; and *Communications* (revised ed., 1966).

106. *The Economist,* 21 November 1846, quoted in J.D. Rosenberg, *The Darkening Glass* (1963), p. 127. See also S. Gordon, 'The London *Economist* and the High Tide of Laissez Faire' in the *Journal of Political Economy,* vol. 63 (1955).

107. See A. Briggs, *Victorian Cities* (1963), p. 59.

108. The sense of the word 'class', as E.P. Thompson points out – and the related study of 'class consciousness' – depends on a sense of social relationships. 'Class happens when some men, as a result of common experiences (inherited or shared), feel and articulate the identity of their interests as between themselves, and as against other men whose interests are different from (and usually opposed to) theirs' (E.P. Thompson, *The Making of the English Working Class* (1963 ed.), p. 9).

109. G. Eliot, *Essays and Leaves from a Note-Book* (Edinburgh, 1884), pp. 229-30 (quoted by Watson, *English Ideology,* pp. 180-1).

5 CONSERVATISM, TRADITIONALISM AND THE BRITISH WORKING CLASS, 1880-1918

Alan J. Lee

I

Even in the heady days of the making of the English working class there was a body of working-class Tories, self-styled 'operative' conservatives, mainly Protestant, many 'Orange'.[1] Their societies spread over Yorkshire, Lancashire and the Midlands in the 1830s and 1840s, fighting the new Poor Law,[2] promoting protection, Protestantism and factory reform. The 1850s and early 1860s, however, were lean years, with Conservatives licking the wounds of 1846. There was little organisational continuity between these early societies and the Conservative Working Men's Associations which appeared in 1867. Put under the umbrella of the National Union that year and made effective by John Gorst in 1871, these were seen by some Conservatives as a means of harnessing the electoral power of the newly enfranchised urban artisan.[3] It was not a wholehearted commitment, however, Disraeli made muted noises of approval, but had little sympathy with working-class organisations as such. There was not much serious interest in working-class issues within the party in the 1870s. The New Social Movement of 1871 was abortive. The Associations reached their peak in 1874, somewhat later in Liverpool.[4] The Primrose League, it is true, claimed to have more than a million working-class 'associate members' by 1890, but the figures were dubious, and the League was justifiably criticised by Ashmead Bartlett's more populist conservative organ *England* for the way it patronised working men.[5] The Liberty and Property Defence League shared this weakness; the Fair Trade League excluded working men from its council; the Anti-Socialist Union was neither clamorous for nor successful in gaining the support of the workers; and the Conservative Party cold-shouldered the Conservative Labour Party (1904-10) and the Trade Union Tariff Reform Association.[6] By the turn of the century the Conservatives were relying increasingly upon a national appeal, shorn of class-specific or other allegiances. Until recently, indeed, despite the survival of the Conservative Trade Union Organisation, the party continued to neglect its active working-class supporters.[7] And yet they existed, amongst the mass of the British workers who were before the First World War Liberal in their politics. Even after the attainment of universal suffrage, and in an age of 'class politics', the Conservative Party has derived about a half of its votes from the working class, about a third of whom have cast their votes for that party.[8]

Attempts to explain such behaviour have tended to rely upon the evidence of opinion polls. In this way we know that the working-class Conservative is likely to live in a non-industrial or county town (rural workers have been unduly neglected[9]), to work in a small plant, to be an owner-occupier or a tenant of a private landlord, not to be a member of a trade union, to have had a middle-class father, and always to have been employed.[10] She (it is less likely to be 'he') might be older than average, will think of herself as 'middle class', and will be disposed to support private enterprise and the established social order.[11] She will tend to be a part of and to share the values of a 'traditional' society, 'a network of face to face groups, based on family, neighbourhood, occupations, associations and status'.[12] Those values will tend to be parochial and deferential, dependent upon a system of ascribed status. Such societies, of course, are not necessarily nurseries for Toryism. They may nurture a strongly proletarian and even radical community, like Methodist Liberal mining communities.[13] Certainly, much of the stuff of 'traditionalism', limited life expectations, matrilocalism and so on, applies to a wider sector of the working class than those of it who vote Conservative. Even 'deference', which in any case seems to apply only to about a quarter of working-class Conservatives,[14] has been criticised as a concept too vague and confused to be helpful in explaining modern British electoral behaviour.[15] It has been suggested, indeed, that it might be better to view Labour voting (if that is accepted as an indication of radical attitudes) rather than Conservative voting as a form of political deviance.[16]

If not very helpful in explaining political partisanship, 'traditionalism' and 'conservatism' remain central to the understanding of working-class ideology. It was this that Marx and Engels complained of when they spoke with exasperation of the 'demoralisation', 'political nullity' and 'bourgeois respectability' of the English worker.[17] The formal structure of party politics has not been the only structure within which working men, or anyone else, have understood politics.[18] Recognition of the incoherence of popular beliefs has to a certain extent been blurred by the use of opinion surveys. Polls and interviews are particularly susceptible to errors of misrepresentation. Not only may respondents wish to please their inquisitors, or be unwilling to disclose their beliefs. They may not be able to formulate their views or even be aware of what their views are on particular subjects, 'for the activity of thought by which we believe something is different from the activity by which we know we believe, so that the one can exist without the other'.[19] The assumption that politics are by nature 'remote and abstract', however, applies only to the formal political system.[20] Much ideological thought is done outside this framework, at home or at work perhaps, but for all its concreteness it is thought that is still 'political'. A mate unemployed, it was once observed, has greater significance than 'unemployment', and may well be, of course, a political perception.[21] Associated with such short-range political perception is the extent of political ignorance. A Conservative canvasser in 1885 found that many agricultural labourers believed there to have been a Conservative government during the previous five years, because their own MP had been a Conservative.[22] Modern surveys do not suggest that such ignorance of the formal system has much diminished. Thus, while it is true that historians of the period before the later 1930s are handicapped by the lack of polls, the result is not as debilitating as some have hinted.[23] Furthermore, it is clear that it is an historical analysis that is needed when dealing with the development and formation of 'class', essentially a dynamic rather than a static phenomenon.[24]

Unfortunately there is a dark age in Britain between the demise of the pollbooks in 1872 and the appearance of the pollsters in the 1930s. There have been some attempts to illuminate it by questioning people about parental political behaviour, but this seems to demand an unrealistic ability of people who have long ceased to be children to recall the politics of often long-dead parents, and similar doubts occur as to the evidence of respondents about their own pasts. This methodological weakness, however, does not mean that socialisation and 'tradition' have not a strong correlation with voting habits. The influence of the family and the context in which the first vote was cast have been seen as crucial determinants of later voting patterns, and the process has been elaborated as a generational one, so that the virtual absence of a Labour Party in the early twentieth century may have reinforced the Conservatives' position when the Liberal decline began, and the depression years of the 1930s may have been the sowing of the Labour harvest of the 1940s and 1950s.[25] But even this approach has to be treated with caution, lest complex experiences are over-simplified. The processes of political socialisation are yet to be properly understood, and seem likely to amount to more than a simple generational transfer.[26]

II

Yet, dark age though it is, it is not impossible to discover a little of how, why and with whom people voted, and possibly even more of their general political attitudes. We know that by 1910 still only some 59 per cent of adult males were registered voters.[27] 'Working-class' constituencies had generally far lower levels of enfranchisement than others, dipping as low as 20.5 per cent and 39.3 per cent in Whitechapel and Everton respectively.[28] Whether or not enfranchisement was the single most important factor inhibiting the rise of the Labour Party before 1918,[29] it is clear that the exclusion of so large a proportion of the working class from the electorate meant that the political attitudes of the working class generally may not have been very accurately reflected in the voting behaviour of the enfranchised workers, even if that were known in any detail. Some have gone as far as to claim that 'although the Tory Party probably suffered absolutely by the [1918] franchise changes, it did not do so relatively, and indeed, for much of the inter-war period it was the working-class party *par excellence*',[30] and this would have been predicated upon a substantial reservoir of pre-war working-class support.

Assessment of the actual working-class vote before the advent of the polls has perforce to be done by assigning a social class to each constituency. As the intention of the 1885 Act had been to separate out 'the pursuits of the people'[31], it is possible to do this, especially for the mining areas, but the categories can have fitted most constituencies only loosely by 1910. Even so the extent of working-class Toryism might be glimpsed from such figures. Of the 124 'predominantly working-class' constituencies, as labelled by Blewett, only twenty-two were consistently Liberal or Labour through the elections of 1885-1910 (and nine of these were in the West Riding). Only three were consistently Conservative (all in Liverpool), but thirty-six were Conservative or Liberal-Unionist more times than they were either Liberal or Labour, and at the high tide of Toryism in 1900 seventy-four of them went to the Conservatives – some, of course, the result of Liberal defaults.[32] Low levels of enfranchisement were partly the explanation, no doubt. Conservatives were returned in all but two of the low-franchise working-class seats noticed by Matthew, McKibbin and Kay, in at least one election, and in a majority of them at more than one.[33] It is clearly difficult, however, to discover whether the minority who voted were representative of the majority who did not. Many of those who did vote Conservative switched to Labour when given the opportunity in 1910.[34] On the other hand, modern studies have shown the influence of a middle-class milieu to be significant in the genesis of the working-class Conservative, so it is perhaps not in the working-class constituencies that one should first look for him. Where, moreover, middle-class influence was strong the working class of the area may have stood a better chance of having been put on the register than in the solidly working-class constituencies. Finally, the total exclusion of women, many of them domestic servants highly vulnerable to 'deferential' or more direct pressures, would also have tended unduly to diminish the representation of Conservatism within the class. Such arguments are difficult to quantify, but would seem to suggest that the extent of potential working-class Toryism before 1918 was at least as large as it proved to be subsequently.

Much of it must be seen as the consequence of specific structural factors. Trivial matters such as the London cabmen's protest at the law restricting the use of cabs at elections, or Parnell's weighty decision in 1885 to instruct his supporters in England to vote Tory, undoubtedly accounted for certain short-term support.[35] Many occupations facing increasing foreign competition, such as the Coventry ribboners, the Nottingham lace-makers, the Boston fishermen and the metalworkers of the Midlands and of Sheffield, favoured protection of some sort and voted accordingly.[36] Personal influence cemented some areas to the Tory Party, that of Chamberlain in Birmingham (but not Coventry), and that of Howard Vincent in Sheffield.[37] Ethnic conflict also contributed to the harvest of Conservative votes in the East of London, over the issue of Jewish immigration, as did anti-Irishism in London and Liverpool (but apparently not in Birmingham or Leeds).[38] Indeed, much of the explanation of voting behaviour (and it must be emphasised that we do not know with any precision who voted in what way), must lie in the micro-analysis of each election, with its own pressures, issues and personalities.

It is, however, at this point that the shortcomings of largely electoral analysis become plain. If we are trying to understand ideological formations, especially during a period (1880s to 1918) when voting was perforce by no means a universal habit among the working class, then explanations of mere electoral behaviour will provide only a part of what is necessary to achieve such an understanding. Furthermore, it may be doubted whether, or how far, it is necessary to look for a close correspondence between formal political allegiance and informal political attitudes. It is important, then, to look more closely at these often incoherent and badly articulated attitudes.

III

It seems helpful to consider them, initially at least, using both the concept of 'traditional society', as defined above, and the concept of 'traditional behaviour', defined by Weber as lying

> very close to the borderline of what can justifiably be called meaningfully oriented action, and indeed often on the other side. For it is very often a matter of almost automatic reaction to habitual stimuli which guide behaviour in a course which has been repeatedly followed. The great bulk of all everyday action to which people have become habitually accustomed approaches this type.[39]

Industrialisation and urbanisation, of course, had considerably eroded the rural basis of traditionalism in Britain by the mid-nineteenth century, weakening both its political representation and its political power. While it has been argued that 'the politics of deference' were drawing to an end in 1867,[40] others have preferred to see that period in terms of 'influence', of one kind and another, and suggest that 'deference' tended to develop after 1872 as the old pressures began to relax.[41] This relaxation led some contemporaries to welcome the growth of party organisation. The prospective Conservative candidate for Bedford in 1885 described the change:

> Owing to the want of an adequate cohesion, men were to be seen voting in a haphazard manner, just as individual whim, individual crotchets, individual resentments, and a variety of other motives might have dictated. Now, happily, all that is done away with. Organisation has taken the place of sporadic enthusiasm.[42]

All the same, the old political morality did not disappear overnight. Factory paternalism persisted in Lancashire, and the reforms had little effect in Lincolnshire, where 'deference' had played little part in farmers' politics.[43] Where it was affected the change was resented by the old hands: 'I felt a righteous hatred for the demagogues who came out of Birmingham at election time, black-coated, gamp-umbrellaed, cotton-gloved à la Stiggins, and interfered with farm hands. This they called farmyard canvassing.'[44] It is difficult to judge how long social-cum-economic 'deference' and pressure lasted in the rural areas. There were still cases of undue pressure being brought by Conservatives in 1910, but by then the counties were of diminishing importance, and in the towns a different pattern had already emerged.[45] It would be wrong, however, to assume that 'traditional' structures and behaviour were confined to the countryside. Most notably in the family, in education, in religion, in work and in 'culture' traditionalism remained significant, at least before 1918.

The family during this period has until recently been studied largely among the middle class, and as an aspect of educational and social reform. It is also, however, the primary unit of social class, and must, therefore, reflect class distinctions. Upon the generally authoritarian nature of the Victorian family as an institution, therefore, subordinating women, children, the weak and the old to the domination of the healthy male breadwinner, was superimposed the economic insecurity of the working-class family, which only served to reinforce such domination. As the family has usually been considered to be a non- or prepolitical group there has been little study of its political influence, but it does at least seem likely that such pressures tended towards introverted, isolated and perhaps even 'privatised' values and behaviour. Even 'radical' families were susceptible. David Kirkwood recalled that his father often spoke of 'winning through', which meant 'surviving, not being starved, not being homeless, not being in debt'.[46] Such defensiveness may have been reinforced by the encroachment of the state upon their own lives, especially when connected with the employment, treatment and education of their children.[47]

Working-class attitudes towards education were divided. The more prosperous and 'respectable' sections of the class gave a general endorsement of the value of and status accorded by education, while the poorer and 'rougher' sections evinced deep distrust of the institutions and the people who ran them.[48] In addition, the values inculcated by the schools, and the burgeoning youth organisations, were heavily 'deferential', authoritarian and nationalistic.[49] As most working-class children left school when they were fourteen, if not before, it might be that the influences of adolescence were stronger, and certainly middle-class concern with working-class adolescence during this period was increasing.[50]

If the effects of traditionalism upon political attitudes are less than clear in the cases of the family and education, however, the same is not so of religion. Religion was perhaps the main source of party division in Victorian politics, and in Lancashire, the notorious home of working-class Toryism, it has been argued that religion was indeed mainly responsible for such voting behaviour.[51] Militant Protestantism was enmeshed with popular anti-Irishism. Here was the English home of Orangeism, the backyard of rabble-rousers like William Murphy and of machine politicians like Stanley Salvidge.[52] It was important in reaping Tory votes, but by 1910 its impact had much diminished outside Liverpool itself. The Catholic working class tended to be Liberal, or when the Liberals attacked denominational education were driven into the arms of Labour with whom they shared a class allegiance. If the Protestant workers wished to make a religious, or, indeed, ethnic point they could, and did vote Tory.[53] Most of the workers, however, had no religious point to make, for the class as a whole was largely indifferent to such matters. The Methodist miners were an exception, and even then religion flourished amongst the activists rather than the rank and file. Nor was Methodism markedly 'traditionalist'.[54] Elsewhere, working-class heathenism was accepted as a fact of life.[55] There was still much superstition and vague religiosity, and some of the apathy was induced, or so it was claimed, by the pervasive class atmosphere of the churches.[56] As one East End furniture-maker put it, 'we felt that there was a God, but that he was no friend of ours'.[57] Attempts to integrate the churches with working-class life met with little success, and attendance at church or chapel was more likely to be associated with upward social mobility than with the downward percolation of faith or doctrine.[58] Estrangement could go even further in the countryside, where even a Tory politician was moved to suggest that the parson was becoming a liability to the party.[59] Amongst older people the waning of religion may have been slower, and there were aspects of family and school life which perpetuated religiosity, if only in a social form.[60] It is likely that the following injunction to 'working people' was more typical of their religious diet than the products of the revived Christian Socialism around the turn of the century, although, of course, no precise measurement can be made.

> Nothing is lost in the Kingdom of nature . . . Nothing is lost in Providence . . . Nothing is more unlike God than waste . . . 'Let nothing be lost' . . . no money, no time, no talent, no opportunity of good-doing or good-getting, no chapter of the Bible, no sermon, no sacrament, no affliction, no success! Make profit, and only profit, from them all.[61]

The self-acclaimed 'working-man's church', the Salvation Army, was characterised by both hierarchical organisation and an authoritarian spirit, as were the youth movements spawned by the churches.[62] To those whom it did touch, however, religion throughout the dark age noted above would have given support overwhelmingly to traditionalist values and attitudes.

Work itself could also be conducive to traditionalism, although the correlation between type of work, size of plant and so on, with traditionalism is by no means simple. The average size of plant before 1918 was smaller than that which emerged from the era of rationalisation and concentration between the wars. The smaller plants were in the older industries, for the most part, where small masters employed a handful of journeymen, and these in the nineteenth century were nurseries for radicalism. This was very much a function of unionisation, however, which was greatest amongst the skilled men. Regardless of size of establishment it was the more numerous semi- and unskilled workers who tended to be politically quiescent. The activity of the 1880s and 1890s, and of the 1910s was, of course, highly significant and important within the movement, but the 'new unionists' were a distinct minority within the unions, as unionists were amongst the working class.[63]

In the cotton unions of Lancashire, which by 1914 constituted something like a sixth of all unionists, the more skilled spinners were prone to support the Conservatives, largely because it had been found easier to squeeze them than the Liberals. Their switch to Labour in the 1900s was a direct consequence of the Conservatives' failure to continue protecting their interests.[64] Even their Tory allegiance, however, had not stopped them, along with other Lancashire workers from being particularly strike prone.[65] The spinners, however, were usually employed in large establishments, and it has been pointed out that these were havens of 'paternalism' until at least the 1880s.[66] This was no doubt encouraged by the spinners who were also shareholders in the firms, and by the greater degree of upward social mobility open to them.[67] The less skilled weavers, on the other hand, who were largely Liberal, were usually employed in smaller establishments, and in closer contact with their employers. They did not, however, share in the ownership of their firms, or have the degree of mobility of the spinners. Clearly, here, there was no simple correlation between either the size of firm or the politics of the employers, and the workers' politics. The unions in cotton as in mining were by this time mainly concerned with wages, unless and until their organisations were attacked as such.[68]

Again, while the typical small shop organisation in the engineering trades tended to breed radicalism,[69] in Birmingham Chamberlain found much support there amongst those dependent upon arms manufacture and fearful of foreign competition.[70] In Sheffield, with a similar industrial structure, the Conservatives managed to hold their own into the

1890s, although here the non-conformist influence was an important aspect of Liberal-Labour co-operation. Subsequently, however, with the focus of working-class politics shifting to the heavier industries, both Conservatives and Liberals lost ground to Labour, until the latter took over in the 1920s.[71]

Some of these differences can be accounted for better in terms of skill, which did not always coincide with differences in size of work-force. It was the unskilled who were subject to more cross-pressures, more dependent upon the goodwill of employer and client, and more threatened by the 'lumpen' elements of Irish and Jewish immigrant labour.[72] In terms of party politics, however, the fact of their greater insecurity and general lack of political socialisation, may well have led them to avoid politics altogether, rather than turning Tory. Modern findings have certainly not pointed to the unskilled as a major source of working-class Conservatism. But it is important, here, to reiterate the general point that political attitudes should not be sought out only in the overt acts of party membership, or even of voting, but in the less formal but still politically relevant areas of life. Given this it is possible to see such attitudes, including the apparently increasing instrumental-ism of the skilled worker, which it has been suggested heralded 'a new notion of work . . . as a limited segment of life',[73] leading to the adop-tion of values which might even be corrosive of 'traditionalism'. It is not, then, the argument here that working-class Conservatism, or other politics, can be wholly explained by 'traditionalism', but that, at least, it is relevant.

Changes in working-class 'culture' can be seen in a similar light. In contrast to an earlier period of arguably more authentic working-class culture in the first half of the nineteenth century,[74] it has been argued that by the latter decades of the century the working class had become more introverted and defensive.[75] Middle-class contemporary opinion, and later students, have tended to see the development of its best known cultural institution, the music hall (and its successor the cinema), as evidence of the foisting upon the working class of a surrogate middle-class culture founded upon and sustained by commercial motives and profits.[76] The more marginal of the working class may have been susceptible to such influence, partly as a result of improved standards of life and rising expectations. An acute contemporary analysis of the cheaper Lancashire music halls in 1900 noted that the songs

have indeed no individuality. And the cause of this is surely to be found in the fact that they do not come spontaneously from the people, but are brought to them by purveyors who belong to another class. The music of the poor in our own day, and in the last generation seems to be a debauched form of the music, often trivial enough in itself, of the richer classes, manufactured wholesale, like the tawdry imitations of jewels with which the eyes of the poor are dazzled and deceived.[77]

Whether authentically or spuriously working-class, there can be little doubt that the image of society produced by the halls by the turn of the century was a mixture of Conservatism, traditionalism and a certain sullen acceptance of the established order.

There had, however, been attempts to politicise the 'new' working-class culture. The development of the working-men's clubs in the 1860s, in part an attempt to undermine the tyranny of the pubs, was closely bound up with party politics. The Club and Institute Union was nominally neutral in politics, but was dominated by Liberals; whilst Radical and Liberal Clubs affiliated to it in the 1880s it is noticeable that Conservative ones did not.[78] The political division was also evident in the regional distribution of the clubs, with the CIU weak in Lancashire, where the Conservative Working-Men's Clubs predominated.[79] The Conservatives, however, were not enthusiastic supporters of their own clubs, many of them owing a conflicting allegiance to the breweries' pubs. In 1884, for example, two Conservative MPs blocked a bill which would have secured for the clubs the protection of the Registrar of Friendly Societies.[80] In general the clubs tended to be found and dominated by middle-class initiative and leadership, with the working men doing the chores, such as canvassing,[81] and as political organisations of the working class they can hardly be said to have succeeded. On the one hand the politicians had to emphasise the importance of 'social' activity in attracting members in the first place, while, on the other, they had quickly to remind members that 'clubs are pledged to certain political principles'.[82] The complaint of the Bedfordshire Conservative Club in 1896 was familiar: 'we regret to say that it is difficult to induce the great majority of members to take an interest in politics, except when elections are imminent'.[83] In 1906 Franke Solbe, secretary of the Association of Conservative Clubs,

regretted to say that on current questions of the day, the individual Radical Clubman was better informed than the individual Conservative Clubman: he displayed more interest in political work and his services were more promptly and prominently recognised than on our own side. In many Conservative Clubs it had to be admitted that the political enthusiast was regarded as a 'bore', and cold water was thrown on his efforts to help forward the very cause that the Club was founded to further.[84]

The message seemed to have had little effect, and it was, indeed, difficult to prevent Radical infiltration because insufficient political discussion ever took place to disclose the fact![85] Even had the Conservative Clubs been greater political mobilisers than they seem to have been, it would remain unclear whether their members had been made Conservative by joining the clubs, or had joined the clubs because they were Conservative. The idea that the lure of the billiard table would seduce them into voting Conservative was probably never seriously entertained. The clubs were, for all their political inertia, really for activists; their purpose lay not in conversion but in organisation, and in that their success was limited, so that for the large majority of working-class Conservatives it is a matter of looking at the source of the harvest, rather than at the manner in which it was reaped.

These then are some of the ways in which the structures of the family, education, religion, work and culture have made traditionalism a significant factor in the formation of working-class ideology. In many cases, it must be admitted, no simple association with political attitudes emerges. In many, but not all, cases such traditionalism was common to the lives of most of the working class, and most of the working class neither voted for nor counted themselves as Conservatives. But support for all parties amongst the organised working class has almost always been economistic in nature, not the attempt to secure 'the whole produce of labour', but to obtain 'a fair day's wage for a fair day's work'. Labour leaders could be as 'deferential', 'respectable' and as 'traditionalist' as any of their *confrères* who voted Conservative. One recalls Engels's complaint that 'even Tom Mann, who I regard as the best of the lot, is fond of mentioning that he will be lunching with the Lord Mayor. If one compares this with the French, one realises what a revolution is good for after all.'[86] And it is true that *ouvriérisme* was not the hallmark of the British labour movement; *épater le bourgeois* was not for them. Merely because such attitudes did not result in uniform political behaviour, however, does not mean to say that they were insignificant. Similar ideological foundations may result in different party affiliations, especially when the ideological distance between the parties is perceived not to be great, and it was so perceived by many people, not only working men. There was, and seems still to be a lack

of coherence between formal political attitudes and more general political orientations. Many modern studies of the working-class Conservative have noted that while giving general endorsement to the established
order, he will protest against the way it immediately affects him, and
this kicking against the pricks may take the place of a more general
heaving against the yoke.[87] In such cases unionists, communists, immigrants or even a bad boss will be blamed for any shortcomings of the
system. It may also lead to a rejection of party politics in general. As
Reynolds put it in 1911:

> political opinion is a matter of class and class experience; it bears
> close upon the hard facts of life; and has behind it the fellow-feeling
> that exists between those who live hand to mouth, and who work
> for masters . . . Party divisions [on the other hand] are created by
> outsiders.[88]

It was precisely for these reasons that Reynolds found Tariff Reform
properly 'Radical', because it cut across party divisions, and although
he might be said to have been grinding a political axe here, his argument
has a ring of truth about it. Most people call upon a wide range of often
contradictory notions to explain political phenomena. Aware of 'class'
they may deny that they belong to any class; or having experienced
conflicts of interest, at work perhaps, they may maintain belief in a
wider harmony of interests, without ever having heard of Adam
Smith![89]

The significance of those who fail to conform to established and
articulated ideologies should not be lost, and it is more rewarding to
look at working-class Conservatism in a wider context of shared incoherence, than as at some species of ideological leper. Thus, opposition
to big capital and to big labour; the appeal from principle to common
sense; hostility to the state; attachment to the close and familiar,
whether in the context of neighbourhood, family, class, religion or
moral values; an acceptance of the political status quo, coupled with a
distrust of those who maintain it; all these may be found as parts of an
internally consistent ideology, which certain of the working class have
shared with others.[90]

While there is not space to exemplify this in any detail, the case of
George Acorn helps to bring it into focus. He was born in the East End
of London in the later nineteenth century, of a poor, illiterate and
'rough' family. His father had no regular job, and consequently his
mother was always in debt. George went to a local ragged school and

learnt to be self-sufficient at an early age. He shared the local anti-
semitism, but, it seems, escaped from falling into the criminal and semi-
criminal classes around him. His membership of church youth organisations made him ponder an army career, but his parents held the common
view that soldiers were no better than thieves. He therefore entered the
furniture trade, the staple local occupation. Significantly, perhaps, as
soon as he could he set up his own business, but finding it difficult to
sell his products he returned to paid employment. He became a journey-
man, left home and married. He soon became ill, however, as a consequence of his working conditions, and was thus deprived of a chance of
joining the ranks of the labour aristocracy. His view of the system
through which he had come was of

> a great machine that catches up all kinds of classes of workers, and
> mangles their sense of proportion and honesty. It is not for any class
> to blame another, all alike come within its iron cogs, and are thrown
> out like a stray bolt whenever it slackens its infernal speed.[91]

There was, for Acorn, no question of collective action, no class analysis,
virtually no political response at all, and yet here were undoubtedly
some of the ingredients from which working-class Conservatism could
have been made. Other men who were more politically active like the
Liverpool docker George Milligan, or the ex-ILPer Harry Roberts, or a
number of the trade unionists who ended up in the British Workers'
League, also demonstrated an hostility to 'the machine'. They did find
the opportunity to suggest remedies, like a return to 'good masters', or
profit-sharing and co-partnership, which drew them closer to traditional
Conservatism.[92]

The term 'traditionalism' has been used in this essay to indicate what
seem to have been important, although by no means predominant
attitudes amongst the working class. It might, however, be better to see
such attitudes less as an appendage or shadow of Conservatism, than as
proto-populist in character. Traditionalism did not, as we have seen,
necessarily or always cause people to adhere to Conservatism in a party
sense. Traditionalists tended not to be overawed by party labels, and to
show scant regard for the niceties of party distinctions. Those who
evinced such attitudes were, it seems, open to the advances of either
Labour or Conservatism. Such men were nothing if not volatile in their
political proclivities. Many others, of course, failed to attain this level
of political consciousness or activity, but the third of manual workers

who have voted Conservative since the Second World War indicate that
such men and women, uncountable in the ante-Gallup dark age, and
many of them without a vote, were no eccentric fringe, and that their
ideology was not just an interesting paradox. They were rather an integral part of the development of working-class ideology during a period
when the stresses of a maturing economy and the strains of an emergent
formal democracy were having their greatest effect.

Acknowledgment

I should like to thank, in particular, Rodney Barker and the editors for
their always helpful and insightful comments in this essay.

Notes

1. E.P. Thompson, *The Making of the English Working Class* (Harmondsworth,
1968), pp. 916-17; J.T. Ward, 'Some Aspects of Working-class Conservatism in the
Nineteenth Century', J. Butt and J.T. Ward (eds.), *Scottish Themes* (Edinburgh,
1976), pp. 141ff.
2. N.C. Edsall, *The Anti-Poor Law Movement, 1834-44* (Manchester, 1971),
pp. 77-8.
3. E.J. Feuchtwanger, *Disraeli, Democracy and the Tory Party* (Oxford,
1968); P. Smith, *Disraelian Conservatism and Social Reform* (1967).
4. H.J. Hanham, *Elections and Party Management* (1959), pp. 107-9; T.
Lloyd, *The General Election of 1880* (Oxford, 1968), pp. 47-9; Feuchtwanger,
Disraeli, pp. 91ff, 194; Smith, *Disraeli*, p. 258; P.F. Clarke, *Lancashire and the
New Liberalism* (Cambridge, 1971), p. 35; S. Salvidge, *Salvidge of Liverpool*
(1934), pp. 15-16, 26.
5. J.H. Robb, *The Primrose League, 1883-1906* (New York, 1942), pp. 49ff,
58, 63f, 143.
6. N. Soldon, 'Laissez-faire as Dogma: the Liberty and Property Defence
League', K. Brown (ed.), *Essays in Anti-Labour History* (1974), pp. 214f; B.H.
Brown, *The Tariff Reform Movement in Great Britain, 1881-95* (New York,
1943), pp. 33-4; K. Brown, 'The Anti-Socialist Union', in K. Brown, *Essays*,
pp. 234-61; K. Brown, 'The Trade Union Tariff Reform Association, 1904-1913',
Journal of British Studies, vol. 9 (1970), p. 151. For instances of coolness at local
level see M. Blanch, 'Nation, Empire and the Birmingham Working Class,
1899-1914' (Birmingham University Ph.D., 1975), pp. 203ff.
7. R. Douglas, 'The National Democratic Party and the British Workers
League', *Historical Journal*, vol. 15 (1972), pp. 533-52; A. Gamble, *The Conservative Nation* (1974), passim; and an interesting letter from a member of the CTUO
to *The Times*, 1 July 1977, p. 26.
8. E.A. Nordlinger, *Working-class Tories* (1967), p. 13.
9. H. Newby, *The Deferential Worker* (1977), goes some way towards recti-
fying this neglect.
10. Bob Jessop, *Tradition, Conservatism and British Political Culture* (1974),
pp. 144-68.
11. W.G. Runciman, *Relative Deprivation and Social Justice* (1966), pp. 170-87;
Jessop, *Tradition*, pp. 188-91, 195ff;
12. M. Stacey, *Tradition and Change: a Study of Banbury* (1960), p. 16..

13. D. Lockwood, 'Sources of Variation in Working-class Images of Society', *Sociological Review*, n.s. vol. 14 (1966), pp. 249-67. This is reprinted in M. Bulmer (ed.), *Working-class Images of Society* (1975), pp. 16-31, a collection of important critical examinations of Lockwood's thesis.

14. Nordlinger, *Working-Class Tories*, pp. 163-4; R. McKenzie and A. Silver, *Angels in Marble* (1968), pp. 92, 139.

15. D. Kavanagh, 'The Deferential English', *Government and Opposition* vol. 6 (1971), pp. 333-60; Jessop, *Tradition*, pp. 30ff.

16. F. Parkin, 'Working-class Conservatism: a Theory of Political Deviance', *British Journal of Sociology* vol. 18 (1967), pp. 278-90.

17. K. Marx and F. Engels, *Selected Correspondence* (1965), pp. 110, 315, 365, 407-8, 411-12. Cf. also Eleanor Marx to Wilhelm Liebknecht, talking of 'the English workman – than whom (between you and me) a worse crew does not exist', *Wilhelm Liebknecht Briefwechsel mit Karl Marx und Friedrich Engels*, G. Eckert (ed.), (The Hague, 1963), p. 428.

18. See the excellent discussion in D. Scott, 'The National Front in Local Politics: Some Interpretations', I. Crewe (ed.), *British Political Sociology Yearbook*, vol. 2, 'The Politics of Race' (1975), pp. 214-38.

19. R. Descartes, *Discourses on Method* (Harmondsworth, 1960 ed.), p. 54. Cf. also Sir Arthur Helps, *Claims of Labour* (1854 ed.), p. 67.

20. P. Converse, 'The Nature of Belief Systems in Mass Publics', D. Apter (ed.), *Ideology and Discontent* (New York, 1964), p. 213.

21. S. Reynolds and B. and T. Woolley, *Seems So! a Working-class View of Politics* (1911), pp. 137-8.

22. C.E. Rayleigh, 'Canvassing Experiences in an Agricultural Constituency', *National Review*, vol. 7 (1886), p. 180.

23. I. Crewe, 'Do Butler and Stokes Really Explain Political Change in Britain?', *European Journal of Political Research*, vol. 2 (1974), p. 48, n.4.

24. For criticism of the ahistorical nature of recent studies of working-class images see J. Cousins and R. Brown, 'Patterns of Paradox: Shipbuilding Workers' Images of Society', R. L. Davis and J. Cousins, 'The "New Working Class" and the Old', and M. Bulmer, 'Some Problems of Research into Class Images', all in Bulmer, *Working-class Images*, pp. 55-6, 192-6 and 170-1.

25. Nordlinger, *Working-class Tories*, pp. 67ff; D. Butler and D. Stokes, *Political Change in Britain* (Harmondsworth, 1971 ed.), pp. 63-78, 136-49. McKenzie and Silver, *Angels in Marble*, pp. 89ff, failed to find a depression generation, but W. Hampton suggests that this was due to their choosing inappropriate cohorts, and presents evidence from Sheffield to support the general theory: 'Working-class angels', *Bulletin of the Society for the Study of Labour History*, no. 18 (1969), pp. 62-3. Further support is given by F. Bealey, J. Blondel and W.P. McCann, *Constituency Politics* (1965), pp. 171-2.

26. D. Marsh, 'Political Socialisation: the Implicit Assumptions Questioned', *British Journal of Political Science*, vol. 1 (1971), pp. 453-65.

27. N. Blewett, 'The Franchise in the United Kingdom, 1885-1918', *Past and Present*, no. 32 (1965), p. 31.

28. H.C.G. Matthew, R.I. McKibbin and J.A. Kay, 'The Franchise Factor in the Rise of the Labour Party', *English Historical Review*, vol. 91 (1976), p. 727.

29. Ibid., p. 740; but see P.F. Clarke, 'Liberals, Labour and the Franchise', ibid., vol. 92 (1977), pp. 582-90.

30. Matthew et al., 'The Franchise Factor', ibid., p. 747. For evidence of this at municipal level see C. Cook, *The Age of Alignment* (1975), pp. 84-5, where 56 per cent of the worst housed urban workers are reckoned to have voted Conservative in the 1920s.

31. Quoted in H. Pelling, *Social Geography of British Elections, 1885-1910* (1967), p. 9. For a list of the English constituencies classified from the 1911

census see N. Blewett, *The Peers, The Parties and The People* (1972), pp. 488-94.
32. Blewett, ibid. (1972), p. 21.
33. Matthew et al., 'The Franchise Factor', p. 728.
34. Ibid., pp. 740-1.
35. Pelling, *Social Geography*, pp. 12, 16, 425-6.
36. Ibid., pp. 189-90, 202, 210, 213, 232.
37. Ibid., pp. 182, 232-3.
38. Ibid., pp. 53-4, 250.
39. M. Weber, *The Theory of Social and Economic Organisation* (New York, 1964), p. 425.
40. D.C. Moore, *The Politics of Deference* (Hassocks, 1976), p. 12 and passim.
41. R.W. Davis, 'Deference and Aristocracy in the time of the Great Reform Act', *American Historical Review*, vol. 81 (1976), pp. 532-39; idem, *Political Change and Continuity, 1760-1885* (Newton Abbot, 1972); T.J. Nossiter, *Influence, Opinion and Political Ideas in Reformed England, 1832-74* (Hassocks, 1975).
42. J. H. de Ricci, *The Welfare of the People* (1885, 3rd ed.), p. 5.
43. P. Joyce, 'Popular Toryism in Lancashire, 1860-1890' (Oxford University D.Phil. 1975), pp. 3-4, 293ff; R. Olney, *Lincolnshire Politics, 1832-1885* (Oxford, 1973), pp. 231ff.
44. J.A. Bridges, *Reminiscences of a Country Politician* (1906), p. 127.
45. Blewett, *The Peers, The Parties and The People* (1972), pp. 371-6, 404; Clarke, *Lancashire* (1971), p. 249; W. Forwood, *Recollections* (1910), p. 150.
46. D. Kirkwood, *My Life of Revolt* (1935), p. 1.
47. H. Pelling, *Popular Politics and Society in Late Victorian Britain* (1968), pp. 1-18, 174-9.
48. On the softening of this hostility in London see D. Rubinstein, 'Socialization and the London School Board, 1870-1904', P. McCann (ed.), *Popular Education and Socialization in the Nineteenth Century* (1977), pp. 254ff.
49. For a good discussion of this in Birmingham see Blanch, 'Nation, Empire and the Birmingham Working-Class', Chapters 2, 3, 4 and 14. For youth organisations in general see J.O. Springhall, *Youth, Empire and Society* (1977).
50. J. Gillis, 'The Evolution of Juvenile Delinquency in England, 1890-1914', *Past and Present*, no. 67 (1975), pp. 96-126. On the important matter of juvenile gangs see Blanch, 'Nation, Empire', pp. 220, 290-1; W. Goldman, *East End My Cradle* (1940), pp. 87ff; G. Acorn, *One of the Multitude* (1911), pp. 16ff.
51. Clarke, *Lancashire* (1971), passim.
52. For English Orangeism see Joyce, 'Popular Toryism in Lancashire', pp. 183ff; Hanham, *Elections and Party Management*, pp. 303-7; Salvidge, *Salvidge of Liverpool*, pp. 44-7; and R.L. Greenall, 'Popular Conservatism in Salford, 1868-1886', *Northern History*, vol. 9 (1974), pp. 131ff.
53. P. Doyle, 'Religion, Politics and the Catholic Working Class', *New Blackfriars*, vol. 54 (1973), pp. 218ff. For Scotland see P. Fotherigham, 'The Political Behaviour of the Working Class', A. MacLaren (ed.), *Social Class in Scotland* (Edinburgh, 1976), p. 145, and for Wales J. Hickey, *Urban Catholics* (1967), pp. 119ff.
54. R. Moore, *Pit-Men, Preachers and Politics* (Cambridge, 1974), pp. 223ff.
55. K. Inglis, *The Churches and the Working Class* (1963); H. Macleod, *Class and Religion in the Late Victorian City* (1974), pp. 42ff.
56. G. Haw (ed.), *Christianity and the Working Classes* (1906), p. 41.
57. Acorn, *One of the Multitude*, p. 51.
58. Inglis, *Churches and the Working Class*, pp. 21-61, 250ff.
59. Bridges, *Reminiscences of a Country Politician*, pp. 86ff.
60. C. Cannon, 'The Influence of Religion on Educational Policy, 1902-1944', P.W. Musgrave (ed.), *Sociology, History and Education* (1970), pp. 162-79.

61. W.G. Blaikie, *Better Days for Working People* (Edinburgh, 1894 ed.), p. 107.

62. Bramwell Booth, in Haw (ed.), *Christianity*, p. 152; Springhall, *Youth, Empire and Society*, pp. 25, 71-80, 91; Blanch, 'Nation, Empire', pp. 306, 309-10.

63. J. Lovell, *British Trade Unions, 1875-1933* (1977), pp. 24ff; B. Holton, *British Syndicalism, 1900-1914* (1976), p. 144.

64. Clarke, *Lancashire* (1971), p. 43; F. Bealey and H. Pelling, *Labour and Politics* (1958), pp. 16ff, 100ff.

65. K.G.J. Knowles, *Strikes* (Oxford, 1952), pp. 197, 207.

66. Joyce, 'Popular Toryism in Lancashire', p. 5.

67. Clarke, *Lancashire* (1971), pp. 82-3.

68. H.A. Turner, *Trade Union Growth, Structure and Policy* (1962), p. 117; K. Burgess, *The Origins of British Industrial Relations* (1975), p. 215.

69. J. Hinton, *The First Shop Steward Movement* (1973), pp. 56ff.

70. Blanch, 'Nation, Empire', p. 194.

71. E.R. Wickham, *Church and People in an Industrial City* (1957), pp. 135ff, 159f; H.K. Hawson, *Sheffield, the Growth of a City, 1893-1926* (Sheffield, 1968), pp. 286ff; S. Pollard, *History of Labour in Sheffield* (Liverpool, 1959), pp. 197ff.

72. Pelling, *Social Geography* (1967), pp. 424-5. Leadership of the unskilled, however, was increasingly Irish: E.D. Steele, 'The Irish Presence in the North of England, 1850-1914', *Northern History*, vol. 12 (1976), p. 241.

73. P.N. Stearns, *Lives of Labour* (1975), pp. 200-1, and 247, 288, 324-5; cf. also idem, 'the Unskilled and Industrialisation', *Archiv für Sozialgeschichte*, vol. 16 (1976), pp. 249-82.

74. On its decline see L. James, *Fiction for the Working Man* (Oxford, 1963).

75. G.S. Jones, 'Working-class Culture and Working-class Politics in London, 1870-1900; Notes on the Remaking of a Working Class', *Journal of Social History*, vol. 7 (1974), pp. 460-508; S. Meacham, *A Life Apart* (1977).

76. L. Senelick, 'Politics as Entertainment: Victorian Music Halls', *Victorian Studies*, vol. 19 (1975), pp. 149-80; M. Vicinus, *The Industrial Muse* (1974), p. 249.

77. C.E.B. Russell and E.T. Campagnac, 'Poor People's Music Halls in Lancashire', *Economic Review*, vol. 10 (1900), pp. 294-5. For a recent interpretation along these lines see J. Taylor, *From Self Help to Glamour* (Oxford, 1973).

78. *Club and Institute Journal*, 23 November 1883, pp. 75-6.

79. B.T. Hall, *Our Sixty Years* (1922), p. 282; Joyce, 'Popular Toryism in Lancashire', pp. 269, 327-28; Hanham, *Elections and Party Management*, pp. 102-4.

80. *Club and Institute Journal*, 24 October 1884, p. 238.

81. Taylor, *Self-Help to Glamour*, pp. 3ff; Joyce, 'Popular Toryism in Lancashire', pp. 270ff, 249ff; W.F. Rae, 'Political Clubs and Political Organisations', *Nineteenth Century*, vol. 3 (1878), pp. 925-9.

82. *Monthly Circular* of the Association of Conservative Clubs, April 1895, p. 1; July, p. 19.

83. Ibid., January 1896, p. 73.

84. Ibid., June 1906, p. 85.

85. Ibid., February 1910, p. 24.

86. Marx and Engels, *Selected Correspondence*, pp. 407-8.

87. M. Mann, 'The Social Cohesion of Liberal Democracy', *American Sociological Review*, vol. 35 (1970), pp. 429ff; Cousins and Brown, loc. cit., p. 74.

88. Reynolds, Woolley and Woolley, *Seems So!*, p. 164.

89. Cousins and Brown, loc.cit., p. 72.

90. For a discussion in connection with the lower middle class see G.

Crossick (ed.), *The Lower Middle Class in Britain 1870-1914* (1977), pp. 35-48.

91. Acorn, *One of the Multitude*, p. 209.

92. G. Milligan, *Life Through Labour's Eyes* (1911); H. Roberts, *Constructive Conservatism* (1913), p. 15; P. Field, *The Handshake of Capital and Labour, or Tory Radicals* (1912); A. Williams, *Co-partnership and Profitsharing* (1913); J.O. Stubbs, 'Lord Milner and Patriotic Labour, 1914-1918', *English Historical Review*, vol. 87 (1972), pp. 717-54.

6 WORKING-CLASS WOMEN AND MATRIMONIAL LAW REFORM, 1890-1914

Iris Minor

As working-class women had little opportunity to articulate their ideals and politicise their experiences, the social reforms achieved on their behalf were based upon ideological perceptions of their difficulties developed by men and women in other social classes. There is evidence which indicates that many reforms, both directly and indirectly influencing working-class family life, failed to take account of the lack of economic and social resources available to women in the poorest households. Consequently, these reforms were often irrelevant; and sometimes they constituted a cultural assault upon those least willing or able to adopt different ways. In addition the *ad hoc* nature of the reform process ensured that reformers could not anticipate the full implications of legislative changes. An examination of legal intervention in broken or disrupted families illustrates some of the more extreme circumstances in which liberal law reforms and philanthropic social policies tended to aggravate the problems confronting many of the poorest women and children.

In the nineteenth century certain socialists and feminists had provided an important stimulus to the ideas surrounding family law reform and the position of women in society. But although they developed an understanding of the economic and ideological bases of Western marriage, the proponents of radical change failed to persuade the organised labour movement to accept their views. Nor were radicals and socialists agreed about the importance of working-class participation in the reform process. By the early twentieth century the Fabian Women's Group and the Women's Co-operative Guild were making the most consistent contributions to reform proposals specifically directed at working-class wives and mothers; but despite their claims to speak for the majority of these women, neither of the groups could boast that their organisations truly represented them.

Trade unionists, on the other hand, were anxious to avoid adopting reform campaigns which were likely to split their ranks. The male-dominated unions were not prepared to put what seemed to be feminist issues before the interests of working-class men. In some respects the labour movement was being rapidly overtaken by economic and social changes affecting families in the last few decades before the First World War. The quest for national efficiency and the regeneration of the race, coupled with attempts to forestall the impending challenge to the two party system by feminists and the labour lobby, resulted in many politicians being sympathetic to reform proposals made by frustrated officials who wanted to use the existing methods of public administration more efficiently.

All these factors were among the elements influencing the nature and direction of social reform, including the highly specific sphere of matrimonial law reform. The relative lack of socialist leadership and working-class involvement in issues pertaining to working-class women in the family helps to explain why those reforms designed to alter the position of women in society were those which were particularly relevant to middle- and upper-class family property and sexual morality. Besides, socialist reform proposals necessitated political claims against private property, whereas legalistic reforms of claims between individuals were normally easier to effect.

From the late nineteenth century, by a process of amendments and new precedents, the bureaucracies and institutions of the legal system redefined many rights and duties established in matrimonial law. However, the means by which these rights and duties were to be applied among the poorest sections of society were a political issue which remained outside the terms of reference of the legal system. There is evidence to suggest that attempts at such application did not meet with any great success before 1914.

The origins of modern English family law are to be found in the property and sexual relations of the nobility, for whom the common law proved to be inadequate. Following the liberalising pressures of the new rich and the middle classes, the administration of the divorce and separation agreements under the law of equity were to some extent written into the common law by the Matrimonial Causes Act of 1857. The new Central Divorce Court granted the right to a divorce or a judicial separation, provided certain matrimonial crimes were proved to have been committed, and provided a plaintiff could afford the procedure or qualify to have certain expenses waived. However, in spite of the lobby of a small group of women, the new divorce code continued to operate to the advantage of men, and the property and authority vested in them. An aggrieved woman could not apply for divorce on the same grounds as a man; husbands were granted divorces on grounds of uncondoned adultery, whereas wives were obliged to prove this offence in conjunction with cruelty, desertion or sexual crimes. If an aggrieved wife was prepared to settle for a permanent judicial separation, she was allowed similar grounds to a man. However, it was only in the event of a wife being fortunate enough to possess separate property in equity law that she could sue on her own behalf, and that following a suit she could retain capital in her name for her own separate use. The restrictions on both the property rights and sexual freedom of married women not only inhibited the extent to which they had their own legal identity, but also limited the degree to which aggrieved wives could claim custody and control of their children. Any woman found guilty of uncondoned adultery had no right either to maintenance or the custody of her children.[1]

The early women's movements therefore centred upon these issues of property and matrimonial law; but during the 1860s additional campaigns that illustrated equally well the middle- and upper-class women's position in society provided added impetus to a number of pressure groups. By the late nineteenth century the divorce issue was regarded as one of many reasons why votes for women was a necessary reform; once the vote had been won the opinion of women would have to be considered in legislation relating to divorce. However, in the decade before the First World War, during the mounting political frustration and the eventual isolation of the suffragettes, all other women's causes were subordinated to that of obtaining the vote.

The preoccupation of the women's movement with issues originating in the property rights of the individual helps to explain why the branch of law reform relating specifically to propertyless working-class women had developed with the minimum of direct campaigning by the main reform groups during the last quarter of the nineteenth century. Officials of public agencies, notably Poor Law administrators, and interested philanthropists provided the main impetus for reforms that attempted to bring the law within reach of the poorer population, and on the terms which it was thought would meet some of the specific marital difficulties of the lower classes.[2] In 1868 Parliament authorised Poor Law guardians to incur legal costs in enforcing maintenance for deserted families who would otherwise become a burden on the rates. The numbers of deserted applying for help rose, and by the 1880s the guardians and law reformers were concerned to find an alternative way of enforcing maintenance for those who were neither propertied and the subject of a judicial separation agreement, nor truly to be regarded as among the regular pauper class. In 1886, therefore, the Maintenance of Wives Act empowered magistrates in local courts to grant and enforce maintenance orders of no more than £2 a week in the hope that people

who could neither afford the services of the divorce court nor accept
the discrimination of Poor Law intervention, would now use the new
facilities to regularise their arrangements.

Meanwhile public discussion of what appeared to be a common
practice of wife-beating in working-class families led in 1878 to magistrates being given the power of granting swift and cheap separation
orders to women who could prove a specific incident of physical assault.
The subsequent Summary Jurisdiction (Married Women) Act of 1895
made it easier for women to gain the protection of the court since it
was considered sufficient for the plaintiff to prove persistent physical
cruelty; in addition this act allowed a wife a cheap separation order on
the grounds of a husband being sentenced to prison for a period of two
months or more. The other great threat to the stability of working-class
families besides violence and crime was considered to be the related
problem of drink. Section Five of the Licensing Act of 1902 included
habitual drunkenness on the part of either spouse as a ground for a
magistrate's separation order.

The most notable feature of separation orders was the fact that the
moral strictures of the Central Divorce Court were applied. If it could
be proved that a wife had been guilty of uncondoned adultery, no
maintenance or custody of the children would be granted to her following a separation order. However, as will be shown later from the discussion generated by the Royal Commission on Divorce between 1909-12,
it appears that, in so far as the working class was concerned, this branch
of family law did not match reality. It was in many respects morally
unacceptable and economically inapplicable to poorer wives and
mothers.

I

Although feminists and some socialists had provided a stimulus to
changing ideas on marriage and divorce, neither occupied a central role
in the final thrust of agitation leading to the appointment of the Royal
Commission on Divorce and Matrimonial Causes in 1909. Three years
earlier the Divorce Law Reform Union had been formed with the intention of mobilising those who had either a personal or professional
interest in obtaining law reform. The movement avoided wider ideological issues, preferring to rest its case on utilitarian arguments and case
histories.

There had been growing disquiet that the utility of the matrimonial
laws was undermined by the fact that they were not readily applicable
to the domestic affairs and financial resources of the majority of poorer

working-class families. In 1909 the Liberal Government appointed Gorell Barnes, a distinguished judge, to chair the Royal Commission on Divorce. His terms of reference required him to 'inquire into the present state of the law and the administration thereof . . . especially with regard to the position of the poorer classes in relation thereto'.[3] The composition of the Royal Commission included two members chosen for their links with working-class people. Thomas Burt, the Northumberland miner who had sat in Parliament since 1874, could be relied upon to see that at least the views of organised working people would be fairly represented among the witnesses. May Tennant was the only woman member of the Commission, but in view of her earlier reputation as May Abraham in the factory inspectorate, it was hoped that she would ensure that the interests of women in all social classes would be protected. The Commissioners received evidence from representatives of the Fabian Women's Group and the Women's Co-operative Guild, and in the absence of any direct communication with women in the poorer sections of society they also sought information from church groups, social workers and legal administrators who had worked among the poor in official capacities.

Minority and Majority Reports were presented in 1912, together with a number of compromise proposals as an agreed basis for further reform. One historian has described the work of the Commission as 'a model of relevance, clarity and the thorough analysis of evidence . . . the last in the great Victorian tradition of investigating Commissions'.[4] Yet both reports betrayed two crucial weaknesses: the definition of the problems and solutions were ideologically biased, and there was an absence of any direct communication with sections of the working class other than the more highly organised and artisan minorities.

Although the Minority Report opposed any extension of the grounds of divorce which would have made it easier for people to revoke their Christian marriage vows, its signatories readily agreed with the Majority Report's contentions that on grounds of utility and natural justice the existing divorce code should be applied equally to men and women, and that the administration of the law should be accessible to rich and poor alike. These were well-worn liberal arguments which had long been associated with divorce law reform, and it was the main objective of the Royal Commission to ascertain whether, moral issues apart, there was a general opinion in favour of there being full equality before the law. The Commission's line of questioning was also preoccupied with the problem of protecting administrative and professional interests; for without any due regard for these matters legal reforms of such a magnitude were not very likely to be enacted. On all these points the Commissioners developed some clear impressions upon which to base their recommendations.

The Commission was not, however, so successful in gauging the extent to which those applying for legal separation would have applied for divorce if they had been allowed legal grounds and had sufficient finance to do so. Neither was the Commission in possession of any convincing evidence as to the importance couples placed on the marriage vow, or the types of behaviour most people deemed to be the cause or consequence of a breakdown in marriage. Although it was generally assumed that the terms of the divorce code were the main determinants influencing the terms upon which people were prepared to marry and to conduct their lives within marriage, no supporting evidence was produced. Attitudes of different social classes to marriage and divorce and the complex role of the law in the social and economic system could not easily be gauged from the statistics available for church and civil weddings, nor from the legal grounds given in cases before the magistrates and divorce courts.

Nor was progressive opinion of one mind. One of the most notable features of the evidence on divorce and the poor was that, apart from general agreement that the code should be liberalised, there were some conflicting views expressed by the socialist or politically progressive women's groups. Understandably, therefore, some of the issues relating more specifically to divorce and the poor were the subject of overgeneralisation, and being highly contentious were never incorporated into the general reform proposals.

The Minority Report considered that those favouring an extension of the grounds for divorce had drawn the wrong conclusions from the available divorce and separation statistics. It was pointed out that members of the Divorce Law Reform Union had publicised the fact that roughly half of those granted absolute divorces had remarried. The reformers had then assumed that a similar proportion of those obtaining separation orders would have wished to have been granted a divorce had the resources been available to finance the suit. The Minority Report, however, had been greatly impressed by the very common observation amongst social workers and magistrates that between 50 and 80 per cent of the separation orders were of an entirely temporary nature. The Women's Co-operative Guild suggested that many of these reconciliations were because the poorer wives lacked sufficient food and shelter for their families and were virtually forced to return to their husbands, accepting a life that was tantamount to prostitution. On the other hand there was considerable evidence to suggest that poorer couples quite frequently split up for a week or so at a time, or quarrelled violently, or threatened legal proceedings to enforce maintenance and other responsibilities. Social workers never ceased to be amazed that even after what seemed like a most cruel assault, desertion or blatant adultery, the majority of couples were subsequently found to be living together in a relatively happy state.[5]

The Minority Report drew attention to a crucial inconsistency in the statistics which recorded that as many as 8,000 separation orders were granted every year. During the examination of court officials it was discovered that very often women would apply for a maintenance order following their husband's neglect or desertion, but that the courts automatically coupled these requests with separation orders. It was, no doubt, a way of legally clarifying a husband's position, particularly if Poor Law relief was being claimed, though it began to be suspected that such a policy might not necessarily reflect a wife's attitude towards her husband. By 1907 many police courts had been persuaded not to grant separation orders automatically to wives who applied for maintenance. Although this new method of procedure and classification of the statistics was not universally adopted, it resulted in a marked decline in the numbers of separation orders recorded between 1907 and 1910, from 7,007 down to 4,539. The Minority Report contended that the records of the courts of summary jurisdiction had both exaggerated and misclassified the nature of marital disagreements brought to them. For instance, whilst many wives wanted the law to enforce maintenance, they had not necessarily considered such a situation warranted an order to keep them apart either permanently or temporarily.

The important function of social workers was repeatedly drawn to the attention of the Commission, but no proposals were linked to the administrative reforms suggested by either report. Members of the NSPCC had told of their success in dealing with marital problems which they discovered in the course of their work in child rescue. Some of their officers had helped reconciliations between parents and in so doing the cruelty towards the children had stopped before legal intervention had been initiated. In other cases it had been noted that following a separation and maintenance order the children were often sent round to their fathers to collect the money and the constant aggravation of family conflict resulted in further violence. In some instances the officers had prevented this source of quarrelling by offering to collect and deliver the maintenance money themselves. This had often calmed the resentment between the parties and left the way open to a subsequent reconciliation whilst continuing to ensure the maintenance and protection of the children. Similar success stories were reported by some of the police court missionaries, and the Mothers' Union had proposed that a paid official should be employed by the courts to undertake this work. The idea was to help prevent ill-considered applications to the courts, to effect reconciliation wherever possible, and to assist with the difficulties of broken homes.[6]

The suggestion that social workers should be incorporated into the legal procedure fell on stony ground. Those who were opposed to anything that could act as a barrier between the people and their legal rights made no mention of the possible function of mediation that could be performed by social workers. For example, the Fabian Women's Group proposed that maintenance money should be paid through a court official. It was suggested that the state should then be responsible for monitoring arrears, adjusting orders and enforcing payments. By incurring the responsibility and costs of this function, it was suggested that the state should act in joint guardianship over the children of broken homes.[7]

The Women's Co-operative Guild proposed divorce by mutual consent, the removal of matrimonial cases from the police courts and the introduction of women into the legal administration as ways in which the interpretation and enforcement of family law would prove more responsive to the problems of the poor and of women especially.[8] They too favoured court collection of maintenance and legal restrictions against arrears. There was, however, no mention of the idea of the state acting in joint guardianship over the children of broken homes, but instead there was a suggestion that a system of free legal advice and litigation should be provided wherever necessary. With reference to the idea that social workers should be employed to mediate between estranged couples in order to help them resolve their difficulties, members of the Women's Co-operative Guild were divided. Some of their members had thought that it was an excellent idea, but many others had expressed distrust of any stranger attempting to interfere in such matters. It was thought that outsiders would never be able to understand fully the nature of marital discord between two individuals and any attempt to remonstrate or mediate was likely to be clumsy and to result in further confusion and enmity. Margaret Llewelyn Davies recommended that no provision for mediation should be included in the legal procedure. Nor was the proposal favourably regarded by the Fabian Women, who distrusted the role of officials and voluntary workers if given the power to interfere between individuals and their democratically agreed rights.

It is true that the reaction of working people to the intrusion of social workers depended greatly upon their own assessment of the nature of their difficulties, and the moral implications of any assistance given. Thus the intervention of a police court missionary was very likely to be considered 'impertinent', but other relief agencies were regarded as more acceptable. In view of the divided opinions on the subject, and no doubt allowing for the extreme lack of resources available to courts for the employment of social workers, this area of discussion did not carry any proposals forward into the reforms suggested by either of the Divorce Commission's reports.

Some witnesses, including those of the Fabian Women's Group and the Women's Co-operative Guild, had campaigned to have incurable insanity, alcoholism, marital violence, prolonged imprisonment and venereal disease considered sufficient grounds for divorce. The Women's Co-operative Guild argued that such additional grounds for divorce would help to raise the status of wives and mothers, since husbands might be deterred from behaviour that could lead to the termination of their marriages. They also drew attention to the fact that, if such circumstances developed in wealthy households there were usually resources available for couples to make civilised arrangements for living separately whilst under the same roof. This was impossible in homes where whole families shared one or two rooms, and if wives absented themselves from their husbands' homes they usually lacked sufficient resources to live independently. Their desertion of the home moreover, jeopardised the likelihood of their obtaining a maintenance order or even outdoor Poor Law relief. It was suggested, therefore, that the only solution for the poor was to grant divorces on certain additional grounds and ultimately to allow divorce on demand.

It should be noted that the Women's Co-operative Guild fully recognised that for women 'reforms of the marriage law without change in their economic position may be of little use to many whose lives are being ruined by marriage'. But the majority of their members came from stable homes, enjoyed fair employment opportunities and supportive families and friends, so understandably, therefore, the Guild boldly declared that were they unhappily married 'they would wish to be free, and would risk the economic difficulties'. Margaret Llewelyn Davies assured the Royal Commission that 'the economic question will have to be dealt with, but our attitude towards divorce should not depend upon it'.[9] The Guild were prepared to alter the legal organisation of the family before changing the economic and social foundations upon

which it was based. Their failure to take up even the tentative suggestion of the Fabian Women, to establish guardianship by the state of
broken families, indicates the hesitation with which they greeted proposals for collective social responsibility.

No doubt the fact that the proposals of the Royal Commission were
based on the most tenuous area of agreement helps to explain why
government response was so slow to materialise. There were also very
powerful and vested professional interests at stake, and the Minority
Report had sufficient backing to delay any immediate action. Gorell
Barnes, the chairman of the Commission, died in 1913, and although
his son introduced a bill in that year, the lack of parliamentary time,
followed by the interruption of the war years, delayed further discussion. In 1920 a number of regional divorce courts were finally established, and in 1923 wives were given equal rights to sue for divorce
on grounds of adultery. It was not until 1937 that new grounds for
divorce were included.

The widening of the grounds upon which divorce and legal separation could be granted probably reduced the degree to which the law
tried to impose a particular moral code upon people in very different
social situations and cultural groups. The fact that during the first half
of the twentieth century there was a relative increase in the number of
people suing for divorce rather than separation, and a relative increase
in the number of wives suing for divorce, is usually taken to signify
the very gradual removal of the economic and legal barriers that had
denied people equal rights and access to the law. However, from the
evidence that is available on certain aspects of working-class life before
the First World War, the little progress that was made in these respects
in the last part of the nineteenth and early twentieth centuries was not
achieved without incurring some serious social costs.

II

The terms of reference of the Royal Commission on Divorce undoubtedly restricted the kind of evidence about working-class family life
which could be considered as relevant. It is significant that the greatest
insights into the morality and family life of the poor may be gained
from the observations of social investigators and philanthropists engaged upon their task of explaining, measuring or ameliorating poverty.
Some of the more astute social investigators and philanthropists had
come to the conclusion that it was difficult to make generalisations
about working-class culture and behaviour. It was not simply that there
were so many different status and occupational groups within communi-

ties of varying economic and institutional compositions; the significance of any commonly held values and customs differed during the course of a lifetime and in the context of highly specific economic and social situations.

Following his investigation of the labouring population in London, Charles Booth concluded that although legal marriage was 'the general rule, even among the roughest class' at least at the outset in life, 'non-legalised cohabitation is far from uncommon' among those forming unions in later life. His researchers had described wife-desertion as quite common throughout the different sections of the labouring population. Booth observed that in such cases the men and women paired off again and as a rule were faithful to the new partners. In his opinion, such arrangements constituted a 'form of divorce without the assistance of the Court', and that legalising the procedure would not have any real influence upon the stability of such unions.[10] M.E. Loane, a nursing visitor, was equally aware of the limited influence of a divorce code. It was her opinion that the 'family life of the submerged' at least, could not be purified by divorce, 'for the painfully sufficient reasons that the persons concerned are not married, or entirely refuse to allow themselves to be hampered by that condition'.[11] Richard Free, a London clergyman operating in the East End, observed that it was very common for poor couples not to bother with legal ties, but they were none the less stable as unions.[12] It would appear, therefore, that the lack of facilities for divorce was of little concern to this section of the population.

The absence of divorce facilities was probably only one reason of many why working people often failed to legalise their subsequent unions. For example, a social worker from the Midlands told Loane that few people ever considered it was morally wrong not to legalise second and subsequent unions. She explained:

> They seem to think that one marriage consecrates all subsequent connections – at any rate it entitles them to be considered 'respectable'. They do not think that there is anything wrong in these unions. They tell me without hesitation, 'We haven't been to Church', as if it were some petty formality . . . It is necessary, however, that *both* the parties should have been married before. Connections of this kind would not be formed between people of the same general decency if one of them were a spinster or a bachelor.[13]

Yet Loane had found that widowers and widows she had met in the south-eastern counties usually opted for a second marriage ceremony.

Although the rules governing sexual conduct featured centrally in the divorce code, there does not seem to be any evidence of this being of such great importance in the lives of the working population. Charles Booth had noticed a divergence of standards over the whole issue of sexual relationships outside marriage, and that as a general rule only a minority of working people aspired to hold the same values as those projected in the middle-class Victorian image of 'respectability'.[14] Among the poorer sections of society Booth observed that there was practically no stigma attached to 'immoral' relationships between couples before marriage. Booth noted that if and when a child was expected it was generally accepted with the minimum of pressure from relatives and friends that 'marriage is . . . the girl's right and the young man's responsibility', and such unions would then be legalised.[15] But whatever the ideal was held to be it was found that deviations would be accepted and defended. For instance, George Bourne, who had forsaken his upper-class background to go and live with villagers, noted that it was not always possible for marriage to follow a pregnancy but that once such young people eventually married and settled down they formed stable unions in a community that was not greatly outraged.[16]

Sometimes marriage was consciously resisted not just by the men but by the women too. One clergyman informed Booth that certain people managed to live together fairly peaceably so long as they were not married, but if they marry 'it always seems to lead to blows and rows'. An old lady who had lived with her man for forty years told an anxious missionary, 'he would have married me again and again but I could never see the good of it'. To outsiders it appeared that 'rough labourers . . . behave best if not married to the woman with whom they live'.[17] Whilst Lady Bell was conducting her study of the working people in Middlesbrough, she encountered similar instances where women feared that the legal contract would alter the balance of power in their arrangements, and other cases where it had been generally agreed that it was best to remain an unmarried mother rather than live legally with a worthless or dangerous man.[18] M.E. Loane gave an example of the attitudes of many of the women found to be 'living in sin', when she quoted the case of a mother who was most respectable and hard working. She lived with a man who would have gladly married her, but she steadily refused him since 'she didn't choose to be knocked about, nor to see her children treated bad, neither!'[19] Even when irregular conduct had caused quarrels and gossip, Loane discovered that it rarely resulted in permanent ostracism in working-class communities.

Both the tory romantic Stephen Reynolds and the socialist romantic Edward Carpenter had gone to live amongst working people, and had concluded that the kind of things likely to lead to marital discord were different in working-class households not simply because of their different codes of sexual morality, but because social arrangements required a certain kind of tolerance and understanding to which rigid rules could not be applied. The visitations of bad luck in the form of the trade cycle, seasonal fluctuations, sickness and debt, relieved by the irregular fortune of the bonus or bumper harvest, made life among the poor especially difficult to control and plan. One of the results of this way of life was that the poor seemed often to lack any absolute standards by which they criticised themselves or those with whom they lived, and in consequence were said to be remarkably tolerant of behaviour which in a wealthier class would have been interpreted as cruel, careless and neglectful. However, the apparent absence of any marked demand for divorce was not interpreted by either Carpenter or Reynolds as indicating a toleration of all family conflict. Reynolds did not believe it was simply a case of people not troubling to employ the law; in his view the existing law could not possibly be applied to the majority of family problems that the working people did find intolerable. He argued that the preoccupation of the divorce and separation laws with sexual infidelity reflected the fact that such behaviour threatened the stability of families which rested on private property vested in the male heads of households. But in the case of propertyless classes Reynolds suggested that there were very different things which threatened the security of the home. He explained that among the poor a nagging and quarrelsome wife, or one who could not manage to budget on less than a pound a week, would prove disastrous for the domestic life of a working man, and a father's attitude towards the earnings of his wife or children could be equally difficult for the woman.[20]

Very often 'a good husband' was regarded as being simply the man who gave his wife a regular sum of money for housekeeping.[21] It is important to note that the regularity of the sum was considered much more crucial than its total, and certainly much more so than the sum of money a husband may or may not have kept back for his own personal use.[22] 'A good husband' would also be described as one who never 'laid a finger on the children', and a bad husband would rarely be so called even if he beat his wife provided that drunk or sober he never turned on the children.[23] There is also some evidence to suggest that various degrees of alcoholism and violence were tolerated by wives no matter how debilitating, provided they felt the husbands had 'just cause'. Physical violence and drink were not the preserve of the worst husbands; it was not uncommon amongst wives either, and in many instances the wives understood the kinds of pressures leading to such behaviour.[24]

Reynolds concluded that there were different causes and symptoms of marital discord between couples in rich and poor households, and it was for this reason that he advocated a reform in the divorce and separation laws in order to make them applicable to different classes. It was his opinion that marital violence or infidelity amongst the poor was not necessarily regarded by them as symptomatic of complete marriage breakdown.[25] Yet there were cases of the most severe violence which reached the courts, and which most working people would not excuse as 'accidental' or 'unintentional'. The courts, however, tended to address themselves to the violence rather than to the underlying cause of marital conflict, such as arguments about irregular housekeeping money or the misallocation of a wife's earnings. It was not unknown for a magistrate to consider that a wife's nagging, for whatever reason, constituted 'undue provocation' and this judgement together with a relatively heavy fine was seen by many women to be futile and unjust.[26] Fines or imprisonment could make such women physically and economically more vulnerable and would certainly precipitate the total breakdown of their marriages. It is not at all clear, therefore, that Reynolds was correct in assuming that the reluctance of working people to go to court indicated entirely different priorities in all matrimonial affairs. But what Reynolds was working towards was the idea that matrimonial disputes among the poorer classes (if not the wealthier) could not, without severe injustices, be settled by a legal process which was directed at identifying and judging a 'criminal' and a 'guilty' partner.

It was not that disputes in working-class families lacked concepts of right and wrong; but it is clear that both parties usually agreed that the greatest wrong would be done by intruders misjudging the issues and employing unwelcome external forces in order to make and enforce judgements. Certainly, whenever Frederick Rogers, who had spent much of his life living and working among the more respectable poor, had seen someone obliged to interfere in a fearful marital battle he had observed that the contending parties had usually joined forces and turned against the outsider with 'And, pray, what business is it of yours?'[27] Similarly, on the occasions when Richard Free, the slum clergyman, could not resist going to the help of some woman screaming 'murder!' he had found himself greeted with screams of abuse; and in one instance was asked 'Can't my husband do bloody well what he likes with his own?' Free was also aware that there were circumstances, nevertheless, in which problem families did indeed ask for intervention but clearly rejected the idea of actually prosecuting the offending party.[28]

It was not only women who declined to use the existing laws which failed to give the kind of relief they sought. Thomas Holmes, who had extensive personal knowledge of many people moving through police courts and jails, condemned the Licensing Act of 1902 which had included the new rights of both husbands and wives to separation on account of their spouses' habitual drinking habits. He gave examples of the tragic inapplicability of the law to the problems as understood by so many of the unfortunate husbands themselves:

> I am not exaggerating when I say that hundreds of men have consulted me about their wives' drunkenness, all of them expecting some help or relief from the Act. When I have explained to them exactly how it affected them and what a separation meant, by far the greater number went away sorrowing, and most of them have added; 'I thought she would be put in a Home for a time, where I could pay a little for her. I cannot put her homeless into the streets; I should not be able to sleep if I knew she was out.' ... And this feeling has ... been characteristic of husbands who have suffered intensely and long, and who through it all have been good and patient husbands.[29]

There is also some evidence to suggest that waiving or reducing legal expenses in conjunction with the Poor Law was inadequate to prevent serious financial obstacles to recourse to the law by the poor. Anna Martin lived and worked with poorer working-class women for many years in a settlement at Rotherhithe. She tabulated the matrimonial experiences of a number of working women of irreproachable private lives, whose case histories were well known to her. Of those assaulted by their husbands only a small proportion had sought legal intervention. From this she concluded that for every case reaching court there were probably as many as fifty aggrieved wives who did not pursue such action. In her view, it was not only their tolerance or the inapplicability of the law that explained why so few wives sought legal redress. There were compelling economic and legal reasons why poorer wives were deterred from appealing to the Poor Law to sue husbands for maintenance. The Poor Law could only sue on behalf of a woman who was living separately from her husband; yet not all husbands removed themselves from the comforts of the home even though they failed to provide their wives with money. Many wives suffered poverty in this way for months and years, and had never been able to save sufficiently to leave home, and rent and equip new accommodation for themselves and children. From her discussion with the women Anna Martin concluded that they were very aware that, if in attempting to escape their husbands, the children were to suffer deprivation and hardship they would then run the risk of being prosecuted for child neglect and would be separated from their children.[30]

The reason for inadequate relief for deserted wives was discussed by the Royal Commission on the Poor Laws between 1905-9. Many witnesses believed that husbands and wives often connived in order to get outdoor relief for the women while the men were away, sick or out of work. Complaints were made that often an allowance was made, and after a few weeks the husband returned secretly to the family and the relieving officer would not be informed of this change in circumstances. The common occurrence of brief and frequent marital breakdown led the Local Government Board to recommend in a circular of 1872 that deserted wives should not be granted outdoor relief during the first twelve months of desertion. The Majority Report of the Commission repeated this recommendation.[31] But indoor relief was not always popular with guardians, who often preferred the cheaper method of outdoor relief, and Anna Martin knew of cases where attempts had been made to refer wives back to their husbands in the absence of any legal separation order. Some wives had found themselves in a position of destitution, unable to obtain immediate legal redress and yet refused admission to the workhouse.[32]

There were also many financial reasons why suggestions for elaborate methods of collecting and enforcing maintenance offered little comfort to the poorest wives and mothers. There was some wilful evasion of the law that proved very difficult to counter. Men were known to escape a summons by disappearing so that their wives were unable to give their whereabouts; they could also escape the demands of the Poor Law by moving from one parish to another until they had disappeared without trace. It was not unknown for men to leave reasonably well-paid jobs and take some ill-paid and irregular work in order to plead an inability to pay before the magistrates. Sometimes men would pay less than the sum stipulated and only after long delays would the guardians feel it worthwhile to prosecute for arrears. A number of husbands were always prepared to go to jail rather than struggle to make back payments; for the sentence automatically cancelled the debt.[33] Holmes observed that it was usually much easier for wives to be granted separation orders than it was for them to obtain sufficient maintenance. He stressed that the problems not only arose in the cases of wilful evasion; frequently men earning low or irregular money established second families and they had insufficient resources to meet all their responsibilities. Although the new family rarely had any legal claim, the men preferred to support them whenever possible, and often accepted a prison sentence to rid themselves of their prior responsibilities.[34]

Knowledge of these kinds of circumstances and of the many other factors which influenced standards of family life among the poor served only to harden the extreme positions of both sides in the divorce discussions. In the absence of sufficient material resources and the lack of social work agencies linked to the legal system, supporters of the Minority Report remained convinced that easier divorce would have the most undesirable results for the dependants. Yet the same kind of evidence also confirmed the Fabian Women's Group and the Women's Co-operative Guild in their conviction that only low-cost divorce by mutual consent would rid family law of its class and sex bias. In the absence of strong pressure to have changes in family law linked to the reorganisation of the Poor Law and the other welfare agencies that intervened in working-class family life, the Majority Report merely attempted a compromise between the purely legalistic approaches to divorce. It suggested that the more numerous grounds for legal separation that had been granted poorer litigants in the lower courts should become grounds for divorce in a much cheaper and quicker legal procedure. But this was an administrative solution which evaded the issues of limited family resources, and of the role of the judiciary in operating laws according to moral priorities that were not necessarily shared by the litigants. There was indeed a much wider truth than Reynolds had intended in his statement. 'Divorce for the poor cannot be both punitive and just'.[35]

III

The impact of matrimonial law and reform upon women and children from the poorer families is best understood in the context of an expanding network of social policies, particularly after 1900. These were designed to oblige parents to adopt new and different standards of parenthood; but in view of the scarcity of individual resources and the cultural dislocation implied by law enforcement, it appears that state intervention often exacerbated the difficulties of wives and mothers, especially for those from broken homes.

The pervasiveness of individualism meant that the majority of people only gradually accepted more than the most limited welfare reforms; and this, coupled with a suspicion of state intervention among much of the working class, helps to explain the *ad hoc* and piecemeal manner in which the state extended its functions without displacing the central role of the Poor Law and its discriminatory policies in the late nineteenth and early twentieth centuries.

The laws restricting child employment and compelling school attendance from the 1870s and, between 1906 and 1911, compulsory medical inspection, pensions for the aged, and contributory unemployment, sickness and maternity schemes were all passed by Liberal Governments; pressure from the trade unions and the Labour Party was intermittent and latent rather than constant. Only the feeding of necessitous schoolchildren could be regarded as primarily an achievement of the labour movement. The organised sections of the working class were concerned that any social reforms being considered did not threaten the established interests of trade union and friendly societies, and were thus often unable to agree upon the extent and terms of state assistance. What was common among working people was their distrust of the motives of policy-makers; their dislike of any assistance that was offered on terms which threatened to interfere with their own customs and ways of life; and help that carried moral sanctions which were regarded as unfair because of the limited resources available to them. In a socially stratified working class the concerns of organised groups did not necessarily reflect the attitudes of the poorer and unorganised. Punitive policies were still applied to those who were unable or unwilling to conform to the standards and duties required of them.

The Fabians were not alone in understanding that the more legislation was designed to enforce improved family life, without increasing the available resources, the more society was placing an impossible burden upon the poorest women.[36] Reynolds observed that the 'so-called democratic legislation . . . has increased the inequality, has more heavily penalised poverty, has intruded further and further into their homes, has interfered less tolerably with their own habits and customs'.[37] Anna Martin traced the way in which since the late 1880s the tightening network of legislation, particularly regarding the wider legal definitions of parental cruelty and neglect, had enforced conflicting claims upon wives and mothers to such an extent that they had insufficient time and resources, or support from the men, to fulfil them. In addition, it was becoming apparent that the impact of social policy, which had been intended to supplement the functions of the family, introduced conflicting demands on all members of the family group and sometimes seemed to threaten the very basis upon which mothers especially had traditionally operated within the household.[38] It is not surprising, therefore, to learn that the poorer women expressed little faith or interest in respect of practically every form of state intervention. For instance, Anna Martin concluded that although policies had been intended to assist and encourage working-class families their impact upon the women in the poorest families served only to aggravate their difficulties. She declared:

> The politician, the philanthropist, and the educationalist seized the opportunity of carrying a reform urgently needed in the interests of the whole community, but wrung the greater part of the cost out of the flesh and blood of the mothers . . . Probably few people realise into what intolerable positions the unrepresented working-class mother is constantly being driven by the law givers of the country.[39]

Socialists, Fabians, feminists and democrats of all political parties had failed not only to capture the imagination of working people in respect of the potential of state intervention, but also to take account of the opinions and experiences of the most vulnerable sections of society. Democrats of all parties preferred to adopt policies based on compromises between conflicting interest groups and the exercise of individual choice in the party system and market economy. But it was difficult if not impossible for the existing political system to be responsive to the opinions and reactions of the least articulate and economically ineffective sections of the community. As Martin observed of the women in her settlement: 'They are not as yet class-conscious, and are far too much engrossed in their hand-to-hand struggle with poverty, sickness and sin, even to realise what outsiders say of them. And so judgment goes by default.'[40] Although a few social scientists and social workers were concerned to understand the social implications of state intervention, their evaluations were of limited influence, in part because of the existence and nature of political parties none of whom catered specifically for the poor.[41]

The dilemma of radicals and socialists therefore was that although they believed that conscious participation of the people was crucial to the ultimate success of social and political change the pre-1914 reform campaigns seldom attracted any persistent or broad-based support from working people; and the reforms that were achieved did not produce wives and mothers who were capable of articulating and politicising their experiences and demanding that the social costs of 'progress' should fall elsewhere in society.[42] Hence the poorer wives and mothers continued to suffer the economic and emotional strains aggravated by the *ad hoc* legislation of the nascent welfare state. It seems reasonable to argue that in the absence of welfare reforms directed specifically at the difficulties of broken homes, the so-called 'progressive' matrimonial law reforms of the late nineteenth and early twentieth centuries served only to increase their vulnerability. Socialists as ideologically diverse as William Morris and H.G. Wells had anticipated the destruction of existing society before the majority of people had been prepared to embark upon major social reconstruction. Certainly there was much in their reservations about the reform process that leads one to reconsider the adequacy of the preparations for 'tomorrow's voyage'; or to ask: whither? And for whom?

Notes

1. Erna Reiss's *Rights and Duties of Englishwomen* (Manchester, 1934) remains the best account of the changing legal status of women in the nineteenth and early twentieth centuries. For a detailed account of the implications of the laws relating to children within the family see T.E. James, 'The Development of the Law Relating to Children in the Nineteenth and Twentieth Centuries' (London University Ph.D. thesis, 1957), especially ch. 4.

2. For a number of issues relating to women and the poor law see E.M. Ross, 'Women and Poor Law Administration 1857-1909' (London University M.A. thesis, 1955-6).

3. *Royal Commission on Divorce and Matrimonial Causes*, PP 1912-13: vol. XVIII, Cd. 6478, p. iii.

4. O.R. McGregor, *Divorce in England* (1957), p. 26.

5. There is a summary of evidence on these points in the Minority Report, Cd. 6478, pp. 176-7.

6. Minutes of evidence from Evelyn Hubbard, vice-president of the Mothers' Union, and others; 1912-13: vol. XIX, Cd. 6480, pp. 189-206. For evidence of Rev. E.S.G. Savile as secretary of the Church of England Men's Society see PP 1912-13: vol. XX, Cd. 6481, pp. 324-8. See also minutes of evidence given by R.J. Parr, director of the NSPCC; ibid., pp. 133-45; and from other officials of the society: ibid., pp. 145-8 and 429-33.

7. Minutes of evidence from Ethel Bentham who had been chosen to represent the 200 or so members of the Fabian Women's Group. ibid., pp. 30-8.

8. Minutes of evidence from Margaret Llewelyn Davies, ibid., pp. 149-71. Eleanor Barton, wife of the secretary of the Sheffield ILP, also gave evidence (ibid., pp. 171-3), which did not differ greatly from that of the Co-operative Women's Guild main report. For biographical sketches of these two women, see J.M. Bellamy and J. Saville (eds.), *Dictionary of Labour Biography*, vol. 1 (1972).

9. See answers to qq. 37,021-3 and 37,006 (Cd. 6481).

10. Charles Booth, *Life and Labour of the People in London, Final Volume* (1903), pp. 41-2.

11. M.E. Loane, *The Common Growth* (1911), pp. 286-7.

12. Richard Free, *Seven Years Hard* (1904), p. 127.

13. M.E. Loane, *The Next Street But One* (1907), p. 72.

14. Booth, *Life and Labour*, p. 45.

15. Ibid., pp. 44-5.

16. George Bourne [George Sturt], *Change in the Village* (1912), pp. 39-41.

17. Booth, *Life and Labour*, pp. 41-2.

18. Lady Bell, *At the Works* (1907), pp. 240-2.

19. M.E. Loane, *An Englishman's Castle* (1909), p. 103.

20. Stephen Reynolds, *A Poor Man's House* (1908; 1928 ed.), p. 493; cf. Edward Carpenter, *Love's Coming-of-Age* . . . (Manchester, 1896), pp. 45-7.

21. Magdalen Pember Reeves, *Round About A Pound A Week* (1913), pp. 13-15, 193.

22. M.E. Loane, *From Their Point of View* (1908), p. 39; Bell, *At the Works*, pp. 79-80; E. Rathbone, *How the Casual Labourer Lives* (1909), pp. vii-ix, xii.

23. M.E. Loane, *The Queen's Poor* (1905), pp. 18-20 and *An Englishman's Castle*, pp. 108-9.

24. Loane, *An Englishman's Castle*, pp. 108-9.

25. Reynolds, *A Poor Man's House*, pp. 488-9, 491.

26. See for example the comments of Ada Nield Chew, *Common Cause*, 2 May 1913, p. 54 and 12 September 1913, p. 887.

27. Frederick Rogers, *Labour, Life and Literature* (1913), pp. 303-4. See also, Thomas Wright, *The Great Unwashed* (1868; 1970 ed.), pp. 131-2 for similar impressions.

28. Free, *Seven Years Hard*, pp. 143, 161-2.

29. T. Holmes, *Known to the Police* (1908), pp. 57-60, 63-4.

30. Anna Martin, *Mothers in Mean Streets; or Toad under the Harrow* (1914), pp. 6-7.

31. *Royal Commission on the Poor Laws and Relief of Distress*, PP 1909: vol. XXXVII, Cd. 4499, pp. 157-8.

32. Martin, *Mothers in Mean Streets*, p. 8.

33. Ibid., pp. 7-9.

34. Holmes, *Known to the Police*, pp. 29-30.

35. Stephen Reynolds, 'Divorce for the Poor', *Fortnightly Review*, vol. 88 (1910), p. 493.

36. For example, from her experience of working-class households in Middlesbrough, Lady Bell stated (*At the Works*, p. 245): 'It is no good postulating imaginary conditions in discussing whether we can achieve a desired result; . . . and my conviction is that there will never be more than a certain proportion of women who can carry the immense burden allotted to the working woman by the conditions of today.'

37. Reynolds, 'Divorce for the Poor', p. 487.

38. See Anna Martin, *The Married Working Woman* (1911), in which she wrote (p. 30): 'The women have a vague dread of being superseded and dethroned. Each of them knows perfectly well that the strength of her position in the home lies in the physical dependence of husband and children upon her, and she is suspicious of anything that would tend to undermine this. The feeling that she is the indispensable centre of her small world is, indeed, the joy and consolation of her life.' See also Pember Reeves, *Round about a Pound*, pp. 231, 224-6; Anna Martin, *The Maternity Benefits*, published by the National Union of Women's Suffrage Societies (1911); idem, 'The Mother and Social Reform', *Nineteenth Century and After*, vol. 73 (1913); idem, 'Working Women and Drink' part I, ibid., vol. 78 (1915) and part II, ibid., vol. 79 (1916).

39. Martin, *The Married Working Woman*, p. 36.

40. Ibid., p. 5.

41. E.J. Urwick, *A Philosophy of Social Progress* (1912; 2nd ed. 1920), pp. 5, 7-8, 13-18, 23-4, 91, 219-20, 222-40.

42. Some of the Fabian Women who had failed to interest many of the leading socialists in the questions of votes for women, and other related issues regarding the specific position of women in society, became aware of the implications of such reforms as the endowment of motherhood. See the Group's *A Summary of Six Papers and Discussions upon the Disabilities of Women as Workers* (1909), p. 6. Their *A Summary of Eight Papers and Discussions upon the Disabilities of Mothers as Workers* (1910) noted that perhaps such paternalistic reforms 'would amount to socialism for men, but for most women would involve a subordination to the patriarchal family' (p. 5). Ada Nield Chew, a regular contributor to the suffragist journal, the *Common Cause*, came to the conclusion that this was one of the chief dangers of the current social reforms confronting women in all classes: 'The Problem of the Married Working Women', *Common Cause*, 27 February 1914, pp. 909-10. She echoed Anna Martin's dread of paternalistic reforms, and did not, therefore, see the socialist reformers as leading the way towards women's liberation.

7 'THE INSTRUMENTS OF THE PEOPLE'?: THE PARLIAMENTARY LABOUR PARTY IN 1906

David E. Martin

'I see', wrote the Prince of Wales to Edward VII on 20 January 1906, 'that a great number of Labour Members have been returned which is rather a dangerous sign, but I hope they are not all Socialists.'[1] A.J. Balfour, the defeated Conservative leader, also looked with disfavour on the new Labour Party and its thirty members; Campbell-Bannerman, the Liberal Prime Minister, Balfour wrote to Lady Salisbury, 'is a mere cork, dancing on a torrent which he cannot control and what is going on here is the faint echo of the same movement which has produced massacres in St Petersberg, riots in Vienna, and Socialist processions in Berlin'.[2] But *The Economist* of 27 January 1906 was more complacent. It allowed that the Labour MPs would bring to the House of Commons a large amount of direct knowledge of social and industrial questions and if treated with 'firmness and sympathy, they may well prove a useful element in our Parliamentary system'.

While established opinion was caught in an uncertain mind, the labour movement, for a short time at least, was jubilant. All sides had favoured greater working-class representation in Parliament, apart from the few socialists who shared William Morris's view that the Palace of Westminster ought to become a storehouse for manure. An influential section of trade unionists, however, believed that increased representation could be achieved within the Liberal Party. But these men, about twenty of whom were elected in 1906,[3] had become a less significant force, especially since the passing of the TUC motion of 1899 which led to the establishment of the Labour Representation Committee in 1900. The LRC, though operating a secret electoral agreement with the Liberal leadership, was also applying Keir Hardie and the ILP's policy of a trade union-socialist alliance. This strategy softened the already rather woolly socialism of the ILP but did ensure the vital finance that the trade unions were able to provide. The tiny Marxist grouping, organised as the Social Democratic Federation, though withdrawing from the LRC in 1901, acknowledged the importance of the establishment of a party of labour; it seemed a step towards Engels's programme of a distinct working-class party, built upon trade union strength but eventually moving to a revolutionary position. The even smaller Fabian

125

Society had also, while still hoping for a revived and collectivist Liberal Party, recognised the organisation and financial power of the trade unions to support labour candidates at general elections.[4]

Thus from its outset the Labour Party embodied a number of aspirations that were sometimes incompatible. Historical writing reflects these differing approaches. Historians of Liberalism have tended to minimise the importance of the early Labour Party. It has been argued that 'the Liberal Party was essentially in good health down to 1914' and that the Great War explains its collapse and the almost fortuitous rise of Labour.[5] Another school of thought strikes a mildly heroic tone, with a whiggishness that has labour and progress marching forward arm in arm. One Labour intellectual has viewed his party as a 'battering ram' created to 'break down the walls of social oligarchy which surrounded Parliament'; two others describe the pioneers as out to win 'freedom from injustice, ugliness and squalor'.[6] From the Conservative side comes the assertion: 'The Labour Party was founded with the intention, not of gaining justice for the working classes, but of establishing their dominance over all other classes.'[7] And a very different analysis has been made by Marxist historians who find the modern Labour Party rooted in opportunist ideology and parliamentary careerism.[8]

I

This paper seeks to reappraise the early Parliamentary Labour Party in terms of its members. In doing so it draws upon the collection of biographical material begun by G.D.H. Cole which after his death in 1959 was passed on to John Saville.[9] The purpose is not one of political biography, although there is a case for shedding some light on those secondary figures who were associated with Hardie, MacDonald, Henderson and Snowden. Rather it is to suggest certain key aspects that made the Labour Party what it was and enabled it to replace the Liberals as the party of reform.

The thirty-strong Parliamentary Labour Party contained men of differing opinions. As the Prince of Wales had hoped, not all were socialists: eighteen probably considered themselves as such.[10] When it came to the election of a leader, Hardie, the socialist veteran, obtained only one vote more than David Shackleton, who was regarded as being foremost a trade unionist. Several other areas of disagreement were to emerge in the party's first few years (and subsequently). Nevertheless, the personnel of the party shared much common ground, perhaps most strikingly in their social origins. In a political system that, apart from the Irish and a handful of 'Lib-Labs', had long been dominated by the two main upper-class parties, the arrival of a group of working-class members drew much comment. Some of this was a little fanciful, as when the *Observer* of 21 January described them as 'toilers with horny hands'; in fact their wage-earning days in factory and mine were often long past. Trade union officialdom in particular had provided higher paid, more secure and less physically arduous work. Of the thirty, twenty-three were active trade unionists and eight of them were or had recently been general secretaries of their union.[11] Yet collectively they could claim many years of genuine working-class life. In the first place their origins were working class, as Table 1 shows. (The only possible exception was T.F. Richards whose father was an unsuccessful book canvasser.) The classification of occupations presents difficulties, but it does seem that a disproportionate number of their fathers were skilled workmen compared with the working class as a whole. In conse-quence these families would be better off than average, though having a trade did not always prevent unemployment and other hardships. If in childhood they escaped first-hand experience of privation, they would have seen its effect on neighbours; Charlie Duncan, for example, recalled that the drunken scenes he had witnessed in his youth had converted him to teetotalism. The experience of others was more direct. Will Thorne's father died in a drunken brawl; his mother married another heavy drinker whose violent temper decided Thorne to go on the tramp. Will Crooks and Walter Hudson both had childhood spells in the workhouse. MacDonald and Hardie shared the disadvantage of illegitimacy. Stephen Walsh's parentage was also obscure: at the age of four he was found wandering and eventually raised by an uncle. After the death of his mother, James Parker was also taken in by relatives.

In most cases their formal education was meagre and often ended at an early age: the mid-Victorian economy offered many poorly-paid jobs to children whose families often depended on such extra earnings. Frequently boys would enter their father's occupation, and this was the case with several of those who became MPs. Others had by their early teens worked in several jobs, and this too was an occupational pattern shared by many working-class boys who drifted from one 'blind alley' to another. Thorne's boyhood jobs were so numerous and disagreeable that at the age of fifteen he vowed to do all he could to prevent other children from suffering the same hardships.[12] J.R. Clynes, the son of an evicted Irish peasant who became a labourer in Oldham, often recalled that as a ten-year-old he had to get up at 4.30 a.m. to go to work as a little piecer in a cotton mill; his wages, as a half-timer, were

	Birthplace	Father's occupation	Own occupation	Estate
G.N. Barnes (1859-1940)	Lochee, Forfar	engineer	engineer	£ 3,129
C.W. Bowerman (1851-1947)	Honiton, Devon	tinplate worker	compositor	£ 3,668
J.R. Clynes (1869-1949)	Oldham, Lancs.	labourer	cotton spinner	£ 9,816
W. Crooks (1852-1921)	Poplar, London	ship's stoker	cooper	£ 1,863
C. Duncan (1865-1933)	Middlesbrough	engineer	engineer	£ 3,883
A.H. Gill (1856-1914)	Rochdale, Lancs.	cotton spinner	cotton spinner	£ 3,750
T. Glover (1852-1913)	Prescot, Lancs.	coalminer	coalminer	£ 673
J.K. Hardie (1856-1915)	Legbrannock, Lanarks.	coalminer	coalminer	£ 426
A. Henderson (1863-1935)	Glasgow	labourer	ironmoulder	£23,328
J. Hodge (1855-1937)	Muirkirk, Ayrshire	iron puddler	steel smelter	£ 2,837
W. Hudson (1852-1935)	Richmond, Yorks.	railwayman	railwayman	£ 169
J.H. Jenkins (1852-1936)	Pembroke Dock	shipwright	shipwright	£ n.t.
F.W. Jowett (1865-1944)	Bradford	mill foreman	powerloom weaver	£15,890
G.D. Kelley (1848-1911)	Rushington, Lincs.	cooper	lithographic printer	£ 3,388
J.R. MacDonald (1866-1937)	Lossiemouth, Elgin	ploughman	private secretary	£25,418
J.T. Macpherson (1872-1921)	Poplar, London	ironworker	steel smelter	£ n.t.
J. O'Grady (1866-1934)	Bristol	labourer	cabinet maker	£ 9,228
J. Parker (1863-1948)	Authorpe, Lincs.	farm labourer	warehouseman	£ 9,652
T.F. Richards (1863-1942)	Wednesbury, Staffs.	book canvasser	shoemaker	£ 264
G.H. Roberts (1868-1928)	Chedgrave, Norfolk	shoemaker	printer	£ 7,110
J.A. Seddon (1868-1939)	Prescot, Lancs.	nailmaker	shop assistant	£ n.t.
D.J. Shackleton (1863-1938)	Cloughfold, Lancs.	powerloom weaver	weaver	£ 7,288
P. Snowden (1864-1937)	Cowling, Yorks.	weaver	civil servant	£ 3,366
T. Summerbell (1861-1910)	Easington, Durham	coal trimmer	printer	£ 1,574
J.W. Taylor (1855-1924)	Monkwearmouth, Durham	blacksmith	colliery mechanic	£ 998
W. Thorne (1857-1946)	Birmingham	brickmaker	gasworks labourer	£ 7,187
S. Walsh (1859-1929)	Liverpool	n.t.	coalminer	£ 7,927
G.J. Wardle (1863-1947)	Newhall, Derbys.	n.t.	railway clerk	£13,995
A. Wilkie (1850-1928)	Leven, Fife	coalminer	shipwright	£11,302
W.T. Wilson (1855-1921)	Undermillbeck, Lancs.	tailor	carpenter	£ 1,896

n.t.: not traced. The occupations given are those on birth certificates in the case of fathers, and the main, early manhood, ones for the MPs.

2*s* 6*d* a week.[13] At eleven T.F. Richards began work as a half-timer in the file-cutting trade and, like Clynes, became a full-timer at twelve. He too retained memories of early hardships, such as going to work without food and then pretending to his fellows that he had already enjoyed a 'splendid breakfast'.[14] David Shackleton and George Wardle both began as half-timers in textile mills at nine; A.H. Gill did the same on his tenth birthday; George Barnes entered a jute mill at eleven. When the majority of these future MPs were growing up, in the third quarter of the nineteenth century, it was normal for working-class children to begin work at an early age, but on entering political life their early experiences were often turned to good account.

The working lives of the Labour MPs gave them, collectively, direct experience of many forms of industrial labour; Table 1 gives some indication of this, though only principal and not all occupations are given. Geographically, too, they covered a wide part of Britain, with some concentration in the North and Scotland.[15] In two of the best known cases — MacDonald and Snowden — youthful effort led to membership of a higher social class, and some of the others had similar ambitions. G.H. Roberts had hopes of a career as a teacher only to be told he had not the strength; after two years as a pupil teacher G.D. Kelley contemplated becoming a clergyman, but to no avail, and, like Roberts, he was apprenticed to a printer. Thomas Summerbell entered the same occupation but on losing his job in 1894 with the introduction of linotype machinery he set up his own small business. The general secretary of the Durham Colliery Mechanics' Association, J.W. Taylor, also had a printing firm which he operated with his brother. But, although many of them were ambitious, almost all the early MPs had worked for several years among the industrial labour force. A characteristic pattern then was for advancement in their trade union. At the same time, many developed an interest in political questions, often in association with the Liberal Party. Some achieved election to local councils, school boards, boards of guardians and, as it became policy to create more working-class JPs, appointment to the magistrates' bench. The public speaking and committee work that this involved was useful experience; T.F. Richards observed that in nine years on the Leicester Town Council he was 'unconsciously qualifying . . . for Parliament'.[16] Local politics also built a reputation among the electorate; for example, Thorne had been a West Ham councillor since 1890, Summerbell had been elected to the Sunderland borough council in 1892 and in the same year Fred Jowett defeated Conservative and Liberal candidates to become a Bradford city councillor.[17] Such duties often required day-time attendance, something that was made possible in at least two cases — Jowett and Crooks — by a 'wages fund' raised by supporters. But it was most commonly facilitated through a full-time post as a trade union official.

Here, indeed, was a break with the mass of the working class. As a salaried brain-worker the trade union bureaucrat belonged, in the Webbs' phrase, 'neither to the middle nor to the working class'.[18] The Webbs went on to quote from an account by an artisan the risk that there was of the full-time official becoming estranged from his members. Living in a 'little villa in a lower middle class suburb' he could come to look down on the workmen he passed as he walked to his office in 'tall hat and good overcoat, with a smart umbrella' and to despise as incapable the unemployed.[19] Certainly, in dress and manner the representatives of labour did not lack respectability; even Hardie, whose comparatively flamboyant appearance on entering the Commons in 1892 had contributed to the coining of the epithet 'Queer' Hardie, seems to have given little offence. G.H. Roberts and Duncan gained reputations for dandyism, but most of their colleagues had the demeanour of sober artisans in chapel.

If during many years as trade union and minor civic functionaries the Labour MPs had not grown grey, most of them had at least entered into middle age. Ten of them were older than Hardie, the father figure of the movement. At the time of their election to Parliament in January 1906 the average age of the group was forty-six, compared with an average of forty-nine for all members of the House of Commons.[20] Before gaining, in the phrase they often favoured, 'parliamentary honours', their lives had often exemplified Smilesian virtues of persistence and self-denial, and even if early struggles were sometimes overcoloured when recalling the way they had 'got on', it cannot be denied that their achievements were considerable.

Of course, these very achievements distinguish them from the mass of the people that they were seeking to represent. Though they had important first-hand knowledge and experience of working-class life, some of their attitudes and ideas were untypical. One not unsympathetic observer characterised them as 'not the representatives of the democracy, but the weapons of the democracy . . . They are the instruments of the people . . . men of a definite and even pedantic class; men whose austere and lucid tone, whose elaborate economic explanations smack of something very different from the actual streets of London.'[21] Moreover, their intellectual horizons were somewhat wider. Many were familiar with the writings of Ruskin and Carlyle, those two Victorian moralists whose strictures against bourgeois values were to be found in most middle-class libraries. The popularity of these authors was brought out by W.T. Stead's survey of the books that had influenced Labour MPs.[22] Referring to this survey, the social conservative W.H. Mallock developed the interesting point that the representatives of labour drew much of their ideology from outside their class.[23]

Yet, though it does give some interesting insights into the ideas that played on the minds of these MPs, too much should not be made of Stead's survey. They were directed to think in terms of literature and were astute enough politicians to know that Shakespeare, Dickens, Ruskin, Carlyle and the Bible were 'sound' and that popular working-class reading such as the *Illustrated Police Budget* and *Winning Post* was to be frowned upon.[24] And though specifically asked about books, a number of MPs denied that their influence was strong. Thomas Glover replied that it was everyday experience in the mines that had counted with him; Shackleton referred to the *Manchester Guardian* and his practical experience as a trade union official; John Hodge too thought he had learned more from newspapers than books; to Henderson the best book was 'life' and even such an intellectual as Snowden declared that men had taught him more things than books. Though more widely read and consequently possessing knowledge of subjects unfamiliar to the average worker, the Labour MPs were not separated from him by any mental gulf. Lady Bell in her inquiry into the reading habits of Middlesbrough ironworkers found that of two hundred households, fifty read novels only; fifty-eight read newspapers only; thirty-seven houses had inhabitants who were fond of reading and in twenty-five they read books 'absolutely worth reading' — and these included Shakespeare, Dickens and Ruskin.[25]

As a whole, the Labour MPs were more given to religious practices than their constituents. O'Grady (who cited Marx as an influence) was the only practising Roman Catholic — an indication of the still largely Nationalist sympathies of Catholic workers of Irish origin who were numerous in parts of Britain. Only two were Anglicans, but several had non-conformist associations and some were lay preachers. An interesting study by K.D. Brown has pointed to a discrepancy between the eighteen MPs who claimed membership of non-conformist churches and the eight listed in the denominational press. The press mentioned Crooks, Gill, Hardie, Henderson, Hodge, Hudson, Jenkins and Taylor, but not Barnes, Clynes, Glover, Parker, MacDonald, Macpherson, Richards, Seddon, Shackleton and Wardle.[26] Some of the latter group nevertheless do seem to have had close associations with non-

conformity and their omission from the various yearbooks and direc-
tories is surprising. In any case, it is significant that almost two-thirds
of the Labour Party should claim, however tenuously, non-conformist
beliefs.

By contrast, it is generally agreed that the working class were inatten-
tive to religious observation. Yet they did practise what has been
termed four-wheel Christianity — travelling to church in a pram for
baptism, a coach for marriage[27] and a hearse for burial — and they
often sent their children to Sunday schools. There were pockets of
infidelism, much indifference towards organised religion, and some
areas where the chapel, if declining in its influence, was still strong. A
contemporary was probably near the truth when he claimed:

> The poor are always 'religious' even to superstition . . . There is little
> agnosticism, still less deliberate atheism among them . . . Mr
> Blatchford's recent attempt at a resuscitation of 'determinism' has
> utterly failed to provoke any genuine response amongst the poor . . .
> It is against the 'Churches', not against Jesus Christ, that the minds
> of the labouring poor are set.[28]

By employing the language of religion a more subtle propagandist than
Blatchford could exploit these vague beliefs, as did Philip Snowden
whose oration 'The Christ that is to be' combined the religiose and
political. An anecdote of Snowden's encapsulates this phenomenon.
He told of a socialist in the Bradford area, a man who declared himself
willing to go to the stake for his socialism as the martyrs of old did for
their religion, and who advised visiting speakers to 'keep it simple, and
then when tha'rt coming to t'finishing up tha' mun put a bit of "Come
to Jesus" in like Philip does'.[29]

Closely associated with non-conformity was temperance. All four of
the MPs who had sat in the Commons before 1906 — Hardie, Shackleton,
Crooks and Henderson — had temperance associations, though Hardie's
went back to his Liberal days and his formal links had lapsed. But
Crooks, a Congregationalist and Shackleton and Henderson, both
Wesleyans, were active in the cause. On being re-elected to the Commons
in 1906 they were involved with an organisation that sought to persuade
labour that liquor was an enemy. This was the Trades Union and Labour
Officials' Temperance Fellowship. Henderson was its president and
Shackleton the treasurer, MacDonald and T.F. Richards belonged to its
executive committee and among its vice-presidents were Barnes, Crooks,
Duncan, Gill, Hodge, Snowden, J.W. Taylor and Walsh. There were

differing attitudes between socialists who held that drink was a symptom of poverty and those who saw it as a cause of destitution. The
appearance of Labour MPs on temperance platforms, often in the
company of Liberals, was a central complaint in Ben Tillett's outspoken pamphlet of 1908, *Is the Parliamentary Labour Party a Failure?*
He declared that instead of fighting capitalism and unemployment,
'Messrs. Henderson, Shackleton, Snowden and others . . . have gone out
of their way to play sneak on the working class'.[30] The support for
temperance within the Labour Party was not commonly shared by
working men, most of whom were regular and often heavy drinkers.
The production of beer reached a record level in 1900, though it
declined after the turn of the century and took up a smaller proportion of working-class expenditure.[31]

The strength of the non-conformist and temperance components
in the Labour Party in part reflects the amount of support it had in the
north, where these traditions were more vigorous than in other parts of
the country. Few votes were to be lost through these associations — the
drink interest was solidly Tory — but, especially where Liberal goodwill
was involved, some were to be gained. A 'drunk and incapable' conviction recorded against Pete Curran shortly before the January 1910
election almost certainly contributed to his defeat, and it is significant
that Hardie and Snowden counter-attacked Victor Grayson not so
much by discussing issues as by insinuating that he had been intoxicated
when making the speech that led to his suspension from the Commons.

At prayer and in its reading, the strongest impression created by the
early Labour Party is one of vague good intentions in so far as its wider
philosophy was concerned. Like the good Samaritan they felt that the
weak should be helped; they favoured a state-supervised minimum for
the sick, aged and injured. Hatred of capitalists was more common in
the more secular circle of the SDF; humanitarian socialists of the kind
found in the ILP hated the exploitation and ugliness of capitalism, but
it often seemed as though they looked for a Pauline conversion (a word
applicable to both religion and socialism) from their opponents; social
classes might be reconciled in that earthly Jerusalem of which they
dreamed; in the biblical language of the day, 'the wolf also shall dwell
with the lamb'.

Though their language sometimes echoed that of the pulpit and was
conciliatory, when fighting elections Labour candidates were shrewd
enough to emphasise their special appeal to working-class voters. Thus,
J.H. Jenkins claimed in his election address in 1906 that, 'as a working
man . . . I have gained a thorough knowledge of working-class require-

ments, and I am in a position to voice their opinions'.[32] At Newcastle
Walter Hudson declared he was a candidate 'because the industrial
workers of the country required representation at Westminster'.[33]
But Labour candidates also aimed at targets familiar to the hustings.
There were few votes in praising foreigners; the South African War had
aroused hostility to the Chinese and the Jews at a time when Jewish
immigration was already being attacked. Nor were men raised in the
heart of the Empire free of jingoism. Jenkins pledged himself not only
to work for the restoration of HM Dockyards to their former position,
but also for them to be extended. He was contesting Chatham and
probably also mindful of creating employment, but patriotic notes
were sounded in constituencies with fewer martial associations. Seddon,
for example, left no doubt about his loyalties in an election address at
Newton; the Conservative Government, he said, 'introduced un-English
methods, reversed the most cherished traditions of the British race, left
an indelible stain on the honour of old England, and shook the British
Constitution to its foundations'.[34]

On the other hand, internationalist attitudes were strong among ILP
members and the humorous patter of the moderate socialist Will
Crooks struck a chord among working-class audiences who were sceptical about the Empire; one observer described him

> recounting the difficulties of the Imperialist Missionary down in
> Poplar: to the first woman: 'Don't you know you belong to an
> Empire on which the sun never sets?' And the reply: 'Wot's the good
> of talkin' like that? Why, the sun never rises on our court'. To the
> second: 'You've got to learn to make sacrifices for the Empire'. —
> 'Wot's the good of talkin' about sacrifices when we can't make both
> ends meet as it is? Both ends meet! We think we're lucky if we get
> one end meat and the other end bread'. To a third: 'If you don't
> agree, you're Little Englanders'. — 'If I'm to pay another twopence
> a pound for meat, my children will soon be Little Englanders!'[35]

Labour candidates were mostly as conventionally patriotic as any
others, though few had specialist knowledge of foreign and imperial
affairs, or much desire to acquire it.

II

There had been labour leaders similar in character to those who took
the Labour Party whip in 1906, and they had usually been Liberals.
Indeed, many of those designated Labour in 1906 had had Liberal and

'Lib-Lab' phases in their careers. Why did they not, like Howell, Broadhurst and Burt a generation earlier, remain with the Liberal Party instead of becoming associated with a relatively impecunious and insignificant committee for labour representation? Many years of socialist propaganda had borne some fruit and wider economic changes had had an effect, and these points will be returned to below. But part of the answer lies in the nature of early twentieth-century Liberalism.

As Pelling has argued, local Liberal associations were often loath to adopt working-men candidates, despite the advice of leading Liberals who since the 1867 Reform Act had sought to incorporate the labour movement into their party. This undoubtedly estranged some politically ambitious trade union leaders from Liberalism.[36] But at the national as well as the local level, many Liberals viewed the rise of labour with some distaste. It is true that the radical wing of the party claimed to represent the interests of the working man. Thus Lloyd George in a speech at Cardiff on 11 October 1906 perorated:

> But if a Liberal Government tackle the landlords, and the brewers, and the peers, as they have faced the parsons, and try to deliver the nation from the pernicious control of this confederacy of monopolists, then the Independent Labour Party will call in vain upon the working men of Britain to desert Liberalism that is so gallantly fighting to rid the land of the wrongs that have oppressed those who labour in it.[37]

On the same date, at Glasgow, his equally vigorous Cabinet colleague, Winston Churchill, developed a similar argument, claiming that 'the fortunes and interests of Liberalism and Labour are inseparably woven'.[38] Certainly, Churchill and Lloyd George were two strong, if at times unstable, figures who were trying to compel their party to support the collectivist 'New Liberalism', and it has been argued that C.F.G. Masterman — that pessimistic and curiously ineffectual politician — was with them in this task.[39]

Yet it is doubtful that the 'New Liberalism' was as attractive and vigorous as it is sometimes said to have been. Lloyd George's call for an attack on landlords, peers and brewers scarcely raised issues of special interest to the English working class and socially-interventionist policies were perhaps only marginally more appealing. R.H. Tawney's generalisation of 1912 was probably close to reality:

> The middle and upper class view in social reform is that it should

regulate the worker's *life* in order that he may *work* better. The
working class view of economic reform is that it should regulate
his *work*, in order that he may have a chance of living. Hence to
working people licensing reform, insurance acts, etc. seems beginning at the wrong end.[40]

Moreover, the debate over social reform has often led to the unprogres-
sive sections of Liberalism being overlooked. On the formation of
Campbell-Bannerman's government Hardie criticised its 'seventeen
land-owning peers and sixteen place-hunting lawyers'[41] and with some
of these the 'New Liberals' had to work. An indication of the problems
faced by the Lloyd George-Churchill combination is given by Lucy
Masterman, who in her diary on 22 October 1908 noted that the Cabinet 'distrust everything they advance'.[42] John Burns, brought in as the
first working-class Cabinet Minister was ironically one of its more
reactionary members: he was more widely condemned as a lost leader
who had betrayed the labour movement than regarded as an acknow-
ledgement of its interests. Also in the Cabinet were traditionally-minded
libertarians like John Morley, much criticised for his opposition to the
legal eight-hour day, and representatives of non-conformist traders such
as H.H. Fowler who as a minister, according to his private secretary,
had not 'the patience to suffer Radical and Labour Members gladly'.[43]
The 'New Liberals' were not numerous compared with both the
older Whiggish elements in the party and the old-fashioned believers in
individualism. Men of property — as almost all influential Liberals were
— were apprehensive about the masses. The party was haunted by the
ghost of the old Liberalism that had been so powerful in mid-Victorian
Britain. Yet its attitude to political democracy, the extension of which
had given it great impetus, was ambiguous; sections were wary of full
manhood suffrage and hostile to votes for women, while plural voting
and the manipulation of the electoral register before the revision courts
were normal practice. There was a wide variation from constituency to
constituency in the proportion of adult males who were able to vote in
parliamentary elections and the majority of the disenfranchised were
working-class men. About 60 per cent of adult males had the vote in
the 1906 election, and among working men the proportion was somewhat lower.[44] Moreover, workers who had the vote often faced difficulties in exercising it because of the nature of their occupations; as
Shackleton pointed out in a Commons debate, groups such as railway
servants, workmen in the building trades and engineers were often
away from home on polling day.[45]

At the local level, Liberals were often unable or unwilling to adapt to the rise of labour. In many cases industrial disputes and the continued growth of trade unions provided areas of disagreement.[46] Tensions of this sort were noticed by the veteran trade unionist Charles Bowerman who reasoned that if an employer, 'however sympathetic with the workers' movement he might be', would never be invited to become secretary of a trade union, no more should he be expected to represent labour in Parliament.[47]

There was in the 1900s an argument that had been developed over many years and was employed by all types of socialist. It held that the Liberal Party was the embodiment of the mid-Victorian bourgeoisie, but that the power of this class was being challenged by labour; that Liberal commitment to individualism could not resist the tendency towards collectivism and that peace, retrenchment and reform were shibboleths that had become obsolete. In the words of *Justice* (6 January 1906): 'Liberalism as a creed and as a force is played out', and was being replaced by socialism. Behind the rhetoric of political debate lay an accurate critique of the pressure that was to contribute to the break-up of the Liberal Party.

MacDonald, the Labour Party's chief theoretician, adopted this view of Liberalism. In writings that try to establish a theoretical case for a party of labour, MacDonald's dialectic was pseudo-biological: socialism was an evolutionary force that would eventually replace the existing form of society. Liberalism had its virtues, but its epoch was past: 'Socialism', he wrote, 'marks the growth of Society, not the uprising of a class. The consciousness which it seeks to quicken is not one of economic class solidarity, but one of social unity and growth towards organic wholeness.'[48] But despite MacDonald's avowals, it was what he termed 'economic class solidarity' rather than the organic 'growth of Society' which was the main force behind the steady growth of the Labour Party. And the expression of this solidarity was the trade unions.

The importance of the trade union movement in the foundation and subsequent growth of the Labour Party has always been recognised. What has perhaps been under-estimated is the strength, in Lenin's phrase, of 'trade union consciousness' by 1900. This consciousness was to command attention during the period of 'labour unrest' in the three or four years before the outbreak of the First World War, but it had long been forming. In 1901 the gainfully employed male population of the UK was about 11½ million. If those in middle-class professions, the armed services and boys ineligible for trade union membership are

excluded — roughly 25 per cent of the total — the number of adult
working men may be estimated at around eight million. 1,873,000 of
them belonged to trade unions.[49] Their influence was proportionately
greater than their numbers. Trade unionists were often among the most
active members of the working class when it came to the organisation
of local political and other bodies. Where trade unionists had secured
shorter hours it meant that they had more free time compared with
other workers (as well as enjoying the prestige that their ability to
improve conditions brought). Moreover, a knowledge of the 'industrial
democracy' of their society and often of the local trades council was
useful in political and social organisation. Unionisation was concentrated in certain key areas and industries, including engineering and
other metal trades, mining, construction, textiles and transport. Trade
unionism was weak or non-existent in 'parasitic' and smaller trades
which were usually of marginal importance within the economy.

These are among the reasons why skilled unionists were to the fore.
But 'new unionism' also had an impact, although among the unskilled
trade union membership was not a constant feature. A period of unemployment, whether because of illness, dismissal or depression of
trade, could soon lead to lapsed membership when even the small
weekly payment required by the general unions could not be spared
from the family budget. Among the unions of the unskilled, turnover
of members was very high, and many workers must have had a period
of membership of a trade union and continued to think in terms of the
movement's objectives. Again, some branches of industry were not
unionised, or only partly so, with some areas or factories unorganised;
here too there was often a potential for trade unionism which a spark
in the form of an industrial dispute might lead to the sudden establishment of a strong branch. (The fact that trade union membership more
than doubled between 1900 and 1914 shows this potential.) Finally,
many employers refused to recognise the unions, though in such circumstances workers still may have had a sense of collective action.
'Economic class solidarity' or 'trade union consciousness', therefore,
were potent factors in the growth of labour representation, greater
perhaps than the numerical strength of the trade unions would suggest.

It is usually accepted that changes within the economy were tending
to increase the workers' sense of solidarity. Work determines class.
More time is spent at work than in any other waking activity and it is
there that attitudes to fellow workers and to the rest of society are
most often moulded. Yet studies of the work process are lacking for
the early 1900s. The frequent surveys of the working class were social

surveys, drawn up by visitors to the home or by commissions of inquiry that did not even penetrate so far. This can be explained largely by the interest in poverty, as with Booth's great investigation of London and Rowntree's study of York. Other observers following the same tradition have little to offer about the work situation and the ideology it engendered (Florence Bell's *At the Works* is a tantalisingly mistitled social survey with only a few generalisations about Middlesbrough's ironworks). Significantly, too, it was usually women who were interviewed; their husbands, if present, remained silent, perhaps as an unspoken rejection of the middle-class intruder. Investigators who 'submerged' themselves were usually fascinated by the low life of London – the pauperised slum-dweller, not the artisan or respectable workman. The few exceptions were unusual individuals: Stephen Reynolds who lived among Devon fishermen, highly literate men like Alfred Williams and George Sturt, and Robert Tressell, whose brilliant novel, *The Ragged Trousered Philanthropists*, is set in the political backwater of 'Mugsborough', a good class holiday resort.

There is, therefore, a lack of material about the formation of working-class attitudes, understood from the inside. But the forces that were influential can be outlined. In the late nineteenth century British industrialists felt themselves under increasing pressure from foreign competition. One response was to attempt to increase productivity. This took the form not only of introducing new techniques but also of tightening up on the labour force. Newer industrial processes removed some of the older skills and with them the differentials of status and pay. Units were becoming larger with amalgamations and economies of scale, and workers were increasingly likely to have to deal with salaried managers rather than a paternalistic factory or workshop owner. There was widespread disquiet about the changes that were taking place.[50] Trade unions were the main form of defence against these changes, yet they reinforced some of them; once a 'trade union rate' for a job had been negotiated with management all workers received it, despite variations in individual skill. The individual's bargaining function was replaced by a collective one, with all that such collectivism implied in terms of uniformity, solidarity and group consciousness. Some employers became more hostile towards trade unions (often invoking the law) and press criticism grew also.[51] In this process of polarisation, the LRC gained in strength; within twelve months of the House of Lords judgement in the Taff Vale case, 127 unions, representing 50 per cent of the TUC's membership, had affiliated.[52]

In the shorter term, the Liberal Party was also a beneficiary of these changes. Liberal candidates were able to gain support in 1906 by emphasising free trade — the 'big loaf' was a shrewd slogan with bread the main item of working-class diet — and by pledging themselves to end Chinese 'slavery' in South Africa and support a Trade Disputes Bill, both regarded as issues of special interest to the working man. But in the longer term they were to lose their working-class base, as Liberalism was also to lose the support of most of the propertied class, which had been moving over to the Conservatives for some decades.

The growth of electoral support for the Labour Party must not be exaggerated. As Table 2 shows, in all but six of the seats won in 1906 there were straight fights with Conservative candidates or only one Liberal standing in double-member constituencies, although it should be noted that the pact with the Liberals was generous to the LRC only in so far as it allowed its candidates a chance to win Conservative seats or hold on to ones already gained. Nevertheless, the issues emphasised by most LRC candidates were very similar to those in Liberal programmes,[53] and in some constituencies Labour appeared to be little more than the trade union wing of the Liberal Party. It is also true that in some regions Labour had little strength while many workers remained Conservative.[54] But in a country of slow political change something significantly new was taking place: even at the time of a sweeping victory there were signs that a major party was in danger of losing its basis of support.[55] With the electoral agreement with the Liberal Party a matter of secrecy, Labour could be both gamekeeper and poacher; at the same time it could both co-operate and criticise. Among socialists of the SDF and *Clarion* type, attacks on Liberalism were often violent — the typical prominent Liberal might be apostrophised as 'Adam Sweater' (with his Tory counterpart, 'Sir Graball d'Encloseland').[56] And though such unparliamentary invective was eschewed by Labour MPs, they were able to put pressure on the party that had helped to elect them.

III

In 1906, then, the Labour Party was a party largely of trade unionists as was inevitable given the only practicable system for the selection and financing of candidates and their organisation. And where the leadership of trade unions held to their links with Liberalism, many rank and file activists were pressing for them to change over to Labour. In coal-mining, where the old leadership was 'Lib-Lab', the membership narrowly defeated a motion to affiliate with the Labour Party in 1906 but by May 1908 this decision was reversed by 213,000 votes to

Table 2: Electoral Results, 1906

	Constituency won in 1906	Previous representation	Nature of opposition	Result
Barnes	Glasgow, Blackfriars	C	C,L	LRC
Bowerman	Deptford	C	C,L	LRC
Clynes	Manchester, N.E.	C	C	LRC
Crooks	Woolwich	LRC	C	LRC
Duncan	Barrow	C	C,L	LRC
Gill	* Bolton (a)	C	C	LRC,L
Glover	St. Helens	C	C	LRC
Hardie	* Merthyr Tydfil (a)	LRC,L	2L	LRC,L
Henderson	Barnard Castle	LRC	C	LRC
Hodge	Gorton	C	C,L	LRC
Hudson	* Newcastle (a)	2C	2C,L	LRC,L
Jenkins	Chatham	C	C,L	LRC
Jowett	Bradford, W.	C	C,L	LRC
Kelley	Manchester, S.W.	C	C,L	LRC
MacDonald	* Leicester (a)	2C	2C,L	LRC,L
Macpherson	* Preston (a)	2C	2C,L	LRC,L
O'Grady	Leeds, E.	C	C,L	LRC
Parker	* Halifax (a)	C,L	C,L	LRC,L
Richards	Wolverhampton	C	C	LRC
Roberts	* Norwich (a)	C,L	C,L	LRC,L
Seddon	Newton	C	C	LRC
Shackleton	Clitheroe	LRC	C	LRC
Snowden	* Blackburn (a)	2C	2C,L	LRC,C
Summerbell	* Sunderland (a)	2C	2C,L	LRC,L
Taylor	Chester-le-Street	L	C,L	LRC
Thorne	West Ham S.	LRC	C	LRC
Walsh	Ince	C	C	LRC
Wardle	* Stockport (a)	C,L	2C,L	LRC,L
Wilkie	* Dundee (a)	2L	2C,2L	LRC,L
Wilson	West Houghton	C	C	LRC

* (a) Constituency returning two members.

168,000.[57] Richard Bell of the Amalgamated Society of Railway
Servants came under so much pressure to move into line with the two
other ASRS MPs — Hudson and Wardle, both members of the Labour
Party — that he gave up both his seat in the Commons and general
secretaryship in 1910. Often it was the socialists in the Labour Party
who pressed in these directions, making the most of disputes that
involved Liberal manufacturers and insisting on the need for independent representation for the working class.

The majority of the working class were not socialists, but the agitation of those who were struck some responsive chords. As a contemporary observed, the 'Trade Unionist does not, as the Socialist does, see
the end of common action from the beginning, but he is looking in
the same direction'.[58] Much of working-class culture was embodied in
the trade unions; they were its main institutional form. Social changes
were intimately related to economic changes as the working class,
despite all its gradation and subtleties, became more cohesive. The
growth of towns increased the size of working-class neighbourhoods in
which families might identify common interests and values.[59] Politically, it was a party of labour that came closest to representing such
trends within society.

Critics might point to much that was opportunistic, narrow,
moderately reformist (and even reactionary) in the ideology of the
Labour Party. It was pragmatic and influenced by other social classes,
'labourist' and weak in theoretical precepts. But such characteristics
were to be found also among its supporters. For all their inadequacies,
the thirty MPs of 1906 were closer than their political rivals to the
working class; they did not have to try to change their basic character
in order to embody proletarian attitudes. In the pardonably ardent
words of a socialist trade unionist lies a central truth of the advent of
the Labour Party:

We now have men to represent us who know what it is to *feel* the
pinch of poverty and the uncertainty of employment, whose homes
for years have had the grim spectre of a rent lord hovering over them
if work should fail, and who realise the depth of the shadow that
falls in the evening of life, when grey hairs become a curse and men
and women are no longer useful in the production of wealth for
profit.[60]

Such a platform was of sufficient appeal to take votes from the Liberal
Party without being so far-reaching as to appear outside conventional

politics. It articulated the need for economic and social reform and the rising expectations of the working class. As an instrument of the people, the Labour Party was neither a torrent nor a battering ram; it was closer to being a respectful but compelling petition.

Notes

1. Quoted in Harold Nicolson, *King George the Fifth* (1952), p. 94.
2. Quoted in B.E.C. Dugdale, *Arthur James Balfour*, vol. 1 (1939 ed.), p. 329. Joseph Chamberlain wrote of 'the labour earthquake': letter of 23 January 1906 printed in *The Autobiography of Margot Asquith*, vol. 2 (1922), p. 82.
3. The return of these 'Lib-Labs' has sometimes led to confusion about the actual size of the Labour Party, for which see the discussion by Trevor Lloyd, 'Lib-Labs and "unforgivable electoral generosity" ', *Bulletin of the Institute of Historical Research*, vol. 48 (1975), pp. 255-9. Twenty-nine LRC-approved candidates were elected; on entering the Commons they declared themselves the Labour Party and were joined by J.W. Taylor, an ILP member who had won Chester-le-Street with the support of a union not affiliated to the LRC.
4. For the ideas held about labour representation before 1906, see P.P. Poirier, *The Advent of the Labour Party* (1958); H. Pelling, *The Origins of the Labour Party*, 2nd ed. (Oxford, 1965); F. Bealey and H. Pelling, *Labour and Politics 1900-1906* (1958); F. Engels, *The British Labour Movement* (1936), pp. 18-21, 33-75 (articles reprinted from the *Labour Standard*, 1881, in which Engels estimated that the working class had the power to gain forty or fifty representatives in the Commons); The Fabian Society, 'To Your Tents, Oh Israel!' *Fortnightly Review*, vol. 54 (1893): this article, written by Shaw and the Webbs, calculated that the larger unions might easily finance fifty labour candidates.
5. Roy Douglas, *The History of the Liberal Party 1895-1970* (1971), p. 2; cf. also Trevor Wilson, *The Downfall of the Liberal Party 1914-1935* (1966), pp. 16-18, 23 and P.F. Clarke, *Lancashire and the New Liberalism* (Cambridge, 1971), p. 394.
6. R.H.S. Crossman, Introduction to Walter Bagehot, *The English Constitution* (1963 ed.), p. 41; W.T. Rodgers and Bernard Donoughue, *The People into Parliament* (1966), p. 182.
7. Patrick Cosgrave, *Spectator*, 1 March 1975.
8. T. Rothstein, *From Chartism to Labourism* (1929), esp. pp. 281-97; for the best sustained statement of this view see Ralph Miliband, *Parliamentary Socialism* (1961); another full-scale study from a similar viewpoint is David Coates, *The Labour Party and the Struggle for Socialism* (1975).
9. The collection is kept at Hull University and provides the basis of the *Dictionary of Labour Biography*. Where references are not individually identified, this is their source. I am grateful to Dr Joyce Bellamy, who has done much to build up the collection, for assistance in consulting it.
10. Bealey and Pelling, *Labour and Politics*, p. 276.
11. H.A. Clegg, et al., *A History of British Trade Unions since 1889*, vol. 1 (Oxford, 1964), p. 387; W.D. Muller, *The 'Kept Men'? The First Century of Trade Union Representation in the British House of Commons 1874-1975* (Hassocks, 1977), p. 5.
12. The problem of boy labour was one that became increasingly recognised in the 1900s. The study by Arnold Freeman, *Boy Life and Labour: the Manufacture of Inefficiency* (1914), was based on evidence from Birmingham (where Thorne spent his early years) but drew its conclusions nationally.

13. *Christian Commonwealth*, 9 February 1910; J.R. Clynes, *When I Remember . . .* (1940), p. 5.

14. 'How I Got On', *Pearson's Weekly*, 26 April 1906.

15. But the Scottish element was less strong than C.F.G. Masterman implied in *The Condition of England* (1909; 1912 ed.), p. 122. In this passage Masterman argued that the Labour MPs were untypical of the working class.

16. 'How I Got On', *Pearson's Weekly*, 26 April 1906.

17. The extent to which labour was making an impact on local politics is problematical, mainly because of inadequate statistics and questions of definition. Many trade unionists were elected with Liberal support, but others, especially socialists, were genuinely independent. In 1900 the ILP annual report recorded that members of the party included sixty-three town councillors, four county councillors, thirty-six urban and three rural district councillors, sixteen parish councillors, eight citizen's auditors, fifty-one members of boards of guardians and sixty-six school board members (G.D.H. Cole, *British Working Class Politics 1832-1914* (1941), pp. 150-1). This is an area that would repay further investigation. A recent study of borough council elections in England and Wales (excluding London) counts 136 successful labour candidates in 1905 and argues that contests at local level did not take place within a framework of Liberal-Labour co-operation, or 'Progressivism': many seats won were taken from Liberals; see M.G. Sheppard, 'Labour at Municipal Elections 1901-1913' (Warwick University M.A. thesis, 1976). There is some confirmation of this view in a study of municipal voting in the 1906-14 period, which suggests that anti-socialist pacts were made between some local Liberals and Conservatives but that a decline in Liberal support took place, to the benefit of Conservative rather than Labour candidates. (C. Cook, 'Labour and the Downfall of the Liberal Party, 1906-14' in A. Sked and C. Cook (eds.), *Crisis and Controversy* (1976), pp. 38-65.)

18. S. and B. Webb, *History of Trade Unionism* (1920 ed.), p. 467.

19. Ibid., p. 470. The subsequent development of some of the thirty had an opportunistic, if not careerist, aspect: Shackleton left the Commons in 1910 to take a post as a senior civil servant; Barnes, MacDonald, Parker, Roberts, Seddon, Snowden and Wardle all ended their political lives outside the Labour Party. Most colourfully, O'Grady, the son of Irish immigrants, became Governor and Commander-in-Chief of the Falkland Islands. Many also left relatively substantial estates (see Table 1).

20. The average age of Labour MPs has been computed from the dates of birth given in Table 1; that of the whole House is estimated by J.A. Thomas, *The House of Commons 1906-1911: an Analysis of its Economic and Social Character* (Cardiff, 1958), p. 25.

21. G.K. Chesterton, 'Introduction' to George Haw, *From Workhouse to Westminster: the Life Story of Will Crooks, MP* (1907), pp. xv-xvi.

22. Stead wrote to 'Lib-Lab' as well as Labour MPs and got forty-five replies which he printed as 'The Labour Party and the Books that Helped to Make It' in the *Review of Reviews*, vol. 33 (1906), pp. 568-82.

23. W.H. Mallock, 'The Political Powers of Labour: Their Extent and Their Limitations', *Nineteenth Century*, vol. 60 (1906), p. 211; cf. also Mallock's four-part article, 'The Intellectual Condition of the Labour Party', *Monthly Review*, vol. 25 (Oct., Nov., Dec. 1906) and vol. 26 (Jan. 1907). For a modern treatment of the influence of Ruskin and Carlyle on the early Labour Party, see R. Barker, *The Labour Party and Education* (Oxford, 1972), pp. 5-7.

24. The lists of some MPs bring to mind the definition of a classic as a book that everybody wants to have read and nobody wants to read; Will Crooks in his reply seemed to think that Ruskin wrote *Alton Locke* and the present writer has in his possession James Parker's copy of Thorold Rogers's *Six Centuries of Work and Wages,* one of the books he claimed to have influenced him: it shows no signs

of having been read. See too the view of Frederick Rogers, *Labour, Life and Literature: Some Memories of Sixty Years* (1913; ed. D. Rubinstein, Brighton, 1973), p. 275.

25. Lady Bell, *At the Works* (1907), ch. 7.

26. K.D. Brown, 'Non-conformity and the British Labour Movement: a Case Study', *Journal of Social History*, vol. 8 (1975), pp. 113-20.

27. Though the proportion of civil marriages was increasing, during this period they accounted for less than one fifth of all ceremonies; in 1906 they amounted to 188 per 1,000: *Sixty-Ninth Annual Report of the Registrar General . . . PP* 1908: vol. XVII, Cd. 3883, p. xxi.

28. F.L. Donaldson, 'The Church and the "Labour Church" ', in W.H. Hunt (ed.), *Churchmanship and Labour: Sermons on Social Subjects* (1906), pp. 93-4. For Blatchford's atheism see L. Thompson, *Robert Blatchford: Portrait of an Englishman* (1951), ch. 13.

29. Philip Viscount Snowden, *An Autobiography*, vol. 1 (1934), p. 82; cf. also Colin Cross, *Philip Snowden* (1966), p. 35-7.

30. The temperance lobby replied by printing anti-drink statements made by Tillett in his younger, teetotal days. For the controversy in full, see the file in the Labour Party Library, LP/TIL/08.

31. A.E. Dingle, 'Drink and Working-class Living Standards in Britain, 1870-1914', *Economic History Review*, 2nd ser., vol. 25 (1972), pp. 609-10.

32. *Chatham, Rochester and Gillingham Observer*, 6 January 1906.

33. *Newcastle Daily Chronicle*, 9 January 1906.

34. *Newton and Earlstown Guardian*, 19 January 1906.

35. Masterman, *Condition of England*, p. 126; cf. Richard Price, *An Imperial War and the British Working Class: Working-Class Attitudes and Reactions to the Boer War 1899-1902* (1972), esp. pp. 234-41.

36. Pelling, *Origins of the Labour Party*, pp. 222-4; idem, *Popular Politics and Society in Late Victorian Britain* (1968), pp. 105-7.

37. *Better Times: Speeches by the Right Hon. D. Lloyd George, MP* (1910), p. 36.

38. R.R. James (ed.), *Winston S. Churchill: His Complete Speeches 1897-1963* (1974), p. 673.

39. E. David, 'The New Liberalism of C.F.G. Masterman, 1873-1927', in K.D. Brown (ed.), *Essays in Anti-Labour History: Responses to the Rise of Labour in Britain* (1974), p. 27. Another discussion of the 'New Liberalism' and the writers who were associated with it does not include Masterman: P.F. Clarke, 'The Progressive Movement in England', *Transactions of the Royal Historical Society*, 5th series, vol. 24 (1974), pp. 159-81.

40. J.M. Winter and D.M. Joslin (eds.), *R.H. Tawney's Commonplace Book* (Cambridge, 1972), p. 6.

41. William Stewart, *J. Keir Hardie: A Biography* (1921), p. 222-3.

42. Lucy Masterman, *C.F.G. Masterman: A Biography* (1939), p. 112.

43. Quoted in E.H. Fowler, *The Life of Henry Hartley Fowler* (1912), p. 500. Morley's radicalism failed to adapt to newer forces; as early as 1892 he complained to Harcourt that, 'the most headstrong and unscrupulous and shallow of those who speak for labour' had 'captured the Liberal party'. Quoted in D.A. Hamer, *John Morley: Liberal Intellectual in Politics* (Oxford, 1968), p. 259.

44. Neal Blewett, *The Peers, the Parties and the People: the General Elections of 1910* (1972) p. 359; H.C.G. Matthew, et al., 'The Franchise Factor in the Rise of the Labour Party', *English Historical Review*, vol. 91 (1976), p. 730. Many fell victim to agents of the two main parties who were active in attempting to remove suspected opponents from the electoral register; for a racy account of such activities in the Pudsey division in this period see J.H. Linforth, *Leaves from an Agent's Diary: Being Some Reminiscences of Thirty Years Work as a Liberal Agent* (Leeds, 1911).

45. 131 HC Deb. 4s., col. 544 (8 March 1904).

46. Martin Petter, 'The Progressive Alliance', *History*, vol. 58 (1973), p. 58; Joseph White, 'A Panegyric on Edwardian Progressivism', *Journal of British Studies*, vol. 16 (1977), p. 149; Alun Howkins, 'Edwardian Liberalism and Industrial Unrest: A Class View of the Decline of Liberalism', *History Workshop*, no. 4 (1977), pp. 147-8.

47. Quoted in an interview with Fenner Brockway in *Christian Commonwealth*, 26 January 1910; cf. G.D. Kelley's explanation of why he had severed a life-long connection with the Liberal Party to become an LRC candidate: *Manchester Guardian*, 28 January, 4 February 1904.

48. J. Ramsay MacDonald, *Socialism and Society* (1905), p. 128.

49. Figures taken from B.R. Mitchell and P. Deane, *Abstract of British Historical Statistics* (Cambridge, 1962), pp. 60, 68.

50. Much information is contained in A.L. Levine, 'Industrial Change and its Effects upon Labour 1900-1914' (London University Ph.D. thesis, 1954); see also the same author's *Industrial Retardation in Britain 1880-1914* (New York, 1967), ch. 5, and E.H. Phelps Brown, *The Growth of British Industrial Relations: A Study from the Standpoint of 1906-14* (1959), ch. 2.

51. The legal counter-offensive is discussed by J. Saville, 'Trade Unions and Free Labour: the Background to the Taff Vale Decision' in A. Briggs and J. Saville (eds.), *Essays in Labour History* (1960). Of the widespread press criticism perhaps the most telling was *The Times* series of articles, 'The Crisis in British Industry', in 1901-2: reprinted by E.A. Pratt, *Trade Unionism and British Industry* (1904).

52. Clegg, et al., *History of British Trade Unions*, pp. 374-5.

53. A.K. Russell, *Liberal Landslide: The General Election of 1906* (Newton Abbot, 1973), p. 78.

54. See the discussion by Alan Lee, ch. 5 above. Though Labour was taking mainly Liberal votes this was not its only source; the voting pattern in parts of Lancashire suggests that Labour candidates obtained up to 15 per cent of their votes from former Conservatives.

55. One contemporary Liberal believed that the ideas of the working class would be dominant in the twentieth century; 'I will', he continued, 'hazard the prediction that the Labour party has introduced into the organism of middle-class Liberalism, now, perhaps for the last time triumphant, the seeds of inevitable disintegration.' 'A Liberal Voter on the Liberal Victory', *The Times*, 31 January 1906.

56. The names are from Tressell, *The Ragged Trousered Philanthropists* (1955 ed.), ch. 48. In fact there were more Liberal landowners than Conservative in the Commons in 1906 (62 to 58, though the landed interest was relatively stronger in the smaller parliamentary Conservative Party). The old parties were also about equal in terms of railway directors and bankers, but coal owners and manufacturers were stronger on the Liberal benches; see Thomas, *House of Commons 1906-1911*, pp. 28-9; cf. T.W. Heyck, 'British Radicals and Radicalism, 1874-1895: A Social Analysis' in Robert J. Bezucha (ed.), *Modern European Social History* (Lexington, 1972), p. 31 and H.J. Perkin, 'Land Reform and Class Conflict in Victorian Britain' in J. Butt and I.F. Clarke (eds.), *The Victorians and Social Protest* (Newton Abbot, 1973), pp. 216-17.

57. Roy Gregory, *The Miners and British Politics 1906-1914* (Oxford, 1968), pp. 29-32.

58. Brougham Villiers, *The Socialist Movement in England* (1908), p. 131.

59. For a recent discussion of some of these changes, see Standish Meacham, *A Life Apart: The English Working Class, 1880-1914* (1977).

60. Charles Coleman, 'The Coming of Labour', *Amalgamated Engineers Monthly Journal*, vol. 2 (1906), p. 20.

8 THE LADDER OF BECOMING: A.R. ORAGE, A.J. PENTY AND THE ORIGINS OF GUILD SOCIALISM IN ENGLAND

Frank Matthews

Critics of guild socialism have often been inclined to dismiss the movement as 'medieval' or 'pluralistic', consigning it under either title to a limbo fittingly occupied by other utopian movements which have been unwilling to come to terms with the 'realities' of modern political life.[1] It is a criticism which tends to arise out of the whole structure and development of British politics. It has often been argued that attacks by left-wing groups on parliamentary Labour are always either premature or useless because they are based on an inability to comprehend the British political process. Since that process is, historically, a gradualist one, innovation must always be gradual and any other method of change must be predoomed to failure. The argument is coherent within its own logic, but rests on an immense condescension towards the intellectual apprehensions of the critical groups. Guild socialists well understood the nature of the British political system and were willing to argue against participation from within on the grounds that such participation must always involve the falsification of ideals and aspirations. For them the political labour movement was wrong at its core simply because it had chosen to work within the system. This meant, using the biological imagery still common to the period, that the infant Labour Party was in decay at its birth, infected by the very organism it had meant to conquer. Any spiritual dynamic the party possessed had dissipated itself in the by-ways of party manoeuvres, and it was this fading central dynamic which the guild socialists perceived as essential in the search for political and social regeneration. So although most guild socialists could well understand the logic of the gradualist argument, particularly as many of them had graduated through the agency of the Fabian Society, yet they found it impossible to sustain any philosophy based on it. And the example of the Labour Party in Parliament after 1906 reinforced a critique the outlines of which had already been formed.

The emergence of that critique is one which is of some historical interest illustrating, as it does, the way in which seemingly haphazard and arbitrary events can combine to produce effects which may be

147

important out of all relation to their origins. In its contribution to the continuing spirit of democracy and free enquiry within the labour movement and in defining areas of concern which politicians do ill to forget, guild socialism was a movement the importance of which is not only out of proportion to its origins, but equally disproportionate to its operative size throughout the period of its active life.

I

It is almost impossible to embark on any discussion of the development of socialist ideas in the period before 1914 without reference to the *New Age* and to its editor, Alfred Richard Orage (1873-1934). He is a man whose contribution both to the literary and the political culture of the pre-First World War period is increasingly acknowledged. Philip Mairet's literary biography, *A.R. Orage; A Memoir* (1936), has more recently been supplemented by Wallace Martin's more comprehensive analysis in *The New Age Under Orage* (Manchester, 1967) and by David Thatcher's extremely interesting chapter on the Nietzschean influences on Orage in his *Nietzsche in England, 1890-1914* (Toronto, 1970). More discursive, but penetrating and useful, is Paul Selver's *Orage and the New Age Circle* (1959).

A superb synthesiser and propagandist, Orage's importance lies in the fact that he came to the *New Age* just at the point where dissatisfaction with the tendencies of the Labour Party was beginning to crystallise for socialists of all classes. The *New Age* was typical of the type of journal which existed precariously on the bounty of the wellintentioned in the period. Originally published in 1894, one of its early contributors was Ramsay MacDonald. Another, some of whose earliest literary efforts appeared in the *New Age*, was G.K. Chesterton. The journal was then edited by A.E. Fletcher whose successor, Arthur Compton Rickett, gave way to the Christian Socialist Joseph Clayton, who was editor and proprietor when Orage and Holbrook Jackson became interested in it. It had always adopted a high tone; often a Christian one and under Clayton developed an independent political policy which its new editors were to continue. It attracted a readership of an independent type well suited to the ideals of Orage and Jackson who were supported by the money of backers then anonymous. Orage was already engaged in the political arena through his membership of the Fabian Society but his earlier intellectual interests and a mature critical intellect had led him to question the Fabian solution to social problems. The search for alternatives made him particularly receptive to the ideas of his friend Arthur Joseph Penty (1875-1937) in the period up to 1907. Later he was more influenced by a man whose active interest in the labour movement was much longer and more consistent. This was Samuel George Hobson (1870-1940). The connection of both of these men with the *New Age* was through personal friendship with Orage, but whereas Orage became acquainted with Hobson in London through the Fabian Society, the association with Penty was of much longer standing and was rooted in their joint activities in the provinces before both men came to London in the early years of this century.

To some extent both Orage and Penty were self-educated. The description 'autodidact' is often used disparagingly by historians, correctly suspicious of the subjectivity and categorisation to which the self-educated may be prone. But it would be wrong to dismiss Orage in particular in so contemptuous a style. He had, after all, a certain degree of education and had been trained as a teacher. But while it is a common enough characteristic of those newly literate to be eager to know, Orage developed that rarer characteristic which is the desire to understand. The whole purpose of his life, once he had clarified this to himself, seems to have been to make a comprehensive frame of reference for it; to appreciate motives and to comprehend purposes. Hence the belief of Middleton Murry that Orage possessed an 'obstinate substratum of belief that there was some secret of control over the Universe; a key by which one could unlock all the doors, and be a master of Power'.[2]

The power Orage sought, however, was not so much power over others as power over self. In his attempts to further this mystical quest he devoted years of serious study to a number of philosophies — Platonic, Vedantic, Nietzschean — until finally, in 1922, he accepted the teachings of Gurdjieff and gave up his editorship of the *New Age* to follow the mentor's guidance in France, at Fontainebleau. Despite this eventual commitment to the doctrine of a man whom many might have described as a mystagogue, the whole tendency of Orage's reflective intellect was towards not confusion, but precision and clarity. So what might be thought of as his excursions into byways were not simply that; rather they were attempts to expand and illuminate experience in the light of the original quest which was towards the comprehending soul working in an environment which would nurture and continuously expand those comprehensions. Orage's view of life seems to have been, therefore, one of ever-changing intellectual horizons in which the expansion of the opportunity to comprehend was seen as part of an endless spiritual quest.

Orage and Penty met in the Leeds Theosophical Society. Penty joined this group in about 1898 when he became conscious of the

deficiencies in his education. He was then in his early twenties and, unlike Orage, he had had no opportunity to enjoy a prolonged education.
Born in York, the son of a builder turned architect, Penty was removed
from school at the age of thirteen and apprenticed in his father's office.
By the age of twenty he had assimilated as much architectural knowledge as his father had to teach and was himself supervising the drawing
office and in charge of the training of apprentices. As he realised how
narrow were the foundations of his general education, Penty began to
look for some means of broadening his cultural prospects. It was
natural, given his inclinations, that he should have turned to the works
of Ruskin and Morris, both of whom had an extensive influence on his
thought and later work. Penty was already an adherent of the arts and
crafts movement in architecture and his own work was particularly
influenced, at this time, by that of R. Norman Shaw. Now readings in
Morris and Ruskin began to reinforce a natural tendency to idealise
medieval works, a tendency propagated by intimate contact with the
architecture of the Middle Ages in and around York.

Penty also attended lectures on the Renaissance given by Arthur
Symonds and he joined the Young Men's Self-Improvement Society,
also in Leeds, at about the same time as he joined the Theosophical
Society.[3] The latter he had joined with no faith in its doctrines, but
rather to put himself into contact with people whose social, religious
and aesthetic experience was wider than his own. Here he began his
friendship with Orage who had also met Holbrook Jackson (1874-1948)
by chance in the same city. Orage carried Jackson and later Penty into
the Plato Group which had come together as an informal society for the
exposition of Orage's views on Platonic philosophy.

The result of the conjunction of three extremely different personalities and talents, united in opposition to the philistines of Leeds, was the
consideration of a number of schemes to publicise their views. Rejecting suggestions both for a journal and for a William Morris Society,
they eventually decided to form the Leeds Arts Club which was to
'cover the whole field of culture and to raise any remotely relevant
issue'.[4] The Club was a 'sensational success' which shook conventional
citizens by expounding the views of Nietzsche, Ibsen and Shaw and
further startled by doing so with a Shavian insouciance hardly palatable
to the respectable bourgeoise who attended. Orage's style at this time
has been described by Gerald Cumberland as 'a wonderful gift of
talking a most divine nonsense — a spurious wisdom that ran closely
along the border-line of rank absurdity', a description which endorses
the comments of other contemporaries.[5] It was, perhaps, less rank

absurdity than an attempt at the apparently paradoxical as the influence of Nietzsche grew on him during the period.

Clearly the manner of its leaders exercised a certain fascination since the Arts Club did not founder and continued to draw outstanding speakers as well as to organise exhibitions which were devoted to all forms of the visual arts. There was, too, a Fabian section which spread the ideas of the society in Leeds and helped to add to the volume of sociological and political ideas which Penty was beginning to absorb — all of which helped to nurture his developing theories. He thus formed his views in a variety of ways and over a period of some years. There had come, firstly, an aesthetic reaction in the course of his early studies. Without prompting he had noticed the contrast — especially pointed in York — between the best medieval architecture and the debased copies of the Victorian. He found himself unable to appreciate why an age which could produce such magnificent building should be regarded as primitive. Pressing still more the dichotomy between his idealisation of the Middle Ages and the realities of his life was the fact that he was trained in an atmosphere of commercial intrigue and speculation. Early in life Penty was brought into contact with local politics and conniving, with the world of the small tradesman and the petty bourgeois, of the grandest effect at the lowest cost. The experience established in him a permanent feeling of distaste for exploitation; for botched and slipshod work as for cheap effects and false economy. His own later work was distinguished by a close attention to design and a scrupulous finish in detail. And his experience of commerce at the local level led him into an analysis of its national effects which helped to form his basic critique of society.

These reactions, combined with the intellectual journey which he had undertaken, roused conflicts in Penty which kept him at a pitch of dissatisfaction for some time. He was tied to a system he despised by his connection with his father's business, but he resented the implications of this connection both for society and for his own practice of his craft. Meanwhile he continued reading, thinking and discussing his ideas with both Orage and Jackson although later Orage and he were to differ totally over Penty's medievalism. By the time that the tensions of his life had forced him to the decision to leave home, Penty was already twenty-seven. He was aware of the difficulties of moving, unestablished, to London but he was tired of the greater difficulties of life at home and, feeling that both grievances and conflicts of personality could never be properly resolved, Penty chose to leave York. The move was initially a cause of some bitterness since he found it even more difficult to establish himself than he had expected, but there is no doubt that ultimately it led to an expansion of his personal and cultural associations.

In 1902 Penty took rooms in Hammersmith where he began work on a book which in relation to the guild movement one may describe as seminal, *The Restoration of the Gild System*. Early in 1906 A.R. Orage, himself gambling on a future in London's literary world, also made the journey south.[6] He and Penty shared a flat in Hammersmith for some time, discussing Penty's ideas as the latter, who never created with ease, worked his way through forty re-writings of his little book.[7]

The association of Orage and Penty at this point is important for the intellectual development of both men; particularly for Orage who was synthesiser rather than creator and seems always to have needed the spur of another's ideas, however obfuscated these may have been, to prompt his own outstanding powers of clarification. He was a natural expositor; a born teacher. This ability amounted to a need to clarify and expound and it created difficulties for Orage who was, on at least one occasion, accused of plagiarism. In his common dealings with colleagues, however, he was a man so well regarded and of such obvious integrity that it is difficult to believe that he could have consciously appropriated another man's work. It is more probable that he, who was often overtaken by the excitement of intellectual discovery, became confused between the hectic spin-off of ideas in his own head and the original sources which had inspired him. And since he seems also to have been a man who longed to produced a great work but who, with the exception of the *New Age* itself, never did so, the rare temptation to be less than incisive in self-criticism may have been too great. There is, therefore, a certain wistfulness in the manner in which he defended himself, later, against two assumptions. First, that Penty alone was responsible for the working out of the òriginal ideas on a guild system and, secondly, that guild socialism was developed out of French syndicalism, and had no native roots of its own.

Writing to Penty in 1913, in reply to an original letter which has not survived, Orage commented:

Long before your book was begun I remember spending hours and hours with you discussing problems connected with the question and, if I remember rightly, I saw a lot of our conversations made use of in your book. Why not? That is what they were for; but you have no right to deny my assistance in the preliminary clearing of the ground . . . Nobody, by the way, can say that the 'New Age' has not given you credit for your book; and it remains.[8]

In another letter, he wrote apropos an article which had appeared in the *New Age*:

> I've made enquiries of one or two readers who know nothing of the matter and none of them has read into A.E.R's article either your co-authorship in the Guild Socialism articles or mine in your book. They conclude that what was meant was (a) that Guild Socialism would never have been thought of but for your work and (b) that Orage was acquainted with you and discussed the subject with you before you wrote your book. There is no suggestion that *I* wrote any part of your book. As you know, I didn't see it in manuscript even . . . By the way, I had in mind my conversations with you *before* either of us came to London. I mean at Harrogate, Leeds and Hinderwell, etc. I don't count the conversation in London. There, I admit, you taught me and I contributed nothing.[9]

Orage's disclaimer of any part in the writing of Penty's book conflicts a little with the evidence of Mrs Penty who held that Orage did see parts of the book and re-wrote one paragraph, but that only. It is not a matter of great significance since it is clear from the letters that Orage was only making a claim for a share in the intellectual origins rather than the actual drafting of Penty's book. More important was the emphasis he laid on the nature of the development of guild ideas from 1906 onwards in a letter which he published in the *Guildsman* for September 1920. Again he was attempting to clarify what he saw as a misunderstanding of the chronology of the movement which had been put forward in an article in the same journal in August.

> Sir,
> Your contributor 'H' may have reasons of his own for fathering the National Guilds Movement on French Syndicalism, but the facts are against him. Mr Penty's 'The Restoration of the Guild System' was published before 1906[10] and much of it was written in draft as far back as 1900, if not before. The development of Mr Penty's local gilds into National Guilds and the substitution of the Trade Union Movement for his Arts and Crafts movement was the work of the *New Age* from 1907 onwards. French Syndicalism, in so far as it affected National Guilds at all, did so only by stimulating a public interest in the question of Labour control; an interest we deliberately

used as a lever for National Guilds propaganda.

As one who, for his sins, has written more, and more continuously on the Guild ideas than all other writers on the subject put together, I can affirm that 'The Fathers that Begat Us' were not French Syndicalists, but English Socialists.

This statement accurately and economically outlined the origin of guild socialism as it took place in Britain. The ideas of Penty and Orage in this respect were complementary. Penty was no publicist, and his turn of mind was more philosophical than political. While it would be inaccurate to make the opposite claim for Orage whose philosophical interests are well known, his search for integration in life led him for a number of years to view socialism, including the guild version of it, as an area of tremendous hope for the realisation of the renewed society. In itself this search would have meant little had it not been for the combination of circumstances which brought Orage and Holbrook Jackson into the editorship of the *New Age*, a task which soon fell to Orage alone as Jackson moved into journalistic areas which were both more sympathetic and more rewarding.[11] The manner in which this occurred has been told elsewhere, but its importance for the history of the intellectual culture of Britain lies in the fact that in Orage the *New Age* gained an editor who quite consciously saw himself as part of a modern and modernising movement. This gave him a prosiliency of imagination which allowed him to tackle most of the 'advanced' issues of the day, the first of these being the question of socialism and its relationship to the Labour Party. Was that party to be socialist and if so, what was that socialism to mean? The new editors were exhorted in the second issue (9 May 1907) to make sure that the socialism they preached should represent a comprehensive analysis. Their correspondent, H. Hamilton Fyfe, begged: 'Above all, don't let the paper be amateurish and faddy. Socialism wants a wider interpretation. It must not be associated with Jaeger clothing and vegetarianism.' Inevitably, of course, as an 'advanced' journal in the period some of its advertisements reveal that support came from just this sort of progressive area. But it was able to arouse interest in articles on women, trade unions, philosophy and socialism, both in its ideal forms and in its practical expression through the Labour Party both in and out of Parliament. And sustained partly by the critique which he had worked out with Penty, Orage was very ready to enter the lists against the deficiencies of Labour in Parliament. From the beginning of his editorship the *New Age* was openly critical of organised Labour politics and of the general tendencies of collectivism. Soon Orage was heavily involved in the Grayson affair where, in Colne Valley, Victor Grayson was adopted as parliamentary candidate by the local branch in defiance of the National Administrative Council of the Independent Labour Party. His subsequent election was rapturously received by left-wing critics of the Labour Party and especially by the *New Age*. This involvement in current controversy affected Orage's relationship with Penty in two ways. It began to force them apart as Orage looked for the means of elaborating Penty's ideas in order to make them viable in modern industrial conditions. In turn this attempt to synthesise repelled Penty, whose political analysis was considerably more static and who was inclined to believe that the solution to the problems of an industrial society had already been sufficiently propounded in his little book.

But there was a more fundamental gap between the two men. While both based a good deal of their philosophical and political theory on man as a spiritual being, their tools of analysis were quite different. Orage is a splendid example of the spirit of enquiry which emerged out of the secularisation of conscience in the closing decades of the nineteenth century. His spirituality is one which is extracted from the responses of man in reaction to his environment, and encouraged by his study of Nietzsche, Orage went on to glorify the possibilities of man working beyond his perceived capacities to create a more supreme synthesis of personality than commonly thought possible. The tendency can be described in the words of a possibly unconscious influence on Orage, the idealist T.H. Green, who believed that the integration of the past history of philosophy with the developments of the modern age was carrying men 'towards the freedom of perfect understanding'.[12]

Whatever might be its potential for Orage, understanding for Penty must always be imperfect, since man was not a perfectible being.[13] It is in this area of fundamentals that Orage and Penty, so closely allied in one respect, diverge. While Orage may always be described as Utopian, that description can never be made to fit Penty. In part, this is because of his rather diffuse religious background. In the classic British manner of class evolution and self-improvement, his family, originally chapel, had later graduated to the established church. They were apparently never intensely religious, and Penty's own belief seems to have been a loosely held deism which allowed him to express religiosity in a variety of ways. But it would be a mistake to imagine that religion meant little to Penty: it is better to view his work as essentially religious. He was, for example, a member of the Church Socialist League in which he met numbers of people with whom he felt a close affinity of ideas. His Christian outlook, although it never held him in any organised sect, still gave a basis to his thought which made it more akin to that of Social Christian movements than any other.[14] He could not imagine a world into which religion or the religious impulse did not enter and he believed, simply, that God did exist. For him this was the constant: forms of religious observance were largely irrelevant and he was perfectly happy to worship with his wife when she was converted to Catholicism after the birth of their children. Christian belief formed the groundwork of his thought and most of his judgements in connection with the guild movement were developed from Christian, and especially medieval, ethics.

What was the system which Penty elaborated? He was hardly an original thinker, and the preface to *The Restoration of the Gild System* clearly acknowledges an intellectual debt to Arnold, Carlyle, Ruskin and Edward Carpenter. But in attempting to devise a means for giving Ruskin's guild ideas a practical basis he hit on the use of the trade unions in a way which implied forms of workers' control while it did not actually suggest them. Penty was attempting to prove in his book that all forms of relationship had been ruined by the onset of industrialism. Medieval guilds had controlled the cupidity and acquisitiveness of mankind, particularly by the use of fixed prices. Capitalist society neither did this nor, obviously, did it seek to. The result was that a neurotic compulsion towards quantity had overcome the earlier stress on quality. Commercialism increased greed and depressed the spiritual energies of man while at the same time it replaced spiritual aspirations by that less desirable social entity, class consciousness. Commercialism had ruined personal relationships and ramified the class system.

Whatever solution collectivism might offer to these problems could only be partial. Penty believed that state ownership of industry would simply reproduce the search for profitability which obsessed private business: 'a government charged with the administration of any industry would become interested in its continuance as a business quite apart from its usefulness or otherwise, or whether or no it had been called into existence by some temporary need of modern civilisation'.[15] The worker would continue to feel as alienated as he might in capitalist industry. The only solution would be to break down that feeling of alienation by re-forming relationships which would be based on an association in the workplace; an identification with relationships and processes which the worker could understand. Industry must be on a human scale.

To achieve this Penty suggested using the trade unions as the core for a reorganisation of industry in which the workers themselves would largely control their own crafts. Expropriation might take place through a process similar to that which the guild socialists were to describe later as 'encroaching control'; an optimistic concept whereby successive, successful strikes would erode the power of management and owners. Penty suggested that this process might in any case be accelerated, if not prompted, by increasing financial stress and the failure of the international economy. As this occurred workers, through their trade unions, would take over particular industries and transform these into modern 'guilds'. Penty wrote: 'it is necessary to transfer the control of industry from the hands of the financier into those of the craftsman — it is evident that the nature of the reforms is such as to place the centre of gravity of the reform movement outside the sphere of politics'.[16] With a purified legislature and a change in industrial functions the individual would be restored to a proper sense of integrity in relation to society and the state. Personal rights would be subsumed into the greater good of the community while the spiritual life of the nation remained of pre-eminent importance.

This is a sketchy outline of a book which was itself neither detailed nor specific. Yet *The Restoration of the Gild System* had an effect quite disproportionate to the quality of its social analysis. The ideas which it expressed are similar to those which constantly perplexed socialists at once more politically active and intellectually subtle. Penty thus forms a link in the chain stretching from social and political theorists of the nineteenth century to those of the twentieth, many of his ideas comparing fairly closely with those of his near contemporary R.H. Tawney. Since Tawney was for a short period a member of the National Guilds League and certainly acquainted with Penty, it is possible that Penty influenced Tawney to some extent, particularly in their joint animus towards the vice of cupidity as it was encouraged by the consuming society.[17]

II

But now it was Orage who became the vital link, a role which stresses the interwoven influence of the two men since it was undoubtedly the *New Age* which vitalised Penty's ideas and which — far the more important point — developed them for a wider public in the period between 1907 and 1914 during which time the term 'guild socialism' came into use. Certainly it was Orage, now influenced by Hobson, who began the synthesis which was to elaborate the idea of welding the guild philosophy onto the more practical, functional basis of trade unionism. Out of this conjunction came the inspiration for the National Guilds

League, which was organised without Orage's active participation. He considered the moment chosen for its formation inopportune and his association with the League was always uneasy and intermittent.

Penty was suspicious of the League for a rather different reason since he did not trust the association of the word 'socialist' with the guild idea. Because of this he and his supporters within the League always referred to themselves as 'National Guildsmen' rather than 'guild socialists'. It was the embryonic divergence of ideas which was later to help in the collapse of the League. And the apparently minor quibble is a major point. It emphasises Penty's insistence on the need for a guild state which was based not on the imposition of doctrine, with whatever tolerance that might be achieved, but rather on the hope of a complete spiritual regeneration of the nation.[18] Only this could give the whole people the will to change the social and economic structure. It was a message which Penty reiterated to the end of his life. On the first page of his last book, *Tradition and Modernism in Politics*, published in 1937, he continued to emphasise socialism as an explosion of moral energy, particularly in the period before 1914: 'Before all things it was a moral revolt and it gave the world a social conscience.'

It was through attacking the lack of moral energy both of Labour in Parliament and of the Fabians as 'mere' collectivists that Orage hoped to open the offensive and display the possible alternatives which a guild system might offer. Yet it was clear in the first issue of the *New Age* under its new editorship (2 May 1907) that the argument was to be articulated in terms of modern political issues and obsessions. An editorial article condemned predatory international capital for forcing Britain into imperialism. It posited the solution in a socialist empire, a heady alternative even for those days of hope. But the theory was repeated in a slightly amended form three years later in the issue of 16 May 1910. In its 'Notes of the Week' there was a discussion of the current position of socialism the weakness of which lay, it argued, in the fact that socialism and the English character are clearly separate categories. The result had been the creation of a clique in socialist circles which perpetuated the dichotomy. The solution was to conjoin the two and to encourage a belief and an understanding that socialists could be and were patriotic and that it was possible to graft the ideas of socialism onto the 'Pax Britannica'. Here was an argument which, though not greatly recurrent, paid more than a tangential tribute to the force of the imperial idea. What was recurrent, and it is a theme which has been stressed by Wallace Martin, was the continuous attempt to argue that the whole direction taken by reforming Liberalism, by the

Labour Party and even by those who thought of themselves as 'socialist' had been wrong and too restricted.[19] It is for this reason that the claim of the *New Age* to deal with what it held to be 'modern' issues and its analysis of the social world is particularly pertinent since it stresses that the philosophy which motivated Orage arose from a sense of potential wholeness which he could not find in any ready-made system.

An important factor which added to the propagandising influence of the *New Age* was its unique position among the journals of the period. Few of the existing labour or socialist periodicals spread the net of their criticism so widely and few appeared actively to seek the means of achieving the necessary transition in society. Of all the journals advocating change in the pre-1914 period only the *New Age* began to develop a practical means to socialism. That it did this, and that it offered a platform for socialists whose bent of mind was generally philosophical or sociological, gave it an added attraction as a forum for intellectuals in the period. Before the *New Statesman*, which did not commence publication until 1913, no other journal offered itself to such a range of heterodox writers.[20] And the tendency of many intellectuals in the period was to regard themselves as socialists in a rather restricted sense since the 'first class mind' could belong only to a progressive party. Writing in the *New Age* Arnold Bennett described his younger self as a radical of the 'Manchester Guardian variety' who became a socialist because: 'When I came to know professed Socialists we were never able to differ in argument.'[21]

The confusion between socialism and radicalism implicit in Bennett's statement was a confusion which bedevilled the young labour movement, but it does emphasise the fact that the high-mindedness and idealism which were traditionally part of the radical presentation were integral also to intellectual versions of socialism. Bennett's conception of himself as a progressive reflects Orage's comment on socialists in one of a series of articles published in the autumn and winter of 1907 under the general title 'Towards Socialism'. In the first of these Orage wrote:

> The world for the Socialist is an everlasting becoming, a perpetual process of generation and regeneration, a continual mounting of life up the ladder of becoming. Hence it follows that the Socialist has illimitable vistas for the future of man . . . If he is satisfied for the moment with demanding the political and economic rights of man, it is only as a step towards other and more lofty demands.[22]

For much of the labour movement even the political and economic demands seemed almost impossible of fulfilment, and Orage's arguments were confined to and appealed to a relatively limited though potentially influential public. Penty, whose own belief in spirituality was more limited to man's ability to express himself through his work — which should preferably be a craft — was unable to follow Orage either at the philosophical or at the political level. As the ideas of the two men began to diverge and their friendship to diminish,[23] Orage became more interested in the political analysis of S.G. Hobson who was beginning to lay a more continuous stress on the need to impose economic change in order to achieve a really socialist society. The socialist solution for Hobson must involve the destruction of the power of capital; a revolution which was only political and not also an economic overturn would inevitably, by being partial, be a failure.

Hobson's role in the socialist movement was both longer and more active than that of either Orage or Penty. It had begun in Cardiff in the late 1880s and progressed through membership of the Independent Labour Party, the Social Democratic Federation and the Fabian Society.[24] His connection with the latter in which Orage too was active, helped to confirm his developing belief that collectivism could only be a partial solution to contemporary problems. Working on a more clearly Marxist basis than many of his contemporaries in the movement — he had read *Capital* in a period when it was not common to have done so — Hobson added to it the ideas which Orage had assimilated from Penty and which both men now began to tease out in order to fit them to the needs of modern industry. In 1907 Hobson had not yet left the Fabian Society, but his continuing association with Orage and the critique of contemporary labour politics which was developed in the *New Age* culminated in a series of articles which he published in that journal in 1912 and 1913. These were edited and published in book form, by Orage, in 1914 as *National Guilds: An Enquiry into the Wage System and the Way Out.*[25] This was the book which Orage was accused of plagiarising. Hobson's name appears neither on the title page nor in the editor's preface.[26]

Between 1908 and 1912 Orage's stance remained well to the left and the issues he supported illustrate this. He naturally publicised the socialist revolt as this was reflected in the Jarrow and Colne Valley by-elections. As a result of the Grayson affair Grayson was not only employed by the *New Age* but for a period in 1908 and 1909 he also became its joint editor.[27] As industrial pressure and the strike wave grew Orage continued his criticism both of the shortcomings of orthodox Labour and of Liberalism, as well as discussing the difficulties of the unions whose alternatives were so limited.[28] Hobson, following a similar path, had abandoned all hope of orthodox Labour after the Grayson affair. Instead, he made one last attempt at the conversion of the Fabian Society. Early in January 1909, he moved a resolution urging the executive to withdraw its affiliation from the Labour Party so that it might concentrate on the creation of a 'definite and avowed Socialist Party'. The attempt was floored by a combination of sentiment from Ethel Snowden and humour from Shaw. Hobson resigned his seat on the executive and took up the tools which lay immediately to hand.[29]

The association of both Orage and Hobson with the Fabian Society and the more generalised effect of the critique promulgated by the *New Age* now began to have an effect in another and indispensable area. The *New Age* had already, late in 1908, made the point that a new generation of serious-minded students was arising whose concern with the social question was greater than their desire to develop mere debating skills.[30] This generation formed the first sizeable university Fabian Groups at Oxford and Cambridge and in the years immediately before the war a number of ex-university men came into the Fabian Society where Beatrice Webb attempted to harness their energies and undercut their critical potential by drafting them into the various subgroups of her Control of Industry Committee.[31] But she and the Society had already been forestalled as an influence by the *New Age*, which many of the young socialists had been reading for a number of years — G.D.H. Cole, Maurice Reckitt, Norman Ewer, Margaret Postgate, for example, among them.[32] Already highly critical of the tendencies of orthodox Labour, particularly critical of Fabianism, many of these young and energetic persons were now thinking along guild lines which Cole, especially, began to investigate with his characteristic precision.

Mairet has argued that Cole's position was finally clarified when he accepted Orage's editorial demolitions of the 'Control of Industry Report' issued by the newly-created Fabian Research Department.[33] Early in 1914 he began to contribute to the *New Age* articles on syndicalism, guilds and industrial change.[34] And early in the following year the National Guilds League was formed.[35] Orage's influence by this point had declined, for he feared that a formalised group would lead to rigidities of outlook and perhaps schism and that this would entirely ruin the spirit out of which guild socialism should grow.

III

With the spirit, too, we are back with Orage's alpha and omega. No one, looking at the existing writings on the guild movement, could fail to be aware that it was the underlying spirit of socialism which its protagonists were trying to release. The development of a parliamentary labour movement based on an uneasy alliance between political labour and the trade unions seemed to many of the critics of that movement to have been the wrong development. It greatly facilitated a practical solution to the problem of fielding a labour side, but the problems it created were perhaps greater than those it solved. The most intractable of these was the inveterate Liberalism of many of the older trade union leaders. It was a Liberalism grounded so largely in the values of self-improvement that the revolution desired by some failed to reach conception, so thoroughly was a contraceptive deference inculcated even in apparently independent labour leaders by the British class system. It is no accident that many of the leaders of the guild socialists and many of their supporting intellectuals were socially ambiguous. The severing of the roots of class allegiance may allow the political imagination to expand wonderfully, but it tends to encourage a belief in the natural logic of all men which it is hard to sustain in the face of day-to-day political reality. By yielding gracefully to the Labour Party the British establishment defused it and eroded its nominal class-consciousness. And although guild socialists were not obsessively class-conscious in their literature they were certainly aware of the calamitous effects of a class-ridden society in the critique of industrialism which they evolved. This was as true of a medievalist like Penty as it was of Hobson or of Cole or any of the more 'modern' publicists of the movement. What they sought to stress, however, was a double message. While believing that something like a total overturn of society was necessary, they mostly feared the corrosive effects of a critique which was articulated entirely in terms of class. Instead they sought to establish their argument by emphasising the need for a society which was organised by function and in which individuals, once the economic stranglehold of capitalism was broken, would be able to attend to the needs of society free of the status obsessions which a class-ridden society inevitably creates. The ideas of the guild socialists arose out of a continuous belief in the value of the individual which has led some of their critics to accuse them of a degree of anarchism.[36] The criticism is understandable since the whole tendency of the guild socialist argument was towards the elevation of the rights of the individual and of the small group as opposed to vast and anonymous organisations, either political or economic. By making man in the workplace both director of his economic and of his political destinies, guild socialists hoped to infuse the renewed society with a spirit of hope and co-operation which would itself be revolutionary. Because of this it is probably more accurate to view the guild socialists as working in a pluralist tradition.[37] The small group ideology which they evolved descends in a more direct line from academics like T.H. Green and J. Neville Figgis than from any more anarchistic thinkers, perhaps because so many of the leaders of the organised guild movement were themselves products of the academic system at a time when the tide of pluralism ran strongly.

As their arguments developed in the course of the decade or so during which the movement functioned, the guild socialists elaborated and extended the criticism which Orage had inaugurated in the *New Age*. It was a criticism which viewed the progress of the labour movement for thirty years past as a progress towards temporisation and compromise; a movement which had lost (if it had ever had) a continuous understanding of the ends to which it was making. So in formulating a theory which described one mode of revolutionary change, Penty, Orage, Hobson and the younger generation of Cole, Mellor, Reckitt and many others, never abandoned a fideistic belief that the most important postulate is an understanding of the informing spirit in the society towards which one is working. Very close in argument to Orage's 'ladder of becoming' is Hobson's analysis of the purpose of guild socialism. It is a purpose fully in accord with Orage's constantly reiterated stress on the need to fulfil the total spiritual needs of man. Hobson's society is one in which spirituality must run hand in hand with a sound economic foundation to produce 'the spiritual State, in which men and women, unhampered by economic confusion and waste, can achieve their cultural destiny'.[38]

This guild socialist critique, basically the same here in the 1930s as it had been twenty years before when it was being elaborated in the *New Age*, was one of extraordinary fertility and influence more perhaps because of its continuous stress on the needs of individuals than because of any unusual subtlety of political analysis. By constantly emphasising the importance of the wholeness of the society towards which any socialist organisation ought to be aiming, it reflected the permanent tension in the labour movement between the potential and the practical. In so far as the practical almost inevitably swamps the ideal, it is a discussion which needs constant refurbishing.

Notes

1. This essay is not attempting an historical outline of the guild socialist move-

ment, or a criticism. There is a number of existing sources for an historical account, most of which are fairly reliable, as also critical. The oldest and by no means the worst of these is Niles Carpenter's *Guild Socialism* (1922). The best modern survey, though brief, is S.T. Glass, *The Responsible Society* (1966). Another older but still useful survey is in H.W. Laidler, *A History of Socialist Thought* (1927), pp. 393-437. An amusing and often perceptive critical account is in Alexander Gray, *The Socialist Tradition* (1963), ch. 16, 'Guild Socialism'. No one should neglect the account in G.D.H. Cole's *History of Socialist Thought* (1956), vol. 3, pt 1, *The Second International 1889-1914*, ch. 4. Cole regarded himself as a guild socialist to the end of his life.

    2. Quoted in Thatcher, *Nietzsche in England*, p. 262. The tendency to believe that some central secret of control in life awaits discovery is not uncommon among the latently religious and may have been encouraged in Orage by his Platonic studies. cf. Thatcher's comment (ibid.) that 'Orage's brand of Nietzscheanism was a mystical one'.

    3. Unless otherwise attributed, evidence for Penty's early life comes from his wife, Violet, who met the author of this essay in a number of interviews in 1963 and 1964. She was formerly Violet Pike, an official of the Ladies' Garment Workers' Union whom Penty met during a stay in America in 1907-8. They were married in 1916.

    4. Quoted in Mairet, *A.R. Orage: A Memoir* (1936), p. 25.

    5. G. Cumberland, *Set Down in Malice* (1919), p. 132. For other comments on Orage see Maurice Browne, *Too Late to Lament* (1954) and Maurice B. Reckitt, *As It Happened* (1941).

    6. Mairet, *A.R. Orage*, p. 30. Orage's break was more psychologically complete in that he left in Yorkshire an earlier career as a schoolmaster and a failed marriage.

    7. Penty not only wrote with difficulty, he first published with difficulty too. As far as the present writer is aware, it has never previously been made clear that Penty published *The Restoration of the Gild System* at his own expense. The book was initially rejected by Swan Sonnenschein who then suggested that Penty might like to support publication himself. This he subsequently did, through the Literary Agency of London. A thousand copies were printed of which only 250 were bound. Penty paid Swan Sonnenschein £43 3*s*. 3*d*. on 8 December 1905. The bound copies were not exhausted until 1908 when a further fifty-one were covered. In November of the following year the remaining unbound copies were destroyed in a warehouse fire. This left only twelve copies in the hands of Swan Sonnenschein. A new edition was never printed. See *Index to the Archives of Swan Sonnenschein & Co., 1878-1911* (1975). Details of the Penty correspondence (publishers' letters only) are found in vols 41-2, 44-7.

    8. Orage to Penty, 27 April 1913. Penty MSS (in the possession of the family).

    9. Orage to Penty, 30 April 1913, ibid.

    10. Orage was clearly working from memory here. *The Restoration of the Gild System* was published early in 1906. It was true that much of it had been written a good deal earlier.

    11. Mairet, *A.R. Orage*, pp. 48-9.

    12. Quoted in Melvin Richter, *The Politics of Conscience* (1964), p. 228.

    13. In this sense, Penty falls into Professor Hacker's category of 'original sin' socialists. See Andrew Hacker, 'Original Sin versus Utopianism in British Politics', *Review of Politics*, vol. 18 (1956), pp. 184-206.

    14. A useful commentary on Penty's social thought is Arthur J. Kiernan, *A.J. Penty. His Contribution to Social Thought* (1941) Catholic University of America, Studies in Sociology, vol. 2.

    15. A.J. Penty, *The Restoration of the Gild System* (1906), p. 5.

16. Ibid., p. 57.

17. Ross Terrill's analytical study, *R.H. Tawney and His Times* (1973), describes Tawney's position as nearer that of a Fabian than of a guild socialist. But his description of Tawney's definition of the functional society is almost exactly that of a guild socialist. 'A society in which industry is established on the basis of social purpose, to which production and accumulation are means, Tawney called a functional society' (p. 160). Such a definition of function was developed by guild socialists particularly under the influence of Ramiro de Maeztu. Tawney was a member of the National Executive Committee of the National Guilds League for the year 1920-21 when A.J. Penty was also a member. Tawney spoke at a Special Policy Conference in December of 1920 and gave a lecture — 'What I Think of National Guilds' — in the South Place Institute on 24 November 1920. See: *National Guilds League, Conference Reports* (and other literature) in Bedford Collection, Box 1, File 2. Nuffield College, Oxford.

18. This was a message which for Penty became ever more important after the Russian Revolution which created a considerable doctrinal split in the NGL and contributed greatly to its eventual decline.

19. W. Martin, *The New Age Under Orage*, esp. ch. 11, 'Guild Socialism'. And see Mairet, *A.R. Orage,* esp. pp. 52-5.

20. A selection of these includes: Arnold Bennett, H.G. Wells, Hilaire Belloc, G.K. Chesterton, J.M. Kennedy, T.E. Hulme, Ramiro de Maeztu, Ezra Pound, Katherine Mansfield, Beatrice Hastings and Florence Farr.

21. *New Age,* 30 November 1907.

22. *New Age,* 3 October 1907. The articles ran from this date until 28 December 1907.

23. Orage's friendship with Penty never ceased, but their separate involvement in different areas certainly encouraged a drifting apart. As Orage became more questing in his search for a solution to the political problem, so his ideas accorded less well with Penty's.

24. See his autobiography, *Pilgrim to the Left* (1938), passim. Hobson had been involved in the labour movement in Bristol where he stood, unsuccessfully, as the ILP parliamentary candidate in 1895 (ibid., pp. 52-4).

25. The articles ran intermittently from 10 October 1912 to 29 May 1913.

26. For a very much less than charitable view of Orage in this period see the pamphlet published by his former mistress, Beatrice Hastings, *The Old 'New Age': Orage — and Others* (1936), p. 42.

27. The joint editorship commenced on 29 October 1908. In February of 1909, Grayson became political editor of the *Clarion.* See Walter Kendall, *The Revolutionary Movement in Britain, 1900-1921* (1969), p. 86.

28. *New Age,* passim; see esp. 'Notes of the Week', 9 June 1910; 16 June 1910.

29. Hobson, *Pilgrim to the Left*, p. 118. See also A.M. McBriar, *Fabian Socialism and English Politics 1884-1918* (Cambridge, 1962), p. 322.

30. 'Socialistic Forces at Oxford', *New Age,* 7 November 1907.

31. For the influence of this committee see M. Cole, 'Guild Socialism and the Labour Research Department' in A. Briggs and J. Saville (eds.), *Essays in Labour History, 1886-1923* (1971), esp. p. 271.

32. See, for example, Reckitt, *As It Happened,* pp. 103-10 and ch. 7.

33. Mairet, *A.R. Orage,* pp. 67-8. This argument applies equally to William Mellor (1888-1942), Cole's close personal and professional associate at this time.

34. *New Age,* 5 February 1914. The first article, 'The Genesis of French Syndicalism — and Some Unspoken Morals' was followed by regular contributions from Cole.

35. At Easter 1915. See M. Cole in Briggs and Saville, *Essays in Labour History,* p. 272.

36. See, for instance, Adam B. Ulam, *Philosophical Foundations of English Socialism* (New York, 1964), pp. 88-9. There is a passing reference to anarchistic tendencies persuading guild socialists to expect too much in the area of creativity from individual workers in A. Gray, *The Socialist Tradition*, p. 457.

37. Kung Chuan Hsiao in his *Political Pluralism* (1927) claims that its anti-monism 'makes guild socialism a definite approach to pluralism' (p. 116).

38. S.G. Hobson, *Functional Socialism* (1936), p. 31.

9 THE NATIONALISATION OF THE BANKS: THE CHEQUERED HISTORY OF A SOCIALIST PROPOSAL

Sidney Pollard

The socialisation of the means of production, distribution and exchange in one form or another has always formed part of the core of the programmes of British socialists. Among these 'means', the banks must patently occupy a prominent place. They had always possessed strategic economic power, and after the breathtaking spate of amalgamations which left at the end of the First World War a bare 'Big Five' to control some two-thirds of the assets of all deposit, joint-stock or clearing banks (the terms become increasingly synonymous) they also showed a high degree of concentration. Conversely, the advantages frequently urged for private enterprise, like competition and individual initiative, were conspicuously absent in the heavily bureaucratised and oligopolistic world of British banking. In consequence, there is a long tradition of proposals for bank nationalisation in Britain, as indeed on the Continent of Europe.

Since the phase of rapid amalgamation c. 1890-1917 the British banking scene has remained remarkably stable, and even before that it was always clear what was meant by the nationalisation of the banks: the Bank of England, the handful of clearing banks, and from time to time, some or all of a penumbra of related financial institutions, like merchant banks, savings banks and insurance companies. In spite of this stability, however, the proposals for bank nationalisation have gone through a remarkable series of vicissitudes, constantly changing, sometimes disappearing from view completely, and always reappearing in a new guise. Their full history, though fascinating, would extend far beyond the scope of a chapter. Here we shall limit ourselves to a small aspect of that history: the reasoning behind the demand to nationalise the banks among what might be called the mainstream socialist parties in Britain. The story has its own intrinsic interest, but it will also lead to some more general reflections.

I

Much of early socialist thought was static, visualising the blueprint of the good society without explaining how it was to be reached. Many of

167

those who did consider the mechanism of change in the first half of the nineteenth century saw it as coming about by the setting up of small co-operative communities, spreading by demonstration and example; total sectoral coverage, but slow geographical spread. The alternative process, of total geographical coverage but slow sectoral spread, taking control of local or central government and socialising sector by sector, had to wait until the 1880s for its consistent advocacy.[1] In one form or another, it has remained the method advocated since.

The Democratic Federation, which in its manifesto of 1883 advocated the establishment of a national bank, 'which shall absorb all private institutions that derive a profit from operations in money or credit',[2] appears to have limited its justification to the moral one: it was wrong to make profits.[3] Elsewhere, its spokesmen added the idea of control (without specifying how that would benefit the workers), the elimination of periodic crises, and the elimination of 'gains of a class which now exercises such enormous influence, and accumulates such vast profits'.[4] There is nothing here that makes out any special case for the banks, and in general much greater attention was paid to the nationalisation of such sectors as land and railways than to banking.[5]

The Fabians in their original statements of the 1880s failed to mention the banks at all. For some, like Bernard Shaw, the purpose of such socialisation as they did advocate was to extend democracy; for most of the others, the objective was efficiency, including the abolition of unemployment and the curbing of monopoly.[6] The Scottish Labour Party, founded after the Mid-Lanark election in 1888, had among its objectives the nationalisation of banking and a state monopoly of the issue of money, and the famous definition by the ILP at its foundation in 1893, to secure the collective ownership of 'all means of production, distribution and exchange' clearly included banking in the third sector;[7] but no prominence was given to it.

This lack of interest in banking continued to the outbreak of the First World War. Thus among all the Fabian Tracts, there was but a single one dealing with the banks: Edward Pease's *Gold and State Banking: A Study in the Economics of Monopoly*. This concentrated on the weaknesses of competitive banks who might be out of step in their credit creation, and on the much greater efficiency, and lower costs, that could be achieved by a single bank which could undertake all transfers by book entries within its own organisation. Pease believed that the natural tendency was for all banks to coalesce into one, which would then have to be nationalised, and would be able to run an internal interest rate policy distinct from the movements of the gold reserve which would be used for external relationships only.[8] Similarly, a wide-ranging study like Emil Davies's *The Collectivist State in the Making,*[9] grouping together banking and pawnbroking as possible publicly run activities, limits itself to the observation that some overseas countries have municipal banks, and that post office banking abroad had wider functions than in Britain. The continental preoccupation with finance capital, ranging from Lenin to Hilferding, appeared to have made little impression in Britain.

Government regulation of economic activities between 1914 and 1918 tended to reinforce the Fabian belief that socialism was creeping in stealthily year by year, and coal and transport, which had been put under government control during the war, were confirmed as prime targets for nationalisers. Sidney Webb's shopping list also included insurance,[10] in part on the somewhat surprising grounds that the accumulated insurance reserves could be used to redeem the vast sums of the war debt; but he ignored the banks. So did *Labour and the New Social Order*, the new statement of Labour Party aims adopted in 1918. Arising out of the same wartime background, it enumerated as subjects for nationalisation several transport, fuel and power industries, each with its own specific justification evidently based on the war-time experience of control[11] but there was no mention of banks and no mention of directed investment.

Soon after, however, the Party's Advisory Committee on Trade Policy and Finance issued a four-page leaflet,[12] which advocated 'the immediate reorganisation of the banking system', including the national-isation of the Bank of England and its extension into branch banking in the towns as a national bank and the development of the Post Office Savings Bank as its agent in the villages. The acquisition of the joint-stock banks was left as a later option. This was backed up by one of the most comprehensive lists of reasons for bank nationalisation ever produced. These included the following: To provide (1) power to con-trol or displace the 'capitalist system'; (2) greater security for deposit-ors; (3) economies in administration; (4) control over the direction of credit, 'having regard to the estimated social utility of the subject of the loan' instead of for 'private and immediate gains', and to extend long-term credits to industry; also (5) to control the level of prices, production and employment 'so far as they are attributable to excesses and defects in the operations of finance': and (6) to reduce the cost to government of having to bail out the banking system from time to time in periods of trouble. All of these were explicitly founded on the war-time ex-perience of government controls, and the accelerating drive towards the creation of a banking monopoly by the amalgamation of the joint-stock banks, as reported by the Treasury Committee on Bank Amalgamations.[13]

Up to 1918, therefore, the interest in banking was sporadic, and the variety of reasons adduced for proposing bank nationalisation also points to a lack of continuity. Where the proposal does emerge, it is clearly tied to some immediate experience: unemployment in the 1880s, and government control, price and credit inflation during the First World War.

II

In the early post-war years interest died down again. The Webbs, it is true, defining banking in a somewhat limited way as 'the service of keeping current and deposit accounts',[14] proposed the nationalisation and municipalisation of deposit banking, largely in the interest of democracy, efficiency (undefined) and greater security for depositors. Capital for industry should be provided by the insurance companies, who were no longer, apparently, required to pay off the national debt. Curiously enough, the Webbs attacked the raising of capital from outside the firm as a recent evil of capitalism (in direct contrast, the 1976 Labour Party bank nationalisation campaign wanted to see the practice expanded). A party report on Major Douglas's social credit proposals, published in 1921, made some reference to the importance of overall credit creation, but only in relation to the unacceptable power of private enterprise units in the placement of treasury bills, and accused the joint-stock banks of favouring large firms unduly at the expense of small in their lending policies. It proposed one single state bank for deposit business, and municipal banks for the savings business.[15]

In general, however, as the Labour Party retreated into administrative gradualism, the nationalisation debate became largely limited to those industries where solidly organised groups of their own workers demanded it, principally the mines and the railways. Nationalisation plans either left out banking altogether[16] or included it as little more than an afterthought. Even a financial expert like Sir Leo Chiozza Money could think of no more potent argument than that socialised banking would have kept down interest rates on war-time borrowing and post-war housing.[17]

It was the deflation and depression of the early 1920s which shifted the focus once more. As the yawning gap between the socialist protestations of the Labour Party leadership[18] and their orthodox financial policy under the pressure of those events became clear, it was the ILP, occupying its role as the socialist conscience of the party, which took the lead.[19]

The inspiration behind the ILP's whirlwind campaign of 1924-6 on this issue was the brilliant mind of J.A. Hobson, whose under-consumptionist or over-saving explanation of the trade cycle had found no favour with the orthodox among his profession, but fitted admirably into the social critique of the ILP. As early as 1923 its *Socialist Programme*, written by Clifford Allen, Fenner Brockway and Ernest E. Hunter, had linked credit restriction by the banks with unemployment, and had advocated public 'control' (but not nationalisation) of the banks and a 'scientific' policy of channelling bank credits towards useful industries and into workers' pockets so that they might be spent rather than saved.[20] A similar resolution, moved for the ILP by Brailsford and seconded by Fenner Brockway at the Labour Party conference in 1924 also advocated the nationalisation of the Bank of England only.[21]

By the time of the adoption of the ILP programme of *Socialism in Our Time* in the spring of 1926, the nationalisation of the banks had moved to the centre of the stage. The key issue was the 'living wage', and to achieve it, the party had now found a solution both to the unemployment problem and the problem of poverty: if more of the national income were given to wage-earners, more of it would be spent and less saved, and the resultant rise in demand would create prosperity and full employment. But such a policy required the control over credit, hence 'the first step for the realisation of [that] policy must be the nationalisation of the Bank of England', whose duty would be 'to ensure a stable price level'.[22] While it might be 'administratively difficult, and politically unwise' to nationalise the joint-stock banks at once, a socialist movement still had to be able to 'govern the pace and direction of the nation's industrial growth',[23] hence they also proposed to encourage and extend Post Office and municipal banking, to nationalise the insurance companies in order to use their investment funds, and to set up a 'National Industrial Bank' and an 'Investment Trust' to channel investments to industry and become the 'planning and directive centre of the nation's industrial life'.[24]

If Hobson provided the theoretical underpinning for such leaders as Brailsford and Wise, another unorthodox economist, John Maynard Keynes,[25] furnished the foundations for an even more remarkable set of proposals, advocated by Oswald Mosley and John Strachey.[26] In his programme, endorsed by the Birmingham Borough Labour Party and ILP, Mosley started with the premises of the authors of *The Living*

Wage, but argued that if the emission of credit was to be used to increase employment, steps would have to be taken to see that it was
not dissipated in higher profits (and savings) or higher prices, and this
could be best done using the credits in direct additional payments to
workers, in the form of the subsidisation of wages in selected firms.
Thus credit creation could be used for, and would become an inherent
part of, economic planning for higher output of the right sorts of
commodities and services at full employment levels. The banks, therefore, would have to be transferred to the public as sources of economic
power, and as agencies to open up enlarged productive opportunities.

Mosley found no immediate echo outside Birmingham and ultimately, in 1930, he was to leave the Labour Government when it
refused to accept a comprehensive plan for dealing with unemployment
based on similar principles, with protectionism added, and he then
quickly moved to the right. Meanwhile, however, the Labour leadership
had also begun to move. A resolution at the Labour conference of 1925
introduced by the NEC urged 'the EC and the Parliamentary Party to
press for the Public ownership and control of the Banking and Credit
System and the encouragement and development of Co-operative and
Municipal Banks'. According to the preamble, the reasoning behind this
demand included the wish to secure public control over 'national
development', over industry and employment; to reduce bank charges;
to retain banking profits for the community; and 'generally to facilitate
the progressive realisation of the Socialist State'. Sidney Webb added to
this the accusation that private banking led to economic instability and
the trade cycle. Neither Webb's introduction nor the ensuing discussion
showed any sense of urgency, though one speaker adverted to the
frequently made charge that Sir Alfred Mond had declared [in a rare
flash of foresight] that the next Labour Government would be brought
down by the banks.[27]

However, the next programme, *Labour and the Nation*, drawn up
under pressure by the ILP[28] and submitted to the 1928 conference,
contained an important section on 'Banking and Currency'.[29] Snowden,
introducing this section on behalf of the NEC, opposed all that the ILP
groups stood for, as well as any thought of using the banks to guide
industrial planning. Assuring the conference that banking was a matter
of but recent interest for the Labour Party on which they were all
ignorant, he was in favour of nationalising the Bank of England – as
long as it was kept out of 'political' control: for once the politicians
got hold of it, they might be tempted to use its power to reduce unemployment from, say, 1¼ million to ¼ million, and a 'terrible price'

would have to be paid for such presumption. The joint-stock banks, however, should not be nationalised for the time being, for a banking monopoly would mean that, once a businessman had his application for a loan rejected by a bank manager, he would have no competing firm to turn to,[30] Hugh Dalton and Pethick-Lawrence, supporting him, both rejected the nationalisation of the joint-stock banks on the grounds that they were unimportant, mere 'outposts' to the citadel of the Bank of England, and despite the urgings of E.F. Wise and Ellen Wilkinson, the NEC version was accepted without a division.

In the following October, conference added the common ownership of the 'means of distribution and exchange' to 'production' in clause 4 of the party constitution,[31] thus catching up with the ILP formulation of 1893. Snowden took the opportunity of lecturing the conference with obvious satisfaction albeit not entirely truthfully, on the fact that the Bank of England alone controlled the bank rate: 'in regard to the . . . Bank Rate, the Treasury has no more control than any individual whom I might happen at the moment to be addressing'. In vain did Frank Wise point out that the Bank represented narrow City interests only, while a high bank rate discouraged enterprise, created unemployment and raised the costs of borrowing by municipalities; in vain did Bevin remind delegates that dear money was quickly followed by demands for wage cuts.[32] There was no division.

Meanwhile the New York crash had ushered in a depression of previously unknown dimensions with which the second Labour administration was utterly unable to deal. The contrast between the new needs and the government's supineness led many socialists to turn to new solutions, particularly those advocated with increasing clarity by Keynes. An alliance of intellectuals and trade union leaders, epitomised by the somewhat incongruous partnership of Ernest Bevin and G.D.H. Cole, together with journalists like Francis Williams, set about educating the labour movement on the relationship between unemployment and credit policy, and the need for the state to own and control the banks in order to enlarge the flow of credit to industry.[33]

Whatever the educative value of the slump, it is clear that it was the fall of the Labour Government, and the manner of its going, ascribed at the time to a 'bankers' ramp', which speeded the conversion of the large majority of the Labour Party to the need to tame and control the banking sector. Suddenly, the nationalisation of the banks was in the centre of the picture, the vital first step to socialism, which was itself looked upon as the sole method of climbing out of the depression. Whatever the truth about the alleged leftward shift of the Labour Party as a result of the debacle of 1931, on the issue of bank nationalisation, the shift, however temporary, was dramatic and real enough.

At the 1931 Labour Party conference, Pethick-Lawrence for the NEC was in favour of public ownership and control over banking and credit. His arguments included the failure of the existing banking system in the slump, even on its own capitalistic terms; the international anarchy caused by the Bank of England's pursuit of a policy independent of the government; and the error of the bankers in wanting to solve the crisis by cutting wages. Bevin saw the issue in terms of power, 'banks versus the people': 'You can talk about socialising your railways and other things; socialise credit and the rest is comparatively easy.' The same view was also taken by J.M. Kenworthy: 'Until we have solved this problem by the public control and ownership of the whole of the credit and monetary system, it is useless for us to talk about nationalising the railways, the mines, or establishing import boards or the ownership of the land or anything of that kind.'[34]

Thus freed, a veritable spate of propaganda on banking and credit now swept the labour movement. The Society for Socialist Inquiry and Propaganda (SSIP),[35] soon to amalgamate with some ILP dissidents and turn into the Socialist League, and the New Fabian Research Bureau, both founded in 1931, were particularly fertile in ideas.

Central were two arguments. The first was the need for total credit control in order to secure full employment (the stability of the price level being now held in little regard), which would require nationalising the Bank of England. The second, to channel the flow of investment to appropriate industries in conformity with the national plan, guided by a national investment board (NIB), which would require the nationalisation of the joint-stock banks. But a whole series of other arguments was put forward in addition. Thus G.D.H. Cole was anxious to keep the nationalised Bank of England of the future out of the hands of the Treasury, since 'it needs to look at policy from the standpoint of trade and industry as well as the State budget'.[36] He would also not amalgamate the joint-stock banks, in order to minimise short-term dislocations, and proposed to transfer their 'frozen credits',[37] with which much socialist writing at the time was concerned, to a new mortgage corporation. A further element in his thought was the justice of using banking profits for social purposes, and the question of power: 'banking and politics cannot be divorced . . . unless the State takes steps to control the banks, the bankers will inevitably control the State'.[38] Colin Clark saw among the functions of the projected NIB not only the planning of home industry, but also the control over foreign investment (which as a matter of fact had been maintained by the Bank of England in an informal way since 1925). It was therefore necessary, in his view, to control also the investment decisions of building societies and insurance companies. G.R. Mitchison believed that the transfer of 'frozen credits' to an 'Industrial Mortgage Bank' would give the government immediate control over some firms, albeit the weakest ones, and the nationalised deposit banks might specialise, each being responsible for a certain group of industries. Medium-term credits of from one to five years were to be the province of a 'commercial credit bank', set up jointly by the joint-stock banks and the NIB. E.F. Wise presented the most consistent set of arguments for nationalising the banking system as the very first step in the transition to socialism. First, in order to 'capture administrative and economic power . . . Let us not forget that the last Government was crippled from the beginning by finance and was finally killed by the financiers' and the next Labour government could once more expect to have a financial panic engineered against it. Secondly, to carry out its 'national plan for economic development'. Third, their object was to end poverty.[39]

The Labour Party NEC itself, in its resolution on 'Currency, Banking, Finance' to the 1932 conference enumerated (1) deflation and unemployment engineered by the existing institutions; (2) the unacceptable powers wielded by the 'financial system'; (3) the need for public control over finance to carry through a 'planned National Development'; and (4) the fear that socialist policies might be sabotaged by the banks. It demanded the nationalisation of the Bank of England, under a minister responsible to Parliament; stable home prices together with the greatest possible stability in the foreign exchanges; and a national investment board to determine the total sum available for investment, its desirable direction at home, and the limits of investment abroad. But it did not mention the joint-stock banks, Hugh Dalton making the somewhat lame excuse that the committee was still examining proposals relating to short-term credit, which might include the deposit banks.

The conference was in no mood for this retreat from 1931. E.F. Wise's amendment to include the joint-stock banks was widely supported, by Stafford Cripps among others. Ernest Bevin, opposing them, used the interesting arguments that the deposit banks with all their frozen credits would be a millstone round their necks; that the acceptance houses and the discount market would, under socialism, be as out of date as a stage coach in the age of the railway or the aeroplane; above all, that the next Labour Government would ignore such a resolution, as it had ignored the resolution on the capital levy, and would make them 'look idiots'. J.C. Wilmot, bearing in mind the nasty Post Office scare during the 1931 election campaign, argued that if the amendment were to be accepted, the Tories would mobilise the millions of small investors against Labour at the next election. Nevertheless, when put to the vote, the amendment was carried by 2,241,000 votes to 984,000.[40] The early nationalisation of both the Bank of England and the joint-stock banks had become explicit official Labour Party policy.

In its 1933 report, *Socialism and the Condition of the People*, the NEC concentrated on unemployment. Among its five major causes was named the deflationary policy of the 1920s. Since an excess of savings over investments leads to a fall in employment, and an excess of investment over savings leads to a boom which is bound to crash sooner or later, the report argues that 'the object of the national control of investment is to make investment equal to savings, and to divert investment into socially useful channels'. For this the NIB would be the 'general staff', rather like the control mechanisms of war-time, but would not control any funds of its own. As for the joint-stock banks, they were accused of lack of co-ordination with each other and with the Bank of England, of wasteful competition (2 per cent of the charges on advances having to be used for running costs), and of lack of social purpose in their lending policies. Thus they should be nationalised and amalgamated into a single powerful banking corporation, while the Co-operative Wholesale Society bank should be encouraged, and foreign and other banks permitted to operate only under licence. The corporation and the NIB would have to conform to the national plan for development. Although some critics, like S.G. Hobson and Christopher Addison, with remarkable foresight expressed the fear that it may well be the banks which would dominate the production plan rather than the other way round, and that the Treasury might block all expansion unless its powers were curbed, the report had an easy passage.[41]

The high point of support for bank nationalisation was reached with the definitive programme, *For Socialism and Peace*,[42] presented in 1934. Basing itself on the arguments of the previous year, it placed banking and credit at the head of the sectors to be taken under public ownership and control, and its provisions relating to banking and currency were reaffirmed in 1935 as the party went into the general election. It is noteworthy, however, that in spite of this apparent consistency, there was no indication in the programme of any other mechanism for economic planning.[43]

Under the umbrella of this official party approval, the large Labour literature of the following years took for granted the nationalisation of the central bank, and the large clearing banks, together with the creation of the NIB.[44] Relatively little was added to theory or argumentation. One official Labour statement brought forward the additional point of the wasteful and sometimes fraudulent speculation financed by the commercial banks.[45] Thomas Johnston stressed that the party as a whole was swayed by the belief that the Labour Government of 1929-31 had been sabotaged by a City conspiracy.[46] An argument weighing heavily with Hugh Dalton was the independent foreign policy, frequently directly contrary to that of the government, pursued by Montagu Norman as Governor of the Bank of England, and his attempt to turn the Bank of International Settlement into a Bankers' International, outside the control of democratic representatives.[47] He also accused the joint-stock banks of falling an easy prey to swindlers, of neglecting medium-term loans, of providing too many easy 'jobs for the boys', and of being anarchic and incoherent and therefore expensive, while the City as a whole was geared to channel loans abroad rather than invest them sensibly at home. To this, Evan Durbin added the need to control the liquidity and the safety of the commercial banks, and 'A Citizen' the fear of the irresponsibility of banks in private hands.[48] Amber Blanco White wanted to prevent the anticipated flight of capital abroad on election victory, but her main argument was the need for a counter-cyclical policy under which the central bank should lend freely to the government at low rates at the bottom of the slump, instead of putting up the barriers to hoard its gold reserve.[49]

However, all of these were minor considerations. Basically, the political drive for bank nationalisation stemmed from the alleged role of the banks in the debacle of 1931; economically, it derived from the growing conviction, before the publication of Keynes's *General Theory*, that a counter-cyclical and employment policy was necessary and possible and required ownership and control of the credit mechanism.[50] At the same time, it is noteworthy that no serious work in depth was undertaken of the kind or quality published by Christopher Mayhew on the related topic of long-term investment.[51]

The honeymoon was not to last very long. *Labour's Immediate Programme*, introduced by Attlee to the 1937 Party conference, did indeed start out with the brave words that 'the community must command the main levers which control the economic machine. These are Finance, Land, Transport, Coal and Power . . . No nation can plan its economic life unless it can control both its finance and its financiers.'

But the nationalisation of the joint-stock banks had been quietly dropped and all that was left was the alignment of the central bank with the practice of other capitalist countries, in the interests of employment; there was no word of socialist planning beyond mention of the NIB. Herbert Morrison indeed, for the NEC, resting his case on the Macmillan Report, affirmed that the joint-stock banks could be regulated 'without improper disturbance' by a publicly owned Bank of England, the unspoken assumption being that it would be the next Labour government's aim to change the system as little as possible. There was a feeble intervention by Ernest Davies, protesting that he did not want to rock the boat or 'ask the impossible of this Executive', but drawing attention to the power of the joint-stock banks to sabotage planning, to embarrass a government by massive selling of government stock and to organise another 'bankers' ramp'; but the NEC's programme was accepted unanimously.[52]

Clearly, the leadership had never believed in the more thorough-going programme of 1934 and the resolutions of 1931-3 that had led up to it. In the internal memoranda in which the NEC hammered out the implementation of the *Immediate Programme* the main desiderata for Labour's policy were stated to be: (1) stability; (2) the development of national resources, including public works; and (3) redistribution of wealth through taxation and the social services.[53] As for the joint-stock banks, Labour policy-makers worked out a most complex and costly structure of supervision, checking and control, some of it copying Nazi Germany, rather than adopt the simple solution of a takeover, which had been thrown out by the 1937 programme.[54] Other leading figures in the Labour Party mainstream had by then also apparently dropped for good any thought of nationalising banks, at least in the foreseeable early stages of a Labour Government.[55]

Over the period 1919-39, at least three phases may thus be distinguished. In the 1920s the experience of deflation and unemployment, still thought of as normally cyclical on the pre-war pattern, induced a strong movement for the control of the credit mechanism, but without much working out of detail. It was the trauma of the world depression and the way in which the fall of the second Labour government had been brought about which gave a temporary ascendancy to proposals for nationalising the whole of the clearing bank system. In this period, numerous subsidiary considerations were added to the central political and planning arguments. From the mid-1930s on the tide receded again, and while the socialist dreams on the left still began with total control over finance, the leadership was moved only by Keynesian

considerations for employment and by the need to follow the rest of
the Western world by taking over the central bank, but no other banking
institution.

III

The positions taken up in the 1930s changed relatively little during the
war years. The left, ignoring the political realities of the official programme, developed its plans on the assumption of a rapid march towards a socialist economy which would need to secure its flanks by an
early nationalisation of all the main banks. John Strachey, for example,
had moved little beyond the Birmingham manifesto. G.D.H. Cole,
another indefatigable campaigner, simply assumed that 'it is plainly
necessary to socialise the deposit banks' and 'it is so obvious that the
banks ought to be brought under public ownership and control (immediately after the war) that I am almost ashamed to spend time on
arguing the case'.[56] His reasons now included the somewhat startling
proposition that since the banks would hold vast quantities of national
debt at the end of the war, financed by them with credit which they
created out of nothing, nationalisation would allow the government to
take over and cancel that part of the national debt held by them. In
the heady days of war support for such sanguine assumptions of wholesale change came even from so magisterial an authority as Schumpeter:

> The Bank of England is no doubt quite ripe for nationalisation . . .
> In commercial banking, concentration and bureaucratization seem to
> have done full work. The big concerns could be made to absorb as
> much of independent banking as there is left to absorb and then be
> merged with the Bank of England in the National Banking Adminis-
> tration, which could also absorb savings banks, building societies and
> so on without any customer becoming aware of the change except
> for his newspaper.

This might represent a 'substantial gain'.[57]

Official Labour, however, saw things differently. A spate of internal
discussion papers, mainly circulated among the Post-war Finance Subcommittee of the NEC, noted that 'the British Banking System is the
most efficient in the world' and gave many other signs of ignorance of
banking, but held to the three basic pre-war proposals: the nationalisation of the Bank of England, the setting up of the NIB, but nothing
more than regulation for the privately-owned deposit and other banks.[58]
In the war Keynesian convictions were strengthened, and the Party was

emboldened to insist that the Bank of England, when nationalised, should come directly under the Chancellor, who should also have 'statutory power, as has been voluntarily agreed during the war, to require any bank to lend him any sum he likes, for as long as he likes, and on what terms he likes' by means of treasury deposits.[59] But the manifesto of Dominion Labour Parties of September 1944, *From a People's War to a People's Peace*, and British Labour's own programme, *Full Employment and Financial Policy*, presented to the 1944 conference,[60] merely stressed stability and the maintenance of employment.

The election manifesto of 1945 made no advance on the *Immediate Programme* of 1937. Herbert Morrison stated before the party conference in 1945 that there had to be a separate case for nationalising each industry rather than a general case for a socialist economy.[61] As for banking, the Bank of England was to be nationalised; the rest merely 'harmonised with industrial needs'. Even though the Bank of England was shown to be grossly biased towards the City's foreign role, and neglectful of British producers' interests,[62] the Labour Government in fact left the governor in office and made few other changes after nationalisation. It continued to rely on the Bank's traditional mechanisms for steering the credit policies of the privately owned banks, adding only the somewhat involved proviso, that 'The Bank was empowered, if it thought it necessary in the public interest, to request information from and make recommendations to, bankers and if so authorised by the Treasury, to issue directions to any banker for the purpose of securing that effect be given to any such request or recommendation'. The Bank of England Nationalisation Act, therefore, came as something of an anti-climax: neither government nor opposition could muster much enthusiasm for the necessary parliamentary debates.[63]

According to an acute French observer, 'in this crucially important area Labour's policy was cautious, not to say timid. The desire to avoid further disturbing an economy that had already suffered so many shocks prevailed over hopes of change, and some would say, over the party's declared objective. One may well feel that a major asset in creating effective planning was virtually thrown away.'[64] It might also be held that, in view of the contemporary nationalisation of some of the major French joint-stock banks, the cause for British caution was to be found in the fact that the British system had suffered too few shocks, not too many.

After the Bank of England was nationalised on 1 March 1946, it became clear very quickly from the public utterances of successive governors that whatever ultimate power the Treasury might have acquired over banking, the City had meanwhile also acquired a firm foothold inside the government. As a political issue, however, banking faded from public view. In internal debate, Labour looked at banking from time to time, but decided to leave it alone since deposit banks were firmly under the central bank's control; the other banks were too complex to be disentangled and meanwhile were earning useful foreign exchange.[65] Such oblique references as occurred in its programmes, as in *Let Us Win Through Together* in 1950, were wholly Keynesian and detached from any notion of socialist planning or any struggle for power. Clearly, in the party's official view, an acceptable equilibrium had been reached with the nationalisation of the Bank of England. Britain now had a true central bank like everyone else, though it was more under the influence of financial interests, and less under government control, than most; but the remaining banks were to stay privately owned with the exception of the tiny co-operative sector.

Thus the period 1940-51 saw the fulfilment of the programme of the moderate leadership of the late 1930s. The Bank of England was brought under direct Treasury control, in line with other Western nations, but the clearing banks were left undisturbed. The justification was partly in terms of power, but mostly in terms of employment policies. The former belief in the need for control over all banks in the interest of direct planning, to stop speculation and fraud, and for the many other reasons given, seemed to have evaporated entirely.

IV

The lull lasted about twenty years. In that period one would look in vain for any specific references to the banks in *New Fabian Essays* or in the statements of faith by party leaders, let alone in the official programmes,[66] and elsewhere there was only a ritual mention. Nor was this self-denying ordinance shaken by the repeated wrecking of British economic policy by the actions of international (and domestic) bankers and speculators.

Occasional resolutions to the annual party conferences had been squeezed out by the timetable, and when a resolution just managed to appear in 1971, obliging the party 'to include proposals to nationalise all banking and insurance companies' in the next election manifesto, and the NEC to report to the 1972 conference on 'the public ownership of all the banks, insurance companies and building societies',[67] it came as something of a surprise. More surprising still was the large majority with which it was accepted (possibly boosted by the recent selling off of profitable sections of publicly-owned industries to private owners by the newly elected Conservative Government), against the ill-concealed hostility of the NEC, who had omitted all references to banking in its own shopping list of industries to be nationalised.[68]

The resulting 'Green Paper', produced by a subcommittee of the NEC for discussion within the Labour Party in 1973, listed three reasons for the proposals to transfer the financial institutions to public ownership: inefficiency in their services to the customers, inefficiency in allocating national resources, and perpetuating inequality in wealth and power. In later discussion, this list was expanded to mention wasteful overlapping of branches; the lack of competition among the oligopoly of the 'Big Four'; too much finance for speculation, and too little for industrial development; and too little interest shown in the management of the firms which the banks supported. The Green Paper proposed to nationalise the English, Scottish and Northern Irish clearing banks, the British overseas banks, and three of the largest finance houses. The banks would form the 'British Bank' which would hive off specialist sections for routine banking, a 'development bank' for medium and long-term finance on the German and Japanese model, and an 'overseas bank'.[69]

This discussion paper ran into trouble from the start, in part from the trade unions of banking employees who were immediately suspicious of attempts to increase the 'efficiency' of branch banking; in part because it left out any references to planning, which was the concern of another subcommittee; and in part because of the hostility in principle from the parliamentary leadership. Internal discussions, therefore, continued during the two elections in 1974, while the programme *Labour and Industry: the Next Steps*, presented to the Blackpool conference of 1975, promised to channel more institutional funds into industry to boost the limited funds available from ploughing back firms' own profits, in accordance with the 'National Plan'. Further, the National Enterprise Board would take on some 'merchant banking' functions and might also be used to 'expand the public sector in banking'. Significantly, there was also a backward glance at the nationalisation of the three major joint-stock banks in France which had helped the success of the French planners.[70]

By now, four years after the initial resolution, the issue could not be dodged any longer. Before the next conference, the Home Policy Committee had commissioned a number of research papers which showed Britain to be the only advanced country, with the exception of the USA, without a major public banking sector, yet despite the favour shown to private banking, Britain also had the least competition among banks. At the same time, it was also shown to what large extent the rapid industrial expansion abroad was maintained by channelling outside funds to industrial firms. Thus nationalising at least part of the banking sector had become respectable, and two new and powerful arguments were added to the armoury of the bank nationalisers: the slow growth of British output compared with other countries and the need to plan and expand industrial investment.

Both arguments were heavily stressed in the NEC report to the 1976 conference.[71] Bankers and members of the Stock Exchange were accused of having devoted too many resources to non-productive purposes and to speculation, to the buying and selling of existing assets rather than the creation of new funds, and of having sought security rather than higher returns. Banks should see their role in the strengthening of the foundation of the British economy, rather than attempting to secure short-term gains. The City was also criticised for its incompetence in neither foreseeing nor stemming the financial scandals and collapses of the early 1970s, and the divided loyalties of the Bank of England as long as the City remained in private hands were also noted: the Bank may have been nationalised thirty years ago, 'it has yet to be socialised'.

Among the proposals were a compulsory 'Investment Reserve Fund'[72] to be ploughed back by every company and spent only under the direction of the Bank of England; an enlarged nationalised sector, made up of the Giro, the National Savings Bank, the Paymaster General and possibly the Trustee Savings Banks; and the nationalisation of the Big Four clearing banks, the top seven insurance companies and one merchant bank. 'All experience' of the mixed economy had shown that 'there is no substitute for public ownership when it comes to engineering a radical change in attitude to investment priorities'. In order to maintain consumers' choice and competition, the French model should be followed and the nationalised banks should preserve their separate identities.

The majority in favour of these proposals was large enough to force their inclusion in party policy, although there were significant abstentions, including some general unions with members in banking. Outside the party, the proposals relating to certain named banking and insurance firms were greeted by a chorus of protest, from some expected and also some unexpected quarters,[73] and Prime Minister Callaghan at once denounced the proposal as an 'electoral albatross', though he admitted that Labour would have to ensure that 'the banking system . . . is genuinely responsive to the needs of manufacturing industry'.[74] There was thus a direct conflict between the majority of the NEC and the parliamentary leadership, and at the time of writing there is still deadlock within a divided NEC[75] though other methods of harnessing finance to industrial planning are being mooted.[76]

Thus the last phase has seen the most rapid changes in fortunes for the policy of nationalising the banks: twenty years of silence, followed by a sudden re-emergence of interest and remarkably widespread support within the labour movement. Moreover, the argumentation has changed abruptly several times within the brief span of barely six years. From the old quest for planning and power, it switched to City scandals and speculation, settled on the poor productive and investment record of the United Kingdom, and lately it has come back to employment, and turned specifically to the unique opportunity offered by North Sea oil for a once-for-all massive and directed investment effort. This time, the campaign has been backed by much more detailed and specific research; it is a sign of the declining fortunes of Britain that much of it has looked abroad for inspiration; and, possibly for the first time, some of the leading protagonists, at least, are aware of the rapidly shifting grounds on which they hold to the constant policy of the nationalisation of the banks.[77]

V

Even a condensed survey of this kind may leave the reader with the impression that there was no history of the proposal to nationalise the banks: it emerged and disappeared from time to time as a component of different policy packages, without being firmly based on a tradition of its own. That impression of absence of continuity would have been strengthened, had space allowed a more detailed treatment, and there is indeed an element of truth in it. If a similar impression, though with vaguer outlines, can be derived from the history of nationalisation itself,[78] the sharper focus of the single banking sector as a target for nationalisation makes the point much more clearly.

More significant still is the discontinuity which can be observed in the justification, rather than the proposals themselves, for even if practical action may be dictated by shifting political constellations, at least the underlying philosophy ought to show some consistency. Yet here the changes are even more bewildering and kaleidoscopic. Beginning with redistributive justice and economic power, we move to efficiency, the maintenance of employment, the prevention of poverty, the control over foreign policy, the planning of industry, efficiency and low cost in banking, the prevention of fraud, the reduction in nepotism, the development of long-term investment, and many others besides from time to time. It is true that some of these are complementary, but others are contradictory, and they do not spring from a common recognisable view of the world or of society. Some, indeed, are anchored in deep conviction; but others are plainly opportunist. Moreover, with the exception of possibly one brief period in the 1930s the Labour Party's parliamentary leadership was never totally convinced of the justification for nationalising the banking sector at all, or rather, it supported it in principle but never in practice, showing all the signs of 'those who win elections with socialist phrases on their lips . . . and then proceed to administer a capitalist society, which they have previously denounced, in as efficient way as possible'.[79]

Plainly, if this particular proposal is any guide, British socialist thought, or the theoretical underpinning of British Labour politics, does not consist in the slow accretion of historical and political recognition of reality: it is, instead, the somewhat disoriented and panic-stricken set of *ad hoc* reactions to a succession of unexpected outside events. Curiously, and significantly too, where a doctrinal tradition does develop, it seems to run the danger of outliving its applicability. Thus one of the major threads running through the history of the 1920s and 1930s is the opposition to the private banking system because of its restrictiveness: its quest for safety was alleged to have induced it to deflate and cut output and employment. Who would not have had sympathy with C.A.R. Crosland's outburst after the war: 'In Britain . . . with an abysmal rate of growth . . . it should be a constant preoccupation of government to bully backward industries into spending money on research, investment, and the development of new products.'[80] Thus the consensus has arisen that government, i.e. Treasury, control over banking means expansion and development, and this has survived even into the 1970s, when it should have become clear after decades of experience that it is the Treasury which is the most restrictive and destructive element in the economy, and that the cutting back of investment and employment is always sharpest where Treasury power is greatest, and can be avoided only, if at all, where the Treasury writ does not run.

If this brief review of the history of bank nationalisation proposals has tended to confirm the beliefs of those who hold that the British Labour movement is a pragmatic one on which the ideological and even programmatic luggage sits but lightly, it possibly holds a lesson for the general historian also. The demand to nationalise 'the banks', meaning throughout, the Bank of England and the joint-stock or clearing banks, is after all a clear-cut and definitive one in British conditions. Yet what difference lies in the objective, the understanding of reality, indeed the reality, the motivation and the dominant ideology, between those who made these demands, say in the 1880s, in the mid-1920s, in the depth of the depression and in the 1970s! It is seen, alternately, as peripheral and central, revolutionary and stabilising, simple and complex, and many other things besides. It is not the only constant term in history behind which, in a changing social context, there hides a multitude of real meanings.

Acknowledgement

I wish to thank Irene Wagner, librarian of the Labour Party, for help in the research on which this paper is based.

Notes

1. Sidney Webb, *Socialism in England* (1889; 1908 ed.), pp. 5-7.
2. *Socialism Made Plain* (1883), no. 6.
3. The Socialist League, established by secessionists from the Democratic Federation, similarly stressed their objection to the 'economic subjection' of man to man: Socialist League, *Constitution and Rules* (1885).
4. H.M. Hyndman and William Morris, *A Summary of the Principles of Socialism: Written for the Democratic Federation* (1884), esp. p. 59.
5. E.g. H.M. Hyndman, *England for All: The Text Book of Democracy* (1881); Robert Harper, *The Nationalization of British Industry, or Compound Profits, Interest and Rent* (1886); Willard Wolfe, *From Radicalism to Socialism* (New Haven, 1975), p. 261.
6. Preface to *Fabian Essays* (1889; Jubilee ed., 1948), p. xxxix, also Annie Besant, 'Industry under Socialism' and Bernard Shaw, 'The Transition to Social Democracy'.
7. William Stewart, *J. Keir Hardie: A Biography* (1921), pp. 44-5; Robert Dowse, *Left in the Centre: the Independent Labour Party 1893-1940* (1966), p. 5.
8. Fabian Tract no. 164 (1912). See also A.M. McBriar, *Fabian Socialism and English Politics 1884-1918* (Cambridge, 1966), pp. 113-14. A somewhat similar idea, typical of the age, for freeing society from its dependence on gold was made by H.G. Wells, who proposed to base currency on the amount of energy available in each locality: *A Modern Utopia* (1904) in *Works*, vol. 9 (1925), p. 71.
9. Published in 1914. See also Brougham Villiers, *The Socialist Movement in England* (1908; 1910 ed.), pp. 177-8, 232.
10. Sidney Webb (ed.), *How to Pay for the War: Being Ideas Offered to the Chancellor of the Exchequer by the Fabian Research Department* (1916). See also idem, *When Peace Comes: the Way of Industrial Reconstruction* (1916).
11. *Labour and the New Social Order* (first version January 1918, revised version in accordance with the resolutions of the Labour Party Conference, June 1918). See also *Labour's Call to the People* (1918) and Arthur Henderson, *The Aims of*

Labour (1918), as well as Ross McKibbin, *The Evolution of the Labour Party 1910-1924* (1974), p. 104.

12. Labour Party, Advisory Committee on Trade Policy and Finance, *Labour Policy in Relation to Bank Amalgamations and the Nationalisation of Banking* [1918?].

13. Cd. 9052 (1918).

14. Sidney and Beatrice Webb, *A Constitution for the Socialist Commonwealth of Great Britain* (1920), p. 168; cf. also Sidney Webb, *National Finance and a Levy on Capital: What the Labour Party Intends* (1919; 1969 ed.), p. 8.

15. Labour Party, *Labour and Social Credit: A Report on the Proposals of Major Douglas and the 'New Age'* (1921). The galaxy of talent on the committee who drafted this document included Sidney Webb, R.J. Davies, Frank Hodges, F.B. Varley, G.D.H. Cole, Hugh Dalton, J.A. Hobson, C.M. Lloyd, Sir Leo Chiozza Money, R.H. Tawney and Arthur Greenwood.

16. E.g. A. Emil Davies, *The Case for Nationalisation* (1920).

17. Sir Leo Chiozza Money, *The Triumph of Nationalisation* (1920).

18. As late as 1924, Philip Snowden still argued for bank nationalisation in order to: (1) reduce costs; (2) give greater security to depositors; (3) transfer bank profits to the State; and (4) give the government control over the price level: *Labour and the New World* (1924), pp. 153-4.

19. Catherine Ann Cline, *Recruits to Labour: The British Labour Party 1914-1931* (Syracuse, 1963), esp. pp. 101 ff.

20. ILP, *The Socialist Programme* (1923), pp. 9-11, 25-8.

21. *Labour Party Conference Report* (henceforth *LPCR*) (1924), pp. 160-1, 165-6. By 1924, the Communist Party, echoed by the National Minority Movement in 1925, was advocating the nationalisation of all banks without compensation: E.E. Barry, *Nationalisation in British Politics: The Historical Background* (1965), pp. 265-6.

22. H.N. Brailsford, J.A. Hobson, A. Creech Jones, E.F. Wise, *The Living Wage* (1926), p. 18.

23. Ibid., pp. 19, 37.

24. Ibid., pp. 45-6; *Socialism in Our Time*, reprinted in Dowse, *Left in the Centre*, pp. 212-15. See also H.N. Brailsford, *Socialism for Today* (1925), p. 96.

25. The extent to which Keynes between the *Tract on Monetary Reform* (1923) and the *General Theory* (1936) was absorbed, anticipated and possibly even influenced by socialist economists outside the circle of orthodoxy is consistently under-estimated by academic historians of Keynesian doctrine, and deserves a study in itself. Cf. G.D.H. Cole, *The Means to Full Employment* (1943), pp. 48-9. But see the contrary view in Donald Winch, *Economics and Policy: A Historical Study* (1969), pp. 344-5.

26. Oswald Mosley, *Revolution by Reason* (1925). An extended commentary was provided in a book by John Strachey, also called *Revolution by Reason* (1925). See also R. Skidelsky, *Oswald Mosley* (1975), pp. 142, 150; H.C. Deb, 5s. vol. 174, cols. 2424-5 (1924); Oswald Mosley, 'The Labour Party's Financial Policy', *Socialist Review*, September 1927, pp. 18 ff. Mosley was aware of the distinction between the Hobson idea of transferring part of a constant national income from those who would spend, and what would later be the Keynesian idea of increasing the national income itself. Cf. *Revolution by Reason*, pp. 16-17: 'At present socialist thought appears to concentrate almost exclusively upon this transfer of present purchasing power by taxation, and neglects the necessity for creating additional demand to evoke our unused capacity which is at present not commanded either by the rich or the poor.'

27. *LPCR* (1925), pp. 262-6.

28. *LPCR* (1927), p. 264.

29. The section *Labour and the Nation: Supplement on Banking and Currency Policy* was at first published separately, but by decision of the 1928 conference was incorporated in the main programme.

30. *LPCR* (1928), pp. 228-32. In his own contribution to the election literature for 1929, Snowden omitted all references to the banks: Philip Snowden, *Wealth or Commonwealth: Labour's Financial Policy* (1929). In the official reply to the Liberal Party manifesto, the Labour Party stressed that it would on no account deal with unemployment by credit creation: *Labour's Reply to Lloyd George: How to Conquer Unemployment* (1929).

31. Ralph Miliband, *Parliamentary Socialism: A Study in the Politics of Labour* (1972 ed.), p. 157.

32. *LPCR* (1929), pp. 227-32.

33. E.g. Ernest Bevin and G.D.H. Cole, *The Crisis: What it is, How it arose, What to do* (1931), esp. pp. 38-42; G.D.H. Cole, *The Next Ten Years in British Social and Economic Policy* (1929), pp. 71-9, 224-46; idem, *Economic Tracts for the Times,* (1932), pp. 52-7; idem, *Gold, Credit and Employment* (1930), pp. 132-48; idem (ed.), *What Everybody Wants to Know About Money* (1933), esp. E.A. Radice, pp. 180, 196-7, G.D.H. Cole, ch. 11; Francis Williams, *Democracy and Finance* (1932). Also, TUC, *Report* (1931), p. 430.

34. *LPCR* (1931), pp. 187-94, 321; Alan Bullock, *The Life and Times of Ernest Bevin,* vol. 1 (1960), p. 497.

35. Margaret Cole, *The Story of Fabian Socialism* (1961), pp. 222-32; idem, 'The Society for Socialist Inquiry and Propaganda', in Asa Briggs and John Saville (eds.), *Essays in Labour History 1918-1939* (1977). Some ideas were developed also within the XYZ Club: B. Pimlott, *Labour and the Left in the 1930s* (Cambridge, 1977), pp. 37, 200.

36. G.D.H. Cole, *The Socialisation of Banking* (SSIP Study Guide 4), p. 6; also idem, *The Bank of England* (SSIP Study Guide 2); *Banks and Credit* (SSIP Study Guide 3); 'Why We Must Socialise the Banks', in *Economic Tracts for the Times* (1932); and *A Plan for Britain* (1933), pp. 9-11.

37. I.e. credits to borrowers who were unable to pay them back.

38. *Economic Tracts,* p. 115.

39. E.F. Wise, *Control of Finance and Financiers* (1933), pp. 1-3; Colin Clark, *The Control of Investment* [1933?]; G.R. Mitchison, *Banking* (1933). Strangely enough, the Socialist League's Programme of 1934, *Forward to Socialism,* which contains a long list of industries and sectors to be nationalised in the first five years of power, omits banking. Cf. Patrick Seyd, 'Factionalism within the Labour Party: the Socialist League 1932-1937', in Briggs and Saville, *Essays in Labour History,* esp. pp. 213, 227.

40. *LPCR* (1932), pp. 188-94; Labour Party, *Policy Report No. 1: Resolution on Currency, Banking, Finance* (1932).

41. Labour Party, *Policy Report No. 5: Socialism and the Condition of the People* (1933); *LPCR* (1933), pp. 157-60, 171-8.

42. Labour Party, *For Socialism and Peace: The Labour Party's Programme of Action* (1934).

43. Ralph Miliband, op. cit., pp. 207-8; Adrian Oldfield, 'The Labour Party and Planning -- 1934 or 1918?', *Bulletin of the Society for Study of Labour History,* no. 25 (1972); David Coates, *The Labour Party and the Struggle for Socialism* (1975), pp. 36-7; G.D.H. Cole, *A History of the Labour Party from 1914* (1948), pp. 278-88, 295-6.

44. E.g. G.R. Mitchison, *The First Workers' Government* (1934); G.D.H. Cole, *Principles of Economic Planning* (1935); John Wilmot, *Labour's Way to Central Banking and Finance* (1935); E.F.M. Durbin, *Socialist Credit Policy* (1934); Labour Party, *Labour's Financial Policy* (1935), pp. 7, 10-12; idem, Study Guide No. 1: *Banking and Finance* (1933).

45. 'Bank Manager', *Why the Banks Should be Nationalised* (1936), p. 7.

46. Thomas Johnston, *The Financiers and the Nation* (1934).

47. Hugh Dalton, *High Tide and After (Memoirs 1945-1960)* (1962), pp. 33-4; idem, *Practical Socialism for Britain* (1935; 1945 ed.), pp. 186, 202.

48. Review of *Practical Socialism,* 1935, reprinted in E.F.M. Durbin, *Problems of Economic Planning: Papers on Planning and Economics* (1949; 1968 ed.), p. 35; 'A Citizen', *The City Today* (1938), pp. 18, 29 (he favoured a 'healthy rivalry' for custom even among the branches of a national bank).

49. Amber Blanco White, *The Nationalisation of Banking* (1934). The author, incidentally, was opposed to the early nationalisation of the joint-stock banks.

50. E.g. E.F.M. Durbin, Hugh Gaitskell, W.R. Heskett, *Socialism and 'Social Credit'* (1935), esp. pp. 31-4.

51. C.P. Mayhew, *Planned Investment: The Case for a National Enterprise Board* (Fabian Society Research Series no. 45) (1939).

52. *LPCR* (1937), pp. 184-6, 277.

53. Labour Party, 'Finance Policy No. 2, Labour's Financial Policy' (November 1938: cyclost.); 'Heads of a Bill on Finance' (December 1938: cyclost.).

54. H.V. Berry and E.F.M. Durbin, 'Finance Policy No. 5, Memorandum on the Nationalisation of the English Banking System' (January 1939: cyclost.).

55. E.g. Hugh Gaitskell, *Money and Everyday Life* [1939?]; Douglas Jay, *The Nation's Wealth at the Nation's Service* (1938).

56. John Strachey, *The Banks for the People* (1940); G.D.H. Cole, *Great Britain in the Post-War World* (1942), p. 88, and his *Fabian Socialism* (1943), p. 62. See also his *A Plan for Democratic Britain* (1939) and *Monetary Systems and Theories* (1943).

57. J.A. Schumpeter, *Capitalism, Socialism and Democracy* (1942; 3rd ed., 1965), p. 230.

58. Especially Labour Party Research Series, R.D.R. papers no. 66, 72, 172, 173, 175, 191, 201, 265, 275.

59. Labour Party, *Full Employment and Financial Policy* (1944), p. 3.

60. *LPCR* (1944), pp. 161-3; Miliband, *Parliamentary Socialism,* pp. 276-7; Cole, *History of the Labour Party,* p. 421.

61. Miliband, ibid., pp. 278-81.

62. Labour Party, *Discussion Series, No. 3: The Bank of England and the Nation* (1946).

63. Dalton, *High Tide and After,* pp. 42-6. The demand for sweeping powers called for in war-time had disappeared.

64. Jacques Leruez, *Economic Planning & Politics in Britain* (1975), p. 43.

65. Labour Party Research Department, R.D. Series no. 130, *Industries for Nationalisation* (July 1948).

66. R.H.S. Crossman (ed.), *New Fabian Essays* (1952); Labour Party, *Forward With Labour* (1955), *Public Enterprise – Labour's Review of the Nationalised Industries* (1957), *Industry and Society, Labour's Policy on the Future of Public Ownership* (1957), *Britain Belongs to You* (1959), *Let's Go With Labour for the New Britain* (1964), *Time for Decision* (1966), *Building A Socialist Britain* (1970); Harold Wilson, *The Relevance of British Socialism* (1964). There is a typical anodyne reference in Douglas Jay, *Socialism in the New Society* (1962), p. 296.

67. *LPCR* (1971), pp. 298-9.

68. Labour Party, *Economic Strategy, Growth and Unemployment* (1971).

69. Labour Party Study Group, *Banking and Insurance Green Paper* (1973), esp. pp. 7, 9, 11.

70. *Labour and Industry: the Next Steps* (1975), pp. 8-10.

71. Labour Party, *Banking and Finance* (1976).

72. Variable in-payments might be used to smooth out fluctuations. TUC-Labour Party Liaison Committee, *The Next Three Years and the Problem of Priorities* (July 1976), p. 8, no. 17.

73. A splendid example of the latter was the pamphlet written by Lord Taylor of Gryfe, formerly of the ILP and Scottish CWS, but now associated with some City interests: *Nationalisation of Banking and Insurance. A Dissenting View*, Labour Economic, Finance and Taxation Association [1977?].

74. Press release, Labour Party Information Department, 24 September 1976.

75. *The Times*, 25 May 1977.

76. E.g. Norman Atkinson, 'Blueprint for a State Bank', *Labour Weekly*, 18 March 1977.

77. Private correspondence with Norman Atkinson MP and John Garrett MP.

78. E.g. Barry, *Nationalisation in British Politics*, passim.

79. John Saville, 'Labourism and the Labour Government', *Socialist Register* (1967), p. 53.

80. C.A.R. Crosland, *The Conservative Enemy: A Programme of Radical Reform for the 1960s* (1962), p. 42.

10 THE LABOUR MOVEMENT BETWEEN THE WARS

Margaret Cole

In the half century before 1914 the labour movement practised a policy of gradualism. Its justification was the general unwillingness of the British ruling classes to go to extremes of repression against large groups of dissentients, and also in no small degree to the growing commercial prosperity which was not too heavily set back even by the depression of the 1880s. There were of course dissentients – those who co-operated with Keir Hardie in the foundation of the Independent Labour Party, for example, and striking miners and engineers; and their opposition was reinforced by the decision of the Law Lords in the Taff Vale judgement, which struck an unexpected blow at trade union funds. But those groups were relatively small and shifting minorities.

There was one element which differentiated the British labour movement from that of other countries. In Britain after the early disastrous ending of Owenism and Chartism, the trade unions grew up before the Labour Party which they ultimately created, so that we do not find in Britain, as we do in some European countries, competing trade unions professing different ideologies – Christian, Communist, Anarchist or what not. In contrast, the American Federation of Labor, under the leadership of Samuel Gompers, took as its simple motto, 'Reward your friends and punish your enemies', and never created a Labour Party – though this did not prevent the unions in the United States from having a history of violent struggle.

The practice of peaceful concession without revolution had one great disadvantage which has not been always fully appreciated by social historians. *As there was no revolution, so there was no essential change in class attitudes and alignment.* This enabled the British Labour Party, in the new century, to be accepted for membership of the International on the ground that though it did not *say* that it believed in the class war it acted as though it did; but it also enabled members of the British upper classes to think and write of the classes below them as though they were a different species – a species of 'natives', to use the language of imperialism, who should be well treated and have their more serious disadvantages remedied where possible, but with whom one could not possibly associate on terms of equality. The strongly persistent class system in education is the clearest institutional example of this; but perhaps more revealing are some of the phrases in common use right up to and during the First World War.

The novelist Charlotte Yonge's description of one of her heroes as inheriting an estate which had 'a great many miners on it' (as she might have said 'blackbeetles') was not by any means obsolete. And it is noticeable that, while local Liberal parties were only too glad to have working men like Arthur Henderson as agents, the national Liberal organisation was scandalised at the idea that a working man should be selected as a candidate for Parliament — save in a very few constituencies in which most of the voters were miners. In the early days of the war tales were spread, and believed, of miners who bought grand pianos out of their excessive wages — it was never explained where, in their one-roomed shacks, the miners found place to accommodate them; and *The Engineer*, the organ of the engineering employers, after persistent agitation had succeeded in securing a minimum wage of twenty shillings a week for women 'dilutees' taking the place of men in the war industries, proclaimed that the result proved, not that women were paid too little, but that men had hitherto been paid far too much. Even after the war was over, 'Poy', the cartoonist of the *Evening News*, drew a picture of Churchill, wearing a flamboyant sample of his headgear, saying to an unmistakeable proletarian: 'You couldn't wear this Hat: You'd look SO SILLY in it!' This state of mind — which, incidentally, played its part in the determination of MacDonald that his first Cabinet should wear full court dress — has not died out today.

The upper and upper-middle classes found strikes particularly alarming; and I can speak to that fact personally, since I was living in Liverpool when the 1911 transport strikes enlarged themselves, with the aid of the city's scavengers, into a kind of miniature general strike; when there were sharp battles (fought largely with pieces of broken bottle) down at the dockside, when the stench of fruit and vegetables rotting in trucks stranded by Edge Hill station spread into the respectable residential districts around Sefton Park; when the destroyer *Antrim* lay as a grey menace in the Mersey; when a cavalry regiment rode through streets empty of trams, and American tourists, decanted from the *Baltic* liner, sat on their Saratoga trunks hoping vainly for porters to appear and bear them away to their hotels.[1] Liverpool was in a panic, and was not comforted when the settlement of the transport strikes was followed by the national strike of miners, by the sinking of the *Titanic* — the *Daily Herald* loudly highlighting the rescue of first-class passengers while so many from lower classes were left to drown — and, finally, by James Larkin's great Dublin strike, which roused even the Trades Union Congress and the sleepy English co-operative movement to help the Irish workers. The ruling classes, all over Britain, were being moved to fight back, when the outbreak of the European war upset all the alignments. The International, except for a tiny fraction, forgot all its earlier anti-war declarations. Ramsay MacDonald, the treasurer of the Labour Party, whom most people had believed to be a pacifist, sent ambiguous messages to recruiting meetings in his Leicester constituency; and for a time the nation seemed unanimous in the pursuit of a war which would be of short duration. Only the handful of determined internationalists and/or pacifists, organised in the Union of Democratic Control and led largely by Clifford Allen, remained as a very ineffective opposition.

This unanimity did not last. As the war went on and on and victory became more uncertain, opposition of many kinds developed, especially to military conscription and state control of industry and agriculture; the No-Conscription Fellowship grew in numbers and strength. But quite quickly inevitable economic forces triumphed. State control was more and more accepted; Lloyd George, though hated in Conservative quarters before the war, became the nation's charismatic leader; and as more and more members of the lower classes were needed to replace the slaughtered thousands and to work all-out to provide their successors with the weapons, uniforms and other materials which they must have, the demands of their representatives had more and more to be met, whatever their discontented betters thought about it. Recent historians of the period have perforce noticed such facts as the growth of the shop stewards' movement (and not only on the Clyde), the mass of negotiation and regulation which allowed high wages and prescribed minima for the 'dilutees' who took over the skilled men's jobs — the working-class version of 'Keep the Home Fires Burning' — in order that their former holders might not find, when and if they returned from the various fronts, that the standard of life for which they had struggled so long and so hard had been destroyed while they were serving their country: but these historians have not sufficiently realised the extent to which war-time conditions raised the importance and apparent power of the working class, together with the plans and projects of the left-wing theorists and propagandists, to which the many soft-soaping reports of the government's huge Reconstruction Committee in its various departments gave partial sanction. The reconstituted Labour Party, with its explicitly socialist programme, *Labour and the New Social Order*, showing that the Webbs and their Fabian allies had given up the hope of 'permeating' the nation as a whole in favour of permeating the Labour Party and its constituent trade unions, indicated how far the rot (as the diehards called it) had gone. And then, in November 1918, came the Armistice, with what seemed to be complete victory, hysterical rejoicing in the streets, and, almost immediately, the 'Coupon' election giving an overwhelming parliamentary majority to the 'Man Who had Won the War' — it is not always remembered how far Lloyd George's policy for the future changed under pressure, even during the brief election period, from advising a comparatively sane and reasonable settlement to accepting the vindictive and eventually disastrous clauses of the Treaty of Versailles.

I

The Armistice was signed: the Treaty, after the long and depressing months of wrangling excoriated by J.M. Keynes in *The Economic Consequences of the Peace*, was signed also. The war, however, did not officially come to an end until August 1921 — a date which can roughly be taken as marking the end of the first of the three periods into which this chapter is divided. This period continued, and even enhanced, the inflation of the war years. Once the fear of defeat (which had recurred, alarmingly, as recently as March 1918) had finally vanished, the 'hard-faced men', in the phrase attributed to Stanley Baldwin, saw their opportunity, and 'trustification' and wildly speculative buying and selling, particularly of cotton textile mills, increased to an enormous extent, being largely financed by the 'Big Five' banks. The cost of living, which had already risen sharply, was thus given another push upwards.

Labour, pending the demobilisation of the huge numbers stored in the armed forces and the dismantling of the 'war industries' — a term which has to be interpreted in a very wide sense — was still scarce; and the government and the principal employers were willing to acquiesce, though not of course without complaint, in labour's efforts to cash in on the situation. A panic fear, almost as hysterical as the Armistice rejoicings, of what *might* be going to happen to British society, contributed in no small degree to this attitude; the diary printed in the December *Monthly Circular* of the Labour Research Department clearly shows the reason. It ran as follows:

November 1	Austrian Revolution
6	German Naval Revolt
7	Bavarian Republic
9	German Revolution. Swiss General Strike

	10	Dutch Labour Disturbances
	13	Danish Labour Disturbances.
		Spanish move towards Revolution
	14	Labour Party leaves War-time Coalition
	17	Hungarian Republic
	18	Portuguese General Strike
	23	London Labour Demonstration refused Albert Hall
December	1	London Labour Demonstration held in Albert Hall

The last two items recall a much-publicised triumph, when the proprietors of the Albert Hall — who had refused to let it for a Labour celebration — were faced with threats by the Electrical Trades Union to cut off the light during its Victory Ball, and by the various transport unions to prevent tube trains and buses from stopping at South Kensington and by taxis to refuse fares — and hurriedly climbed down. The *Herald* (a weekly during the war) celebrated the event with a drawing on its front page of an electric bulb, with a caption in large letters, THE LIGHT THAT FAILED. It looked to some as though 1848, the Year of Revolutions, might be coming again.

The Albert Hall affair was fun and because of the quick victory of the unions it attracted a good deal of public notice; but other developments were more serious. There were strikes in many of the big cities, of which the largest was a general strike in Glasgow in January 1919, which earned some of its leaders short spells in jail; and perhaps the most spectacular two strikes (one before the war had ended) of policemen in the metropolis. There were demands by the Miners' Federation of Great Britain for nationalisation of the mines with some form of workers' control; there was a national railway strike in September 1919 against wage reductions proposed by Sir Auckland Geddes, which had a good measure of success, partly owing to a very effective publicity campaign run by a committee of the Labour Research Department; more immediately alarming was the insistent demand for immediate demobilisation in the army — comparatively few of whose members had been able to vote in the General Election — which produced serious mutinies in more than one camp. Concurrently, the 'Irish war', with the violent suppressive action undertaken by the Black and Tans and the Auxiliaries, was attracting a great deal of vocal attacks on the government; the Labour Party sent its own fact-finding mission to the troubled country.

The coalition government did what it could to defuse these explosive elements. Ireland had to wait for a while; but the menace of mutiny was dealt with by a hasty scrapping of any plans for an ordered de-mobilisation, and the resultant chaotic unemployment mitigated by an 'out-of-work donation' at a weekly rate well in excess of anything that could have been received under the pre-war Insurance Acts (which in any event applied to comparatively few occupations); and by the rapid discharge of most of the women 'dilutees'. This took care of the em-ployment situation until a national system of unemployment insurance could be worked out and put into effect by an act of 1920. Meantime, the Wages (Temporary Regulation) Act of 1918 aimed at preventing wage reductions for a six-month period. The Miners' Federation was bought off by the setting-up of the Royal Commission on the Coal Mines, with wide terms of reference: its chairman was Mr Justice Sankey and its membership divided equally between the two sides of the industry, each appointing three members and three 'experts'; its meetings were held publicly in the House of Lords, and government spokesmen promised that its recommendations would be put into effect 'in the spirit and in the letter'. The remaining main effort was the establishment of a large National Industrial Conference, also repre-senting the two sides of industry, which was opened in February 1919 by Sir Robert Horne, the Minister of Labour. The conference appointed a committee, with Arthur Henderson, the secretary of the Labour Party, leading for the unions (with G.D.H. Cole as secretary) and Sir Allan Smith, chairman of the engineering employers and no friend to high wage demands, leading for the employers. This committee reported to a second conference in April with a fair number of recommendations; but the government made various delaying excuses, and practically nothing came of the recommendations before, in the following year, the labour side of the conference resigned in disgust.

It is interesting to observe, in retrospect, how close the 'intellectuals', including the politicians of the Labour Party, were to the leaders of the industrial workers during this period.[2] Sidney Webb joined the national executive of the party in place of W.S. Sanders, the paid secretary of the Fabian Society, who had gone to the war; and in friendly discussion with Arthur Henderson, particularly after the latter's rude exclusion from the Cabinet over the projected Stockholm Conference, there were drawn up the pamphlet on *Labour's War Aims*, the new constitution of the Labour Party (passed finally in 1918), and the policy pamphlet *Labour and the New Social Order*. The style of the last-named —

including the plethora of capital letters! — would stamp it as Sidney's in the absence of any other evidence; but Beatrice Webb recorded the fact in her diary, and added that Arthur Henderson, far from querying its proposals, complained that they did not go far enough and asked why Sidney had not suggested the nationalisation of many more industries. 'Why', he asked when dining with the Webbs in September, 1919, 'Why should the miners and the railwaymen have the privilege of being socialised? — the engineers and other operatives resented this partiality.' The Webbs thought that he wanted to go too fast; but meanwhile Sidney's performance on the Sankey Commission gained him great prestige among the rank and file of the labour movement, causing him to be selected unanimously in the following July by the Labour Party of Seaham Harbour to be their candidate — notwithstanding a determined effort by the Durham Miners' Association to retain the seat for a miner. 'The explanation', Mrs Webb said to her diary, 'is that these leading men in these isolated pit villages are readers of books and not hearers of revivalist speeches and propagandist lectures.' And by writing regular reports and holding question and discussion meetings in the constituency the Webbs for some years maintained a fruitful and happy relationship with what Beatrice flatteringly called 'the University of Seaham'. Indeed, as her diaries show very clearly, the educated recruits to labour, particularly those who had come over from the Liberals via the Union of Democratic Control, the No-Conscription Fellowship, and the first National Council for Civil Liberties, were playing a considerable part in drafting policies acceptable to the older leaders of the Labour Party, even if a handful of trade union bureaucrats such as Tom Shaw, MP for Preston and leader of the cotton unions, wanted middle-class politicians and 'missionary intellectuals' kept firmly in a subordinate position.

The word 'missionary' refers to another group, mainly of intellectuals, who looked for leadership to Clifford Allen. Allen, a Cambridge graduate who before 1914 had been one of the critics of the Webb influence in the Fabian Society, fell seriously ill as a result of the hardships he suffered as a conscientious objector and became, in effect, the saint of the pacifist and international dissentients. After the war he set himself, with other sympathisers such as Fenner Brockway and the distinguished journalist H.N. Brailsford, to turn the ILP into a real organ of opinion. One of Allen's gifts was that of fund-raising, and he collected from wealthy and not-so-wealthy individuals monies sufficient to put the ILP on its feet, to hire for it offices close to the Houses of Parliament, and to turn its organ, the *Labour Leader* founded by Keir

Hardie, into a journal of intellectual and artistic discussion under the name *New Leader*, with Brailsford as salaried editor – and to contribute financial support to the National Guilds League.

The NGL provided yet another source of intellectual co-operation. It had been formed in 1915, in order to spread the gospel of guild socialism, a system for the conduct of society in which industry would be run by self-governing guilds based on rationally reorganised trade unions in collaboration with a democratic state. This philosophy, first promulgated by the architect A.J. Penty in a book entitled *The Restoration of the Gild System* and further elaborated by S.G. Hobson in a series of articles in the *New Age*, appealed strongly to some of the more reflective leaders of the unions. As it laid considerable stress on local initiative, in contrast to the bureaucratic national collectivism associated with the name of the Webbs, it gained considerable support from the shop stewards and other local leaders who, while the national leaders were hampered by legislation and the war-time Treasury Agreements from calling strikes, found themselves, almost without asking, at the head of left-wing movements among the war workers. The guild doctrine was in due course developed so as to cover industries which were not considered 'ripe' for nationalisation; the solution suggested for such cases came to be known as 'collective contract' or 'encroaching control'. The idea was that the workers in any given plant or factory, organised in 'one big union' or a group of unions, would offer to undertake jobs of production for a negotiated lump sum, out of which they would meet all costs, including that of continuous payment to individual members of the guild, whether or not there was immediate work for them to do – thus eliminating factory by factory or industry by industry the insecurity of the 'wage slavery' against which the pre-war socialists, in the *New Age* and elsewhere, had written so furiously. The workers' organisation would also be responsible for hiring and firing and for the detailed running of the work, and from this beginning would take over more and more functions from the employers and their managers – hence the phrase 'encroaching control'. Such a suggestion, holding out to the manual workers the prospect of a security already enjoyed by many of their 'betters', had a strong appeal for the local organisers, particularly in the munitions centres; and at the end of 1916 the Glasgow branch of the NGL had started a monthly journal called *The Guildsman*, which after the untimely death from pneumonia of the branch's secretary, the engineer John Paton, migrated to London and reappeared as the *Guild Socialist*, edited by G.D.H. and Margaret Cole. Meanwhile, in the latter years of the war and the immediate post-war years, the NGL regularly published detailed schemes for guilds in various industries, in pamphlets which were eagerly bought; and also produced a mocking facsimile of the government's Whitley Report.

The Whitley Report made proposals for some form of what we should nowadays call 'industrial participation', both national and local. But as it contained no suggestions for any real social change, as for example in the *ownership* of industry or property, the left, guild socialists and shop stewards alike, loudly denounced it as a fraud; and though some tentative efforts were made to carry out parts of it, the only Whitley Joint Council to survive into the new era was in the civil service — where there was no question of ownership involved.

Meanwhile, the trade union movement itself, partly stimulated by the intellectuals to whom reference has already been made, was beginning to make efforts to improve its own efficiency. Amalgamations had reduced to some extent the welter of unions of very varying sizes and types which had existed before the war; and some quite strong bodies had been founded; by mid-1920, after much discussion, the Trades Union Congress abolished the weak Parliamentary Committee, which was all it possessed by way of an executive, and replaced it with a General Council organised according to industry. G.D.H. Cole, who was for a brief while the secretary of the newly established Advisory Committees of the reorganised Labour Party, was consulted about the drafting of the necessary constitutional amendments; but had no direct responsibility for the final result. He, with Page Arnot, was simultaneously concerned with the setting-up of a federation of professional workers' associations, which was part of the growing tendency to bring together 'the workers by hand and brain' (as the new Labour Party constitution phrased it); and though the association thus brought together catered for the less exalted of the white-collar workers, the development is of some importance. It was paralleled by the remarkable growth of the adult education movement, exemplified by such bodies as the Workers' Educational Association. The WEA believed in co-operation between the universities and working-class representatives in the running of classes, and accepted financial support from the Board of Education. On the left it had a rival in the Marxist Plebs League, born before the war out of a breakaway movement from Ruskin College, which founded the Central Labour College in London and eventually the National Council of Labour Colleges. The NCLC regarded both the universities and the state and local education authorities as hopelessly involved with the capitalist system, and refused any financial or other assistance from such tainted sources, preferring to seek support from trade unions, of which a considerable amount was secured, from the South Wales miners, for example, and some of the building unions. The rivalry of the two movements did much to stimulate intellectual discussion amongst industrial workers generally: the leading protagonists in the Marxist group included Tom Mann, J.F. Horrabin, the cartoonist and illustrator of Wells's *Outline of History*, Noah Ablett and W.W. Craik from South Wales, and Raymond Postgate, the socialist journalist and historian, who was married to a daughter of George Lansbury.

One should remember also, the emergence of the strongest intellect among those who left school at eleven years old — Ernest Bevin, who became a public figure in the spring of 1920 as 'the dockers' KC' when he bought, and exhibited, on small plates, to a startled Court of Inquiry, the actual amounts of food which Professor Bowley, the economist, had declared to be a ration sufficient for a dock worker who, according to one of the witnesses called by Sir Lynden Macassey, the counsel for his employers, was expected to carry on his own back seventy tons of wheat in a day. The publicity which he received for this inquiry brought Bevin to the front rank among trade union leaders. Another landmark was the appearance in 1921 of R.H. Tawney's *Acquisitive Society*, a book whose witty and eloquent indictment of capitalism as unjust, morally wrong and socially absurd and inefficient had a tremendous appeal to pacifists and socialists alike. And yet another, though of rather a different kind, was the coming together in 1920 of various small left-wing groupings to form the Communist Party of Great Britain. The leaders of the Labour Party, reading such utterances as 'Communists will take Labour leaders by the hand in order to take them by the throat', firmly turned down the repeated application of the new party for affiliation; but a good many on the left, regarding the Bolshevik revolution as the hope of the workers, joined up enthusiastically, and only changed their minds when a year or two later the Third (Communist) International ordered Communists in all affiliated societies to become 'cells' and direct their attention to controlling any social group with which they were connected in accordance with instructions from Moscow.[3]

It should not, however, be hastily assumed that every left grouping, even in the first flush of enthusiasm, accepted Bolshevik principles and practice in their entirety. For example, in the late summer of 1920 the Fabian Society offered the guild socialists a free hand to organise a week of the Fabian summer school — a good example of the willingness of Fabian leaders to give their opponents a chance of stating their case. The guild socialists accepted eagerly, and wound up their week by staging a musical called 'The Homeland of Mystery', based largely on the visit paid by George Lansbury to the USSR earlier in the year, which included a song to a Russian Communist leader ending with the lines:

And always you must say
As you walk your bombstrewn way,
'When the Proletariat dictates and the Proletariat's ME
Why what a very comfortable kind of State that kind of State will be!'

— which was a fairly prophetic observation to have made, three and a half years before Lenin's death. But at the time it was regarded as no more than a joke.[4]

The Building Guild, however, was not a joke, but a real attempt to translate some of the workers' control slogans into actual fact. The principal cause of this development was the shocking state of housing for the working classes and others of low incomes, attested to by many reports both private and official, about which nothing to speak of had been done either during the war or in the years immediately before it. (Agitation on the Clyde had produced the 1915 Rent Act; but that was little more than a plaster which led eventually to troubles more obstinate than those it was designed to remedy.) In an attempt to do something about the housing situation, the radical Christopher Addison, who was the head of the newly-created Ministry of Health from 1919 to 1921, brought into being the Housing Act of 1919, which stimulated the local authorities to embark on house-building schemes by guaranteeing them out of national funds a subsidy to cover all their expenditure on such schemes beyond the product of a penny rate. This was of course an immense inducement, though it was unfortunate that the failure to establish any effective control over the prices of building materials resulted in an orgy of profiteering by the firms concerned and a great increase in the costs of housing. Nevertheless, S.G. Hobson, the entrepreneur and journalist who had written the National Guilds series in the *New Age*, saw the opportunity at once, and got into touch with Richard Coppock, then Manchester organiser of the bricklayers and afterwards secretary of the National Federation of Building Trades Operatives, and succeeded in getting his support for a scheme whereby the building trade unions of Manchester set up a building guild which tendered for housing contracts on a lump sum basis, their offer being

sufficiently high to guarantee a wage for their members — thus eliminating the 'insecurity' of the 'wage-slavery' system. This proposal was
accepted after some negotiation; and this form of collective contract
caught the enthusiastic attention of rank-and-file workers who would
have made nothing of the guild socialist philosophy of 'functionalism',
but knew very well the practical meaning of 'insecurity'. They readily
came into the building guild plan, both in Manchester and elsewhere,
as soon as the proposition had been officially accepted; and the Co-
operative Wholesale Society helped by extending short-term loans
to the Guild in order to finance the schemes until the government
guarantees became operative.

Just about the same time, a Quaker master builder in London,
Malcolm Sparkes, who had been a conscientious objector during the
war and had for a long time been advocating some sort of industrial
partnership, set about forming a London Building Guild, and consulted
G.D.H. Cole and Richard Coppock. After a good deal of discussion,
agreement of a sort was reached and a National Building Guild came
into being, under whose auspices, it was afterwards admitted, some
excellent work was done. In imitation, some much smaller guilds were
formed in the furnishing trades and elsewhere; but their importance
was minor.

The executive committee of the NGL was hesitant about the building
guild, partly from doubts about its organisational ability, and partly
because the naked profiteering in the supply of building materials had
pushed the cost of housing schemes up to a point where their survival
became distinctly doubtful. The NGL felt unable to repudiate so public
an attempt to put its own recommendations into practice; but its
support was half-hearted, and its leaders were not surprised when the
economy drive of 1921 onwards resulted in the ending of the government grant. The guilds had no other resources available; the CWS made
no attempt to provide any; and the whole experiment came to an
inglorious end by 1923, with much mutual recrimination on the blame
for the fiasco — and for any almost inevitable mistakes in the running
of the contracts.[5] One of the causes of the failure, undoubtedly, was
that it was started so late in the day.

II

It is the general belief that Black Friday (15 April 1921) marked the
end of the period of labour 'inflation' and the beginning of a new
period of repression. This, though certainly a picturesque view, is in
fact much too simplified. In the early autumn of 1920, the post-war

inflation 'bubble' began to collapse, as the immediate war-time deficiencies were partly made good and investors came gradually to realise that their hopes of immense profits were myths. Prices broke, and employment fell. In December 1920, the numbers out of work were 858,000, rising by the following January to almost a million and a quarter; and the hastily-cobbled Insurance Act of November 1920, which extended contributory insurance to cover the great bulk of the wage-earning population, provided benefits which compared very poorly with the incomes that had been earned by those who had work, and could only be paid for fifteen weeks in any one year – after which the Poor Law was the only resource left. The condition of the recipients was not made any easier by the frequent shifts in government policy on insurance benefits; at one time growing and evident misery induced an authorisation to pay out additional small allowances for dependants; at another an additional period of payment not covered by insurance contributions was granted. This was called 'uncovenanted benefit', but it was limited to sixteen weeks, after which came the hated 'gap' of five weeks, during which no benefit whatever could be drawn. So hesitant and inadequate were these early steps towards the welfare state.

Naturally, this state of things was bitterly resented by the unemployed, and demonstrations and hunger marches became part of the landscape from October 1920 onwards – the police often interfering to break them up, not always without bloodshed. But neither the trade unions nor Labour MPs did much about it. The unemployed had no trade union, and many of the MPs were elderly trade unionists who saw no compelling reason to trouble themselves with non-union men, even if they had had any practical remedies to suggest. So it was left to the Communist shop steward, Wal Hannington, to organise from 1921 the National Unemployed Workers' Committee Movement – whose political complexion caused it to be anathematised by the Trades Union Congress. Nevertheless, the government was sufficiently alarmed by the unemployed and by the miners' strike described below to pass in October 1920 the Emergency Powers Act, which enabled the government to proclaim a state of emergency, renewable month by month, under which very drastic regulations could be imposed by Orders in Council sanctioned by a (presumably) frightened and subservient House of Commons. This Act was put rapidly through all its stages, while the Miners' Federation was preparing to strike over a complicated wage dispute, and had called upon its partners in the Triple Alliance. Their reaction being sympathetic but lukewarm, the miners struck alone in October, and after nearly three weeks returned to work on a settlement which satisfied very few of them. The government, having previously refused to implement the recommendation of Sankey and six other members of the Royal Commission to nationalise the industry, made up its mind to rid itself of its war-time responsibilities which the rapid fall in the selling price of coal had rendered very costly; and in February 1921, rejecting a proposal put forward by the MFGB providing for a national financial pool in order to preserve minimum standards for the poorer colliery districts, it announced in the King's Speech that government control would end at the end of March instead of the previously fixed date of 31 August, adding that only a modest subvention out of national funds would be available to ease the transition. It was then disclosed what rates the coalowners were planning to pay after control ended. These showed enormous reductions in the rates presently existing — over 40 per cent, for example, in the big district of South Wales, and the Miners' Federation promptly rejected them, only to be faced with a general lock-out. They at once called upon the Triple Alliance for support.

The Triple Industrial Alliance — of miners, railwaymen and transport workers — had been suggested in the euphoric atmosphere of 1913, and had come into shadowy existence two years later. But in order for it to become an effective bargaining and fighting force it would have been necessary for the partners to arrange for all their wage agreements to terminate at the same time; and that was never done or even attempted. Another serious weakness lay in the organisation of the partners themselves; the National Union of Railwaymen, the fruit of a 1913 amalgamation, had competitors within the industry, and the Transport Workers' Federation was not a union at all, but a loose grouping of unions of very different size and character. Consequently, though the NUR and the TWF passed resolutions of support, the attitude of their own membership was at least doubtful; and when, on 14 April 1921 Frank Hodges, the miners' secretary, gave to a meeting in the House of Commons an address which seemed to carry a suggestion that his executive might be willing to discuss some form of compromise, both railwaymen and transport workers changed their minds, and next day, J.H. Thomas of the NUR announced publicly that there would be no sympathetic strike. The locked-out miners kept on with their struggle until the beginning of July, when a vote of their membership sent them back to work at wages which in some cases were only about half what they had been getting in March.

15 April 1921 was Black Friday. It was reckoned, by the whole labour movement, as an appalling defeat, and by a great many as a

shameful betrayal. The *Daily Herald* — which raised a large fund for money to help the miners — called it 'the heaviest defeat that has befallen the Labour movement within the memory of man', and the cartoonist Will Hope drew in *The Communist* a furious picture of 'The Cripple Alliance'. Many of the workers prevented by their executives from striking felt a sense of shame — a fact which certainly influenced events five years later. Inevitably, in the economic circumstances, the defeat led to more defeats. Wages on all sides were seriously lowered — though not without resistance; trade union membership, and conse-quently monies in the hands of the TUC and the Labour Party (and even of the co-operative movement) fell heavily; the *Daily Herald* got into great difficulties and in November 1922 had to be taken over by the TUC and the Labour Party. But all was not servility. In 1922 the engineering employers, having defeated their workers in a long fight, thought it worth their while to include in the settlement a definite repudiation by the Amalgamated Engineering Union of any claim to 'interfere in management' — which plainly shows that the spirit of workers' control was not yet dead. There was considerable resistance — some of it successful — to the 'Geddes Axe' economy proposals of February 1922; and at the end of July 1921 the members of Poplar Borough Council (where Lansbury's son Edgar was mayor) having refused, in the interests of their poor ratepayers, to bankrupt the Council by paying over the large precepts demanded by the London County Council and the Metropolitan Asylums Board, marched in pro-cession with band playing and banner flying, to defend themselves in the High Court. They lost their case; and in September were duly con-signed to Holloway and Brixton prisons — where the prison officers found them an uncomfortable liability. But they refused to give in and before long secured a 'rate equalisation' concession for the whole of London. (An attempt made in the following year to make the Poplar Guardians cut their relief rates met with no greater success; the indi-vidual Guardians were surcharged, refused to pay, and the surcharges were never enforced.[6]) Finally, in the autumn of 1922 the Conserva-tives in the Cabinet decided they had had enough of Lloyd George, threw him out of the Cabinet, and broke up the national coalition; in the subsequent election Labour, turning to politics where industrial action had failed, startled the country by getting 142 members elected to Parliament; there are many living today who can recollect their emotions when the Clyde went Red. These Reds, on the motion of Emanuel Shinwell, made an early impression by rejecting J.R. Clynes, a nice but weak man, for the leadership in favour of Ramsay MacDonald,

whom they knew to be a competent administrator and mistakenly
assumed to be a champion of the left; in the election called by Baldwin
in 1923 the Labour Party came back 191 strong, and their new leader,
with the support of the Liberals, became Prime Minister.

III

Although the Labour Government decided against attempting to introduce any definitely socialist legislation (which would certainly have
resulted in its being immediately turned out), there is a good deal to
be said for it, during the first few months at all events. The most
important contribution was made by John Wheatley, Minister of
Health; he stopped the vendetta against the Poplar councillors, and his
Housing Act did much to remedy the damage caused by the abandonment of Addison's Act. The new government tried to make a start on
remedies for unemployment; it abolished the 'gap', and eased many of
the regulations: and C.P. Trevelyan, as President of the Board of Education, introduced a number of minor reforms. The trade unions, which
were not now feeling revolutionary, were pleased with these and other
small reforms; and a slight improvement in the economic situation
helped to make their members less restive.

MacDonald, certainly, was anxious to prove Labour 'fit to govern' in
more senses than one; a sentiment demonstrated by his insistence that
his ministers should wear court dress, by his inclusion in his Cabinet of
distinguished persons who were not definitely Labour (e.g. Haldane,
Parmoor and Chelmsford — all peers, be it noted), and of his liking for
'society ladies' who produced fascinating guesses about his father: all
this meticulously noted by Beatrice Webb, even while her husband
firmly told her that Mac was the only possible leader, since Arthur
Henderson, with loyalty always ill-rewarded, steadily refused to stand
against him. MacDonald's main interest was in foreign affairs; and in
that field he could be credited, at least in part, with getting the French
out of the Ruhr, making a little more sense out of the reparations
problem by the Dawes Plan, working closely with Herriot when the
latter succeeded Poincaré, and taking at any rate some steps towards an
Anglo-Russian accord and a loan for the USSR. It may be doubted, in
view of his later behaviour, whether he was much of a supporter of the
loan which was, in the event, the main real cause of his fall. This fall,
however, was triggered off by two pieces of blatant idiocy — the prose-
cution of J.R. Campbell, editor of the Communist *Workers' Weekly*,
and its withdrawal, which gave Asquith the opportunity to turn the
government out; and MacDonald's behaviour over the 'Zinoviev letter',

which helped to lose the subsequent election. His colleagues, notably Philip Snowden, the Chancellor of the Exchequer, were aghast at his behaviour; but in retrospect it appears to have done him little harm with the bulk of his party. They swung over immediately, it is true, to industrial radicalism; but after the catastrophe of the General Strike they returned to politics, and to MacDonald as their leader and premier in 1929 — 'a magnificent substitute for a leader', as Beatrice Webb called him.

IV

Several contributing causes led to the General Strike. Perhaps the most important was the action of the Chancellor of the Exchequer, Winston Churchill, in returning Britain to the gold standard in 1925 at the pre-war parity, which was fiercely criticised by Keynes among others; this immediately affected wages and prices, encouraged employers (particularly the coalowners) to look forward to further reductions in wages and the unions to resistance. Second, undoubtedly, was the widespread feeling that the defeat of Black Friday had not been inevitable but brought about partly by cowardice and treachery, and that the labour movement was strong enough to try another round; this happened to coincide with the emergence of several vigorous union leaders, notably A.A. Purcell of the furnishing trades, A.B. Swales of the AEU, George Hicks of the Building Trades Operatives and Arthur Cook, the fiery new secretary of the Miners' Federation. Fred Bramley, secretary of the TUC, died in 1925, but not before the General Council had set about establishing a joint committee with the All-Russian Council of Trade Unions. The third factor was the ILP, now working on a programme called 'Socialism in Our Time' and busy quarrelling with MacDonald; and the group centred round George Lansbury, who had left the *Daily Herald* in 1925 and started his own left-wing journal, *Lansbury's Labour Weekly*. Most of the best known of the *Herald's* writers, including Gerald Gould, W.N. Ewer, G.D.H. Cole and Raymond Postgate, contributed to it. Ellen Wilkinson provided a lively and incisive commentary on Parliament: the paper flourished until the Communists started a *Sunday Worker* which ate badly into its sales; in 1927 it was forced to amalgamate with the *New Leader*, now edited by James Maxton. Lansbury was only partially consoled by being elected chairman of the Labour Party in 1928.

The radical newspaper cartoons of the Australian David Low also helped to form opinion; but what really triggered the whole thing off was the hasty attempt by the mineowners, in the summer of 1925, to force drastic wage cuts on their employees. The Miners' Federation indignantly refused to accept, and called upon their comrades to help. They appealed to the TUC and its constituent unions; and the upshot was that Baldwin realised that if the miners went on strike, after the end of July no coal, whatever its source, would be delivered anywhere, and no transport would run. The government was not prepared to cope with strikes on such a scale; and Baldwin hurriedly announced that a subvention would be paid in order to keep the pits working without wage cuts, while a Royal Commission chaired by Sir Herbert Samuel and including William Beveridge met to consider what could be done about the crisis. 'Red Friday!' cried the Labour leaders in triumph — and then sat back and did as nearly as possible nothing whatever. This was not for want of urging — Walter Citrine, who had come from Liverpool to take over Bramley's job, was one who urged his fellows not to be so supine; but he was then a little-known man, and until his reminiscences were published in 1964, none of the public was aware that that very efficient administrator had even tried.

Nearly everyone knew, though, about the preparations that the government were making. They laid in stocks of coal; they revived the Emergency Powers Act; they invited voluntary help in case there should be a strike, and encouraged the voluntary Organisation for the Maintenance of Supplies; they appointed regional commissioners to oversee the supply of necessities; and well before the period of the subsidy had expired they sent a circular round the local authorities telling them of their plans. Then everyone awaited the report of the Samuel Commission.

That report appeared in March 1926. It turned down general nationalisation and the continuance of any subsidy; but it admitted that the organisation of the industry left much to be desired, and suggested that during a period of discussion mining wages should suffer some reduction, and that the costs of the industry should be considerably reduced. Both sides promptly rejected the proposals of the report. The miners produced the slogan 'Not a penny off the pay, not a minute on the day'. The mineowners, believing that they were in a good position and had government sympathy, delayed making any further offer until the very end of April, when the first lock-out notices had begun to operate, and the Privy Council had already declared a state of emergency under the Emergency Powers Act. Their offer included wage cuts and provisions for a longer working day.

The Privy Council's decision was published in the press on May Day, when a huge conference of trade union executives was meeting in the

London Memorial Hall (scene of the foundation of the Labour Party a quarter of a century earlier), and was awaiting a report from the TUC's Industrial Committee. When the report came, containing the General Council's proposals for co-ordinated union action in support of the miners, it was accepted by delegates representing nearly three and three-quarter millions, while the opposition, consisting mainly of the representatives of Havelock Wilson's National Sailors' and Firemen's Union, amounted to less than fifty thousand. (It must, however, be remembered that, as J.H. Thomas never tired of telling people, any 'sympathetic' strike fell heavily upon workers in the transport trades who were expected to prevent supplies from reaching the establishments involved. It is possible that a recognition of this fact was partly responsible for the decision to call out immediately the iron and steel and metal workers, and those in the chemical and building trades, in order that railwaymen, busmen and dock workers might not feel too much alone.)

The strike — 'the purely industrial struggle', as J.H. Thomas called it — began on the morning of Tuesday, 4 May, and it turned out to be far more complete than the General Council had ever anticipated — or indeed desired.[7] In centre after centre 'all-out' was reported; and local committees, sometimes based on the trades councils, sometimes formed *ad hoc*, took over and ran the whole business, including the issue of permits for the carrying of foodstuffs and hospital necessities, so efficiently as to amaze all observers. There was a good deal of co-operation with the police in the keeping of order; and though there were some clashes, and a good few arrests, there were no deaths and no real fighting; it was an amazingly peaceful demonstration for what the government — and Churchill's *British Gazette* — persistently called 'an organised attempt to starve the people and wreck the State'.

In Eccleston Square the strike leaders, even with Ernest Bevin to direct them, were confused and frightened. By their own action they had deprived themselves of newspaper support — even the *Daily Herald* printers had come out — and they did not trust their own despatch riders (on motor cycles with reports of complete stoppages); they relied more on the very heavily slanted reports in the *British Gazette*, with which the hurriedly improvised TUC paper, the *British Worker*, never caught up. Lloyd George was sympathetic, but Asquith, now Lord Oxford, was strongly hostile, and the British Broadcasting Company, whose chief, John Reith, feared for its independence, took in general the government line. Its most hostile act was to deny to the Archbishop of Canterbury, Randall Davidson, the opportunity to broadcast his proposals for peace negotiations.

Accordingly, when the TUC leaders were faced with a declaration by Sir John Simon — later reinforced by Mr Justice Astbury — to the effect that the strike was unconstitutional and illegal, they were shaken into considering giving in; and when Sir Herbert Samuel, recalled from holiday, drew up a Memorandum and presented it to them (without guarantees of government acceptance) they decided that the time had come to end the strike. The miners refused to budge; but on 12 May a deputation from the TUC (including Thomas and Bevin) went to Downing Street to discuss terms. On being informed that only absolute surrender would be acceptable, they gave way, and called the strike off. All over the country the local committees, many of whom had believed they were winning, were astounded; and when reinstatement was refused, or very harsh conditions imposed on strikers turning up for work, there was a second 'no victimisation' strike which, although it had practically no publicity, was nearly as widespread and a good deal more successful than the General Strike had been. Nevertheless, it was all over — except for the miners. They stayed out, with some small exceptions, until November, when, exhausted, they went back to work, practically on the coalowners' (not the government's) terms. It must be admitted that once Baldwin, 'the man of peace', as he liked to describe himself, had yielded to his own fire-eaters, the miners had really no chance of success. What remained was the aftermath.

It was a very serious defeat. But, interestingly, it did not have so shattering an effect on the membership of the labour movement as had Black Friday. When the Trades Union Congress met in the autumn, there were no such cries of 'treachery' as there had been five years before. The movement turned its attention to achieving political power, its left-thinking element pursuing the policy known as 'Socialism in Our Time' or 'The Living Wage', which had been worked out by a group of ILP members in the years before the strike and had been endorsed by the ILP conference at Easter, 1926. Before that the policy had been rejected by MacDonald, who called the proposals 'millstones for mere show round the neck of the Movement'. In anger at his attitude the National Administrative Council of the ILP had sacked MacDonald in 1925 from the editorship of the *Socialist Review*, thereby coming nearer to the inevitable breach with the Labour Party.

The cost of the strike was heavy. The miners, beaten to their knees, had to submit to the loss of the seven-hour day and the national minimum wage, for both of which they had struggled so hard. Direct government punishment was inflicted by the Trade Disputes and Trade

Union Act of 1927, with its severe restrictions on industrial and political activity. The unions in general were disposed to come to terms with the employers' associations, as was shown most clearly by the Mond-Turner discussions of 1927-8. Between them the employer Alfred Mond and the trade unionist Ben Turner worked out a report, made public in 1928, which revived the ideas of the Whitley Report and the Industrial Conference of 1919 regarding industrial relations. The proposals received some considerable press attention for a while, but nothing really came of them; their impact, in any event, was reduced by the issue, also in 1928, of the violent anti-collaborationist statement known as the Cook-Maxton Manifesto, after its signatories.

For the rest, the decade following the Armistice strikes the present-day historian as one of much emotional unreality. By the end of the war, the fierce anti-war sentiments expressed by some of the war poets and in prose by books like Barbusse's *Le Feu*, Duhamel's *Vie des Martyres*, and Siegfried Sassoon's novels had died down, not to be revived until *Journey's End* and *All Quiet on the Western Front* appeared in the late 1920s. The troubles of ex-officers reduced to touting vacuum cleaners from door to door or going up to universities with their younger brothers and cousins was temporarily highlighted in some of the novels of E.M. Delafield and Vera Brittain's once-praised *Testament of Youth*; but they were fairly quickly reabsorbed and what the bulk of the better-off wanted to do was to forget all about the war, and go off on a wild spree of hectic enjoyment. Any number of nostalgic biographies and autobiographies are extant, recreating for us the delights of that 'golden age' — all pulling a multi-coloured cover over the darker facts of the ruined towns. Even an undergraduate like Hugh Gaitskell, future leader of the Labour Party, on his own confession had to have his nose well rubbed in the issues of the General Strike before he realised what was going on in the world. And had not learned economists declared, as late as early 1929, that a depression was impossible in America because of its vast market?

V

The picture of the 1930s is a good deal simpler, if more horrid — and clearer in the recollection of those alive today. It began with the parliament of mid-1929, elected largely on promises made both by Labour and Liberals to deal properly with unemployment — the Liberals' promises, owing much to Keynes, were a good deal more specific than those of Labour, though unfortunately for them the leaders of the Liberals were still at odds with one another. Labour's general plans were more or less set out in a woolly pamphlet entitled *Labour and the Nation*, which in fact said little more than had been said eleven years earlier in *Labour and the New Social Order*. MacDonald would have been very unwilling to see it more precise; he had already been upset by the suggestion, coming from Bevin, from Wheatley, and from the ILP, that Labour should refuse to take office again without a clear majority. This, said MacDonald, would be regarded by the public as plain cowardice; and there is not much doubt that, in the summer of 1929, he was right. So, with Liberal support, the second Labour Government was formed; one or two half-hearted attempts to change the leadership came to nothing. The 1924 failure was widely held to be MacDonald's misfortune rather than his fault, and many still believed him to be a man of the left.

The Cabinet which he formed should have gone far to disabuse them. He dropped John Wheatley, who had been the main success of the 1924 government, and recruited George Lansbury to take his place as a left-winger. After a struggle, MacDonald allowed Arthur Henderson to have the Foreign Office, to which he had wanted to appoint — of all people — J.H. Thomas: failing that, he made Thomas Lord Privy Seal, charged him among other things with the task of doing something about unemployment, and appointed to assist him a team consisting of Lansbury, Thomas Johnston and Oswald Mosley, who had left the Conservatives during the time of the first Labour Government and was now MP for Smethwick in the West Midlands and in close touch with the ILP — a more unsuitable team could scarcely have been found. Philip Snowden was again put at the Exchequer, where he pleased the more insular of his countrymen and seriously displeased a number of representatives of other countries, by taking an intransigent attitude at the Hague conference and securing a larger share of reparation money for Britain: Sidney Webb, elevated to the peerage (though Beatrice always refused to use the title and hoped he would drop it after he was out of office, which he did not do), was put in charge of the Colonies and Dominions. According to Beatrice Webb's calculation there were seventeen members of the manual working class in the government as a whole — 'a poor lot!' she told her diary — and nine (including Sidney, Snowden and MacDonald himself) from 'the lower middle class', as against fourteen who came from the aristocracy and the 'old governing class' combined. The mixture was much as it had been five years before: it was unfortunate, however, that Margaret Bondfield, the first woman to sit in the Cabinet, was so much in the hands of the least progressive of civil servants as to earn for her government a good deal of unpopularity among the unemployed and those who were concerned with their condition. Sidney Webb, Lord Passfield, was another Cabinet minister who suffered from overmuch trust in 'expert officials'.[8]

For' a while, after that summer election, it looked as though the future might be favourable. The Kellogg Anti-War Pact had been drawn up the year before and signed by the representatives of fifteen nations for a start; Mussolini — whom few people in Britain other than Bernard Shaw took seriously — had been pushed by League of Nations influence out of Corfu. Stresemann in Germany, and Briand in France, seemed to be ready to co-operate in the pursuit of peace; Henderson was pressing his Foreign Office officials in the direction of a disarmament conference; the Young Plan for reparations, fractionally more practical than the Dawes Plan, appeared to be replacing it; and the world in general looked more prosperous and happy. So the new Labour Government could start cheerfully upon a programme of moderate social reform — not socialism, to which the fraction of the Liberals who supported them would never have agreed. It was some little while before portions of their programme such as the repeal of the Trade Disputes and Trade Union Act, the reorganisation of the coal industry, and the raising of the school-leaving age, tangled with unfriendly forces — sometimes, though not invariably, in the House of Lords — and had to be dropped or postponed.

But the sunny weather did not last long. In the autumn of 1929 the American price boom broke, and some Americans in panic took back the funds they had invested in European enterprises. This produced financial disasters in Central Europe, of which the failure of the Austrian Credit Anstadt bank was perhaps the most spectacular; and British bankers and investors found their investments becoming rapidly almost valueless. The September crash of Clarence Hatry was the most spectacular British collapse. The price of primary products fell heavily, leaving the producing countries with hardly any funds with which to purchase British manufactures; and the figures of unemployed, already distressingly high, reached two and a half million by December 1930. For a party which had made so much during the election of its intention to conquer unemployment these were not comforting figures.

So discontent began to grow rapidly. In February, 1930, before the government had been in office a year, Sir Oswald Mosley produced a scheme known as the Mosley Memorandum for solving the unemployment question. This scheme, which had the general support of Lansbury and Johnston, suggested *inter alia* public control of imports and of banking, a 'rationalisation' of industry, and a generous increase in pensions and other allowances, in order to increase purchasing power in the country; when it came before the Cabinet, the fierce opposition of Snowden, the dogmatic free-trader and champion of the gold standard, ensured its rejection. Mosley then resigned from the government though not from the Labour Party; but the battle was joined again at the party conference in October, when the Doncaster divisional party moved for a full enquiry into the Mosley proposals and the motion came very near to being accepted. Mosley was voted on to the National Executive Committee, and J.H. Thomas thrown off. It was evident that Mosley's proposals enjoyed a great deal of sympathy in the Labour Party at large; but being in a hurry (and possibly also aiming at the leadership) he misjudged the mood of the Labour Members of Parliament and produced, in February 1931, a pamphlet entitled *A National Policy*, said to have been drafted in collaboration with seventeen MPs. When the policy of the pamphlet was rejected by the parliamentary party, Mosley announced that he was leaving the Labour Party and founding a new party; four Labour MPs, one being his wife, and one Irish Unionist, joined him. He was set now to form the Fascist movement, though not before an unexpected by-election in Ashton-under-Lyne had enabled a new party candidate to split the vote and let the Conservative win; it is hardly surprising that Mosley was expelled from the Labour Party.

VI

Discontent with the government, having once begun, grew quickly. The most vocal element in it was the ILP which, under Maxton's chairmanship, was moving rapidly to the point of severance from the Labour Party. The main element of contention was the claim of the ILP to have a policy of its own, separate from and sometimes at variance with the established policies of the Labour Party. Neither then nor thereafter had the Labour Party any intention of permitting 'double allegiance'; but its leaders did not make things easier by initiating, in February 1930, a campaign to ban all organisations of which it disapproved, on the principal ground that each and all of them afforded a door through which Communists could enter the party in order to capture it for their own propaganda and policies. Some of these, such as the National Unemployed Workers' Movement and the National Minority Movement (whose purpose was to infiltrate trade unions) were in fact largely controlled by Communists or their 'fellow travellers' — a state of things due mainly to the unimaginative attitude of the Labour Party itself; but others, such as the League Against Imperialism, were nothing of the kind, and towards the end of 1930 a movement got under way the purpose of which was to force the party to live up to its own professed objects rather than to promote a rival programme.

This was the Society for Socialist Inquiry and Propaganda (SSIP) which came into being as a result of a lunch-time discussion during a conference of the Tutors' Association (the body which organised tutors in adult education) by H.L. Beales, Margaret Cole and R.S. Lambert. These three, being much distressed at the growth of unemployment and the passivity of the government, approached G.D.H. Cole, who was then Reader in Economics at Oxford and a Fellow of University College there – as well as being a member of the Economic Advisory Council which MacDonald had set up earlier in the year,[9] but to whose advice he paid little or no attention – and suggested that something ought to be done. Cole secured the support of Ernest Bevin, one of his colleagues on the Economic Advisory Council, and the permission of Lady Warwick to allow Easton Lodge to be used as a venue for early discussions. Accordingly, in the late autumn three weekend gatherings were held at Easton Lodge, to discuss what might be done to ginger up the Labour Party – Francis Meynell, one of those attending, coined the name 'loyal grousers' to describe the nature and purpose of the group. It was a pretty good sample of leaders from the left who turned up. They included ex-writers on the *Daily Herald* such as Lansbury, Meynell and Raymond Postgate; Stafford Cripps and Clement Attlee of the official Labour Party; quondam guild socialists like William Mellor, Ellen Wilkinson and W.H. Thompson, solicitor and conscientious objector; nearly all the young Oxford socialists who had formed the university General Strike committee (many of whom were to hold office in the third Labour government); ILPers like Brailsford and Leslie Plummer; of adult educators Tawney and E.S. Cartwright, the organiser of the Oxford Tutorial Classes Committee; and W.R. Blair of the Co-operative Wholesale Society, whose death in the following year was a real disaster. All these were recruited, not as representatives, but by personal appeal; but the great catch was the trade unionists, Arthur Pugh and above all Ernest Bevin. Bevin was the shining light; his grasp of matters economic and financial amazed the young university men, and when formal discussions were over he practically held court, telling anecdotes of 'The Movement' to an admiring audience. When, at the third gathering, those present decided unanimously to set up a society for the study and promotion of socialism in detail, everybody was delighted to learn that Bevin had agreed to be its chairman.

The SSIP was formally founded in the following summer, at a

conference in the Transport Workers' hall, secured for the occasion by
Bevin. Even before that it had done a good deal of work in arranging
lectures and discussion forums and publishing pamphlets and study
guides, many of both having been written by its vice-chairman. And in
March of 1931 Cole, with the blessing of Arthur Henderson and the
Webbs, had formed another body, the New Fabian Research Bureau,
with Attlee as chairman. The purpose of the NFRB was to do vital
policy research which the Fabian Society itself, growing elderly and
inert under a lethargic secretary, was failing to do, and which the
Labour Party had not got around to doing; and the most active of the
remaining Fabians came in and worked hard for the new body. Kingsley
Martin, who almost simultaneously succeeded the worn-out Clifford
Sharp as editor of the *New Statesman*, also joined the group. E.A.
Radice, one of the young Oxford socialists, was paid secretary to both
SSIP and NFRB in their beginnings; he was succeeded in 1933 by
John Parker, later MP for Dagenham.

SSIP, however, died; it was perhaps too small and too personal an
organisation to survive. But what brought it to an end was not that
fact, but the actions of the ILP. By early 1932, after the heavy electoral defeat of the Labour Party (see below), the ILP had moved
rapidly towards a breach with the official leaders, mainly because of
its determination to insist upon a policy and 'pledge' of its own, and
its opposition to the Labour Party's standing orders. After a good deal
of abortive discussion between Henderson and Maxton, in July 1932
an ILP conference decided by a majority to disaffiliate; but a good slice
of the membership, led by E.F. Wise, an ex-civil servant with much
experience of international trade, felt that this decision would be fatal
and refused to accept it. Cole wished to enrol the dissenters in SSIP;
but before that could happen the ex-ILP members came forward with a
proposition for combining both groups into a new Socialist League —
the title recalling William Morris. As a good few of SSIP's governing
body were themselves also members of the ILP, they carried the day
over the opposition of Cole, who was in bad health at the time. Much
more serious was the insistence of the newcomers that Wise and not
Bevin, should be chairman of the new League; Bevin, though he made
no public disclaimer, was very angry, holding the opinion that both he
himself and the trade union movement which he believed he represented, had been grossly insulted: it confirmed his conviction, based partly
on his experience with Mosley and MacDonald, that 'intellectuals' were
persons who stabbed honest working-class leaders in the back. Although
Frank Wise, whose actions had caused the immediate trouble, died in

1933, leaving the leadership of the Socialist League to Stafford Cripps, Bevin never modified his views: he refused to have anything to do with the New Fabian Research Bureau, and the attitude of the most forceful and in some respects most able mind among the trade unionists was not without influence in the years to come. Cripps, whose tactical judgement was never his strongest point, led the League on a course similar to that which had broken the ILP and finally got it, and later himself and some of his colleagues including Aneurin Bevan, expelled from the Labour Party. It should be noted, if only briefly, that in 1930 the Trades Union Congress, having failed to get the *Daily Herald* on its financial feet, enlisted the help of Odhams Press. The managing director of Odhams was J.S. Elias; he reorganised the paper so as to make it competitive in appeal with cheap dailies like the *Daily Express* and the *Daily Mail*, and within a very short time succeeded both in boosting the circulation to one and soon to two million copies, and disposing of the left-wing editor, William Mellor.

Before the Socialist League was actually formed, the 'Great Betrayal' had taken place. The economic situation went from bad to worse; wage cuts were made and social services reduced; Margaret Bondfield, the Minister of Labour, introduced the hated Anomalies Bill, worsening the conditions of relief for the unemployed; and Snowden, at the Exchequer, refused every attempt to modify his free-trade assumptions. 'No one', said Lord Passfield after Britain had gone off the gold standard late in 1931, 'No one ever told *us* we could do that!' In the spring of 1931 Snowden set up the May Committee, whose report was published in early August; it painted an extremely gloomy picture of the British economy, proclaiming to the world outside that Britain was on the verge of bankruptcy. This impression was heightened by the book by André Siegfried, a French journalist-economist, called *England's Crisis*, which had come out in the spring and was widely read; foreign investors began to call back their money and gold reserves drained away fast. The government did nothing more than set up a small Economy Committee of MacDonald, Snowden, Thomas, Henderson and William Graham, on which committee Snowden pressed for cut after cut, while he and his Prime Minister were going to and fro, consulting bankers English and American, and the leaders of the other parties, in the hope of finding some way out of the mess. At long last, after having consented to a great many cuts, a large minority of the Cabinet jibbed at reducing the pittances paid to the unemployed; the objectors were influenced by the determination of the TUC, whose spokesmen during discussion were Bevin and Citrine, to give no support to cuts of this kind. Parliament was in recess: MacDonald, called back from holiday in Scotland, told the meeting of the Cabinet on 23 August that the economies which as a whole they were prepared to make were not sufficient to restore the confidence of the financial powers, and that he must therefore present to the King the resignations of himself and his ministers. Next day he returned to tell them that he was now head of a national government including, besides himself, Snowden, Thomas and Lord Sankey, and the leaders of the Tory and Liberal Parties — except Lloyd George, who was ill. Anyone who cared to join him would be welcome. He hardly, it was said, seemed to expect that many would; and in fact, apart from the ministers he had mentioned and his own son Malcolm, only about a dozen out of nearly three hundred Labour MPs went with him. It was understood that the King had thought it best that he should continue as premier, and that Baldwin had agreed to serve under him — which he did until 1935.

For financial stability the new regime was formed too late: in September, before the new government had had time to do more than call Parliament together to ratify its formation, and to pass a hasty budget of Snowden's, a fresh draw on sterling had forced the abandonment of the gold standard. Only a little later, at the beginning of October, the Conservative element in the government insisted on a General Election, MacDonald having previously undertaken that nothing resembling a 'coupon' election would be held. The election took place on 27 October; and the ex-Labour ministers — whether or not prompted by an instinct to cover up their own breach of faith — vied with Liberal and Tory speakers in abusing the Labour Party and trying to terrify the electorate. MacDonald appeared on platforms waving a worthless German million-mark note; and Walter Runciman declared that a Labour government would raid the Post Office Savings Bank in order to finance its schemes — a statement which Snowden, who knew it was not true, never contradicted in any way. The 'national' government did not fight on any positive programme; it asked for a blanket 'doctor's mandate' to do whatever should prove necessary — and received it abundantly.

Even *The Times* thought the election results 'astounding'. In the atmosphere of panic, voters (including of course millions of working-class voters) poured out to the polling stations to save their country. Labour membership of the Commons was reduced from 289 to 46 — to which might possibly be added Maxton with two others fighting as ILP candidates, and three more who were standing as independents of the left. The 'nationals' had a majority of 497, of whom seventy were

Liberals of one sort or another and only thirteen National Labour supporters of MacDonald. Among the opposition Lansbury was the only member of the late Cabinet to keep his seat, and among minor ministers there were only Attlee and Stafford Cripps. Lloyd George, with three of his relatives, made a small addition to the opposition ranks.

The election results were of course a disaster for Labour, though the figures rather exaggerate it. The majorities, seen in terms of votes for individuals, were large; but Labour, though losing two million overall, retained a solid faithful lump of over six millions. Those who defected to 'national' candidates were reacting to the propaganda about disaster, and to the incontestable fact that the dissentient ministers had not put forward any positive programme of their own for conquering unemployment; but they were not registering any fundamental disagreement with their own party. The proof of this can be seen in the fact that it was MacDonald's photograph which was turned to the wall, or destroyed, in hundreds of local Labour Party rooms; that the Labour Party conference of 1932 set itself to try to rebuild a real Labour programme; and, more significant, that Labour in local government underwent no such disaster. There was certainly some quite considerable immediate loss; but by 1933 this had been completely made good, and in 1934 Herbert Morrison led the Labour Party to a spectacular victory on the LCC, giving Labour a control which it never lost until the LCC was destroyed — a control buttressed by victory in fifteen of the metropolitan borough councils. These victories showed that there was a vigorous and consistent Labour force in the country at large, which had found in MacDonald and his small coterie a convenient scapegoat for its own shortcomings in political and economic thought.

VII

To those who lived and worked through them, the 1930s were a confusing and a distressing time. In retrospect, however, the pattern becomes simple. The most important element was undoubtedly the gradually increasing menace of the Nazis and the slow conviction of the British people, and even slower conviction of the pacifist labour movement, that the menace could not be stopped without employing physical and even military force. The difficulties in the way of this recognition were certainly formidable. The massive attack in works of fiction upon war conditions had got going with a good deal of publicity at the end of the previous decade, and it was reinforced, as the years went on, by detached 'horror' investigations and reports of what technological advances might be expected to produce in the future – books like *The Merchants of Death*, and *What Would be the Character of a New War*, and above all H.G. Wells's terrifying, and, as it proved, erroneous nightmare of the future in *The Shape of Things To Come* – later made into a film. The effect of these (doubtless well-meant) efforts was to make ordinary people terrified of what might happen to them and their families if war came again; and they were not soothed by Wells's vision, in *The Shape of Things to Come*, of a civilisation preserved by public-spirited aviators. Fear combined confusingly with a fairly widespread belief among those influenced by Keynes that the Germans had been very harshly treated by the victors, particularly by Clemenceau and Poincaré, in the Versailles Treaty and in the years following. Many felt guilty, and were quite ready to believe that Germany deserved to be readmitted to the consensus of nations and to be relieved of some of the penalties imposed upon her. I can well remember coming into the offices of the Socialist League at the beginning of 1933, staggered by the announcement that Adolf Hitler had become Chancellor of the Reich, and meeting only expressions of boredom and remarks like, 'Well, what about it? He's not as bad as von Schleicher, is he?'

The pacifist mood was clearly shown in February, 1933, by the highly publicised action of the Oxford Union, which on the motion of Frank Hardie declared by a large majority that 'this House will under no circumstances fight for King and Country'; and still more definitely in the following October, when John Wilmot won the East Fulham by-election by nearly 5,000 votes over a Tory candidate who was pilloried as a war-monger. This mood was shaken in 1934 when, after Dollfuss had crushed the Austrian Socialists, Hitler in the 'night of the long knives' had caused Roehm and other of his close associates to be murdered. People began to feel that real physical force would be needed to stop the Nazis but they still tended to alibi themselves with the words 'collective security'. At the end of the year the famous Peace Ballot was taken under the auspices of the League of Nations Union. In June 1935, just after the government had made a naval agreement with Germany, the result of the ballot was declared. Over eleven and a half millions declared themselves adherents of the League and only slightly fewer numbers voted in favour of reduction of armaments by international agreement and the prohibition of private armament manufacture: more significantly, nearly seven millions of those questioned said that if one nation attacked another, military measures should be used to make it stop. It is possible that not all of those who voted in the ballot realised its implications; but it is perfectly clear, if the resolutions are taken together, that Britain had committed itself to actual fighting. And at the Labour Party conference at the beginning of October the trade unions drove the lesson home.

At this famous conference Hugh Dalton moved for the executive that the party pledge itself to support aggression against Abyssinia. After the debate had gone on for some time Lansbury, the leader who had done very well in deploying his meagre forces in Parliament, rose and declared that as a Christian and disciple of one who had said that 'those who take the sword shall perish by the sword' he could not support the resolution. His patently sincere eloquence emotionally moved his audience until Ernest Bevin, moving ponderously to the rostrum, delivered a reply of calculated malevolence, in which he said that Lansbury was being dishonest, that it was not capitalism but the trade union movement that was being wiped out, and that Lansbury should be ashamed to take his conscience round from meeting to meeting asking to be told what to do with it.[10] Lansbury endeavoured to reply, but got no further support, and was defeated by over two million votes to 100,000. In great distress, he resigned the leadership; and in two weeks the government, headed by Baldwin, called a General Election. The Labour Party won just over 100 additional seats, Lansbury being returned by an immense majority, and MacDonald was rejected in Sidney Webb's former seat; but the Conservatives still had a fully adequate majority of MPs. Clement Attlee was then elected to the leadership – not a particularly easy task.

For, though the conference had in effect voted for rearmament, not all, even of the majority, were happy about it. A general vote was all very well; but when it came to particular implementation the case was different. For one thing, the whole tradition of the party was against conscription, which in the First World War had been introduced only by breaking more than one official promise *not* to introduce it: it was not in fact accepted by Labour this time until war had all but broken out. The Peace Pledge Union, initiated in October 1934 by Canon Dick Sheppard, a year later had getting on for 100,000 members, all personally pledged never to support or sanction another war. Secondly, the political complexion of the government being what it was, many socialists felt no confidence that if rearmament were voted and the guns and planes and fighting ships were built, when the day of reckoning came and the guns were fired, they would be trained in the right direction – against the dictatorships and not against the working people of other countries. But it is not practicable to turn a rearmament programme off and on like a tap, and the Labour Party, unsophisticated almost to the last, came reluctantly to realise this before Chamberlain had given way to Churchill.

Another problem facing the party leadership was what to do about Russia. The Soviet revolution had been heartily welcomed by both left and centre politicians in the middle classes, including the intelligentsia, and by almost all of the manual workers. Right into the mid-thirties, and especially after the disappointments of the second Labour Government, individuals and groups kept going to visit the Soviet Union and coming back appreciative of what they had found there. The most influential of these, of course, were Sidney and Beatrice Webb who went to Russia in the summer of 1932 and were welcomed, as Sidney said, like 'a kind of minor royalty'. Before they left England, G.D.H. Cole had prophesied that they would like what they found; and when parts of Beatrice's diary were published they proved him to be perfectly correct. Her support of the Soviet Union was not shaken — at least, not openly — by the purges and the trials of the generals, nor even by the Nazi-Soviet Pact signed just before the war, followed by the Russo-Finnish war and the Russian occupation of the states on its western border — all of which very much disturbed the faith of her fellow intellectuals — and she lived long enough to hear the news of the surrender of von Paulus at Stalingrad. But it should be remembered that the rank and file of the movement largely shared the Webbs' view. As one trade unionist said to me, when the Pact was signed, 'Well, I suppose Stalin had got to look after the interests of his own people'. This did not, however, make them love the British Communist Party any better — particularly not when, at the behest of the Comintern, their leaders including, eventually, Harry Pollitt had to eat their earlier words and declare the war to be a sordid imperialist venture.

This enthusiasm for the Soviets derived from the conviction that there was no hope for the people of the Western countries while capitalism endured. So the second main characteristic of the 1930s was a much increased consciousness of the physical miseries of poverty and unemployment, and recurrent attempts, not merely by the left but by many 'persons of goodwill' to do something about it. One of the best sellers of the time was Walter Greenwood's *Love on the Dole*; and again and again there appeared accounts, some factual and some in the guise of fiction, about life in the depressed areas, with up to 60 and even 70 per cent out of work, in contrast to the new light industries that were growing up to the south and east of them. Ellen Wilkinson's portrait of Jarrow, *The Town That Was Murdered*, caught the imagination, and the hunger marchers from Jarrow and other desperate places were often fed and sheltered (despite the hostility of the Labour Party and TUC leadership) in the towns through which they passed. The thoroughly respectable Pilgrim Trust, founded in 1930, published a carefully-researched study of *Men Without Work*; Sir John Boyd Orr gave to conferences meticulous analysis of the miserably poor meals which could be bought with the money paid weekly to the unemployed; poets like W.H. Auden, Stephen Spender and Cecil Day Lewis joined in the outcry. Even the Prince of Wales expressed sympathy with the condition of the miners of South Wales; a fact which might have produced more Labour support for him at the time of the Abdication if Winston Churchill and the Fascist Party had not declared so loudly in his favour. In general, there was visible a strong leftward tendency in the printed word. Allen Lane started the sixpenny Penguin books in 1935, and the Pelicans two years later; in 1936 Victor Gollancz founded the Left Book Club, which was responsible for a great number of cheap books selected by a committee consisting of Harold Laski, John Strachey and Gollancz himself. Sidney Elliott turned the Sunday paper *Reynolds' News* over to a vigorous critical policy; 1937 saw the foundation of the weekly *Tribune* by Stafford Cripps and G.R. Strauss MP, and of the monthly booklet *Fact*, edited by Raymond Postgate. It is slightly ironical that after the worst of the depression the economic condition of the working class, *taken as a whole*, was rising slightly, owing largely to the rise of new industries and the ruin of the primary producers in other countries; but this had little effect on the standard of living in the depressed areas. The strong feeling that something drastic ought to be done about poverty was nevertheless very evident, and resulted in the formation of a whole succession of 'ginger' groupings, including the 'Friday Group' formed originally to discuss the causes of the 1931 debacle, the Next Five Years Group whose chief supporters were Sir Arthur Salter and Harold Macmillan MP, but which included also trade unionists of standing like Arthur Pugh of the iron and steel workers and John Bromley of the National Union of Railwaymen; and the various Unity and Popular Front movements: these, however, were all rendered ineffective by the solid impenetrability of the Conservative and Labour Parties and the permanent split among the Liberals. The Labour Party was looking forward to winning the next election by its own efforts, and would consider nothing else; and even had its leaders been rather more forthcoming, the fierce disagreements in the ranks of the protesting groups would probably have ensured their failure.

In the midst of this confusion, while Mussolini had just driven Haile Selassie into exile under the cover of the Hoare-Laval agreement and

Hitler had marched unchecked into the Rhineland, and not long after MacDonald had yielded place to Baldwin, Francisco Franco flew from the Canary Islands to Morocco in a British plane provided under the auspices of an English sympathiser, and from Morocco crossed to Spain in order to pull rebels in various cities together into a right-wing rebellion against the Spanish republican government. Immediately there appeared to be once more a clear-cut moral issue: a nephew of mine, born in 1922, when I asked him many years after what had been the most memorable event of his youth, replied at once, 'The Spanish Civil War — *Then* we knew what was Right and what was Left, and that Right was Wrong.' The bulk of the membership of the British labour movement was firmly anti-Franco; visitors from republican Spain were cheered to the echo at Labour conferences, forcing the party's executive committee to adopt a more positive line; refugee children from the Basque country were adopted by British hosts; an International Brigade of volunteers for the Spanish war was formed and eagerly joined by individuals from the working and middle classes, some of whom died in battle, as British martyrs in the republican-socialist cause; and the bombing of Guernica brought in masses of small contributions for the republicans.

But, as everyone knows, the effort was fruitless. The British government adhered to the farce of 'non-intervention', under which phrase the German and Italian governments cloaked the continuous supply of war materials to Franco, and piratically sank ships bringing goods — even potatoes! — to republican ports. Léon Blum, the Popular Front premier of France, felt his government too shaky to intervene effectively, thus inducing caution in the actions of his British opposite numbers. The civil war continued for longer than had been expected; but in March of 1939, Madrid at last fell, and the refugees began pouring over the mountains to the refugee camps in the south of France. Only a month earlier, Neville Chamberlain, who had succeeded Baldwin in May 1937, had recognised Franco's government: a year before, Hitler had annexed Austria, and at Munich a little later, with the concurrence of the French and the British, had dismembered Czechoslovakia, sending Chamberlain back home bearing (as he said) 'Peace in our Time.' It was not true, and by midsummer of 1939, when the futile guarantee to Poland had been given, and a fairly bogus attempt made to reach an understanding with Soviet Russia, the British Labour Party at last followed the TUC in realising what was happening, and on 2 September, in Attlee's absence through illness, Arthur Greenwood in Parliament 'spoke for England'.

Class divisions in Britain remained deeply ingrained, but Labour, despite its muddlings and missed opportunities, had emerged as one of the two main parties. Had unemployment and the rise of fascism been tackled with more determination and vigour, and had Bevin been won over to the more progressive side of the movement, the history of the inter-war period would have been a very different and a much happier affair.

Notes

1. For Liverpool, see R.J. Holton, 'Syndicalism and Labour on Merseyside' in H. Hikins (ed.), *Building the Union* (Liverpool, 1973) and for a general discussion Standish Meacham, ' "The Sense of an Impending Clash": English Working-class Unrest before the First World War' in *American Historical Review*, vol. 77 (1972).

2. Margaret Cole, *Growing Up into Revolution* (1949), pp. 58 ff.

3. Raymond Postgate in *How to Make a Revolution* (1934) gives details of Communist tactics in one organisation, the Labour Research Department; for the trade unions, see R. Martin, *Communism and the British Trade Unions: A Study of the National Minority Movement* (Oxford, 1969).

4. 'The Homeland of Mystery' has never been published, but see Cole, *Growing Up into Revolution*, pp. 93 ff, 118.

5. Frank Matthews, 'The Building Guilds' in Asa Briggs and John Saville (eds.), *Essays in Labour History 1886-1923* (1971); G.D.H. Cole, *A Century of Co-operation* (Manchester, [1945]), ch. 17.

6. Raymond Postgate, *The Life of George Lansbury* (1951), ch. 16.

7. See the account of the strike given by G.D.H. Cole in his previously unpublished operetta, 'The Striker Stricken' (1926) in Asa Briggs and John Saville (eds.), *Essays in Labour History 1918-1939* (1977), pp. 57-101.

8. See Drummond Shiels, 'Sidney Webb as a Minister', in Margaret Cole (ed.), *The Webbs and their Work* (1949), pp. 201-18.

9. On paper, the Economic Advisory Council was very impressive. MacDonald took the chair, and among its members were Hubert Henderson, Colin Clark, Keynes, Tawney, Cole, Sir Josiah Stamp, Bevin, Citrine and several businessmen. It was scheduled to meet monthly; but nothing came of its discussions. See G.D.H. Cole, *A History of the Labour Party from 1914* (1948), pp. 231, 236.

10. Francis Williams, *Ernest Bevin* (1952), pp. 193-4; Alan Bullock, *The Life and Times of Ernest Bevin*, vol. 1 (1960) p. 568.

11 SOCIALISM AND THE LABOUR PARTY: THE LABOUR LEFT AND DOMESTIC POLICY, 1945-1950

David Rubinstein

Many contemporaries hoped or feared that the Labour Government of 1945, the first supported by a majority in the House of Commons, would create a socialist society. Labour Party leaders often claimed to be bringing about a peaceful social revolution, a term much in use at the time.[1] Immediately after the government's election King George VI had to give a resolute assurance to the enquiring American president, Harry Truman, that revolutions were not a British institution.[2] The Keep Left group of MPs, on the other hand, asserted in May 1947 that a revolution was exactly what the nation had voted for in 1945.[3] Yet already disillusionment had begun to set in. 'Sagittarius', the *New Statesman and Nation's* penetrating satirist, concluded in the same year:

> The Revolution's wave has passed its peak —
> It only lasted for Election Week.[4]

Soon after the government's fall, its period of office could be seen in perspective not as the beginning of a socialist Britain, but as the end of a long struggle to establish the framework of the welfare state.[5] In this field, as with full employment, its success was striking. There was, however, no hint of either socialism or social revolution in the sense of a significant shift in power relations between social classes, let alone the abolition of classes.[6] In the government's emphasis on social welfare rather than socialism can be seen the extent of the failure of the Labour left between 1945 and 1950.

I

The failure cannot be attributed to lack of left-wing pressure. Constant demands were made, in Parliament, in the socialist press, by the constituency Labour parties and at the annual party conference, for the Labour Party's declared aim of bringing about a socialist commonwealth in Britain to be pursued more vigorously.

One target of socialist critics was the government's social policy, despite its efforts in this field. As early as 12 October 1945 Sydney

Silverman sponsored a motion in the House of Commons calling, in defiance of government policy, for an immediate increase in old age pensions. His motion attracted the signatures of nearly 170 Labour backbenchers.[7] The next month a Labour rebellion in a parliamentary standing committee resulted in a government defeat over its attempt to delay the payment of benefit for industrial injury until the fourth day of injury.[8] On 23 May 1946 Silverman moved an amendment to delete a clause of the National Insurance Bill which limited unemployment benefit as of right to 180 days. Barbara Castle, Jennie Lee and S.O. Davies were among the MPs who joined the attack, claiming that under the bill long-term unemployment was in effect blamed on the unemployed and that the clause was 'a furtive effort' to reintroduce a means test. In a division, thirty-two Labour members voted against the government. W.G. Cove, a former teacher, led a campaign in Parliament and at the Labour Party conference in opposition to the educational policies of Ellen Wilkinson, the Minister of Education, whose hostility to the comprehensive school he called 'a danger to the whole Labour movement'.[9]

There was also much concern within the party over economic and financial policy and a planned economy. Socialist planning was at the centre of the demands made in *Keep Left*, the manifesto signed by fifteen MPs led by Richard Crossman, Michael Foot and Ian Mikardo. Maurice Webb and Barbara Castle were two of the MPs most insistent that the housewife should be protected by delaying or abandoning the 'bonfire of controls' begun by Harold Wilson at the Board of Trade in the autumn of 1948. The bonfire, Webb warned the party conference in 1949, could well become 'the funeral pyre of social justice'.[10] In the House of Commons during the economic crisis of 1947 a number of MPs demanded that sacrifices be shared equally by all social classes, urging the need for higher taxes on profits, control of dividends and the introduction of a capital levy. They condemned the availability of luxury goods at a time of cuts in the rate of construction of new houses and factories.[11] The provision of hotels, expensive shops and fashionable restaurants, Harold Lever claimed on 24 October, had reached 'positively gigantic proportions'. In February 1948 the publication of a White Paper on incomes and prices enunciating a doctrine of severe wage restraint resulted in a letter to the Prime Minister from sixty Labour MPs calling for limitation of profits. This was accompanied by a parliamentary motion led by Ellis Smith and signed by twenty-one MPs, repudiating the White Paper and urging restraint of prices and profits rather than wages.[12]

Many backbench MPs were involved between 1946 and 1948 in a campaign to force the nationalisation of iron and steel upon a government many of whose members were by no means enthusiastic on the issue. At an agitated meeting of the parliamentary party on 11 August 1947 the demand to expedite nationalisation was backed by a petition signed by nearly 150 backbenchers.[13] Outside Parliament *Tribune* was heavily involved with the campaign for steel nationalisation, pointing out in an unsigned article on 8 August 1947 that the issue at stake was nothing less than the control of the economy by capitalists or the government.

Criticism of the government's financial and taxation policy as unfair to the working class, favourable to profits and dividends and hostile to economic equality, reached a climax when Sir Stafford Cripps's budget speech in April 1949 announced reduced food subsidies, foreshadowed charges on the National Health Service and asserted that there was little possibility of redistributing income in the immediate future by increasing taxation. Richard Acland, Ronald Chamberlain, Mark Hewitson, James Hudson, Emrys Hughes, Kenneth Robinson, Thomas Scollan, Ellis Smith and George Wigg were among the outspoken critics of the budget, their attacks reflecting opposition to the whole trend of economic policy rather than to one financial measure alone. Smith, who made consistent demands throughout this Parliament for planning and a comprehensive economic strategy, declared on 7 April: 'We have no Socialist drive or vision of the end we want to achieve, or how to reach it.' The deepest impression was made (also on 7 April) by Hewitson, a trade union leader and a member of the Labour Party's National Executive Committee, who threatened a fight against the Labour Government 'as we have fought in the past against Tories and Tory employers'. Like the backbenchers, many constituency parties reacted angrily and vigorously to the budget. So many letters were sent to party headquarters at Transport House that a special 'budget reply' had to be prepared. One strongly worded letter came from the secretary-agent of the Coventry Borough Labour Party, George Hodgkinson, who wrote that the assumptions of the budget proposals had driven many of the keenest party workers to cease party activity: 'There is a feeling that Sir Stafford Cripps is going the way of Ramsay MacDonald, and in the Budget has shown more patriotism than socialism.'[14]

Another focus for criticism of the government was the failure of nationalisation of industry to act as an instrument of socialism. Sixteen resolutions for the party conference of 1948 and eighteen more in 1949 dealt with democratic control of nationalised industries, supporting workers' participation and the inclusion of more socialists on the boards, and opposing the high salaries paid to board members.[15] When the party policy statement *Labour Believes in Britain* was in draft early in 1949, one of the criticisms made at the Policy and Publicity Committee was that 'the spiritual results of nationalisation' had been less beneficial than had been hoped. At the same period meetings of area groups of MPs with the party chairman, James Griffiths, and the secretary, Morgan Phillips, produced a number of complaints about nationalisation. These involved unacceptable appointments to the boards, the lack of industrial democracy, and the higher prices which, it was alleged, immediately followed measures of nationalisation.[16]

Few if any other subjects aroused such repeated and agonised debates at the party conferences. The demand for more democratic control of publicly owned industry was raised by spokesmen of two leading trade unions, Jim Figgins of the National Union of Railwaymen and Robert Openshaw of the Amalgamated Engineering Union, but the case for giving the workers a major share in the control of the nationalised industries was voiced with even greater feeling by some of the rank and file. One such was Bob Shaw, a goods guard from Nottingham, who told the 1949 conference that the promised new spirit had failed to materialise on the nationalised railways. Frustration had not diminished but increased. The old managers had retained control and the industry was saddled with heavy compensation payments. Shaw's solution was to 'place the workers in control of these railways'. His outburst received a measure of statistical support from a survey undertaken by the NUR journal, the *Railway Review* at the end of 1948, which showed that 45 per cent of the 485 railwaymen who replied to a questionnaire felt that their jobs were virtually unchanged, while another 45 per cent felt that frustration had increased after a year of nationalisation. Fewer than 15 per cent of respondents thought that they had a share in running the railways.[17]

Although the National Union of Mineworkers did not advocate workers' control of their industry, it was clear that dissatisfaction among miners and others was not removed by the transfer of the mines to public ownership. Harold Davies MP wryly told the Labour Party conference in 1948: 'In the mining industry there is the National Coal Board. It has been said that the difference between the National Coal Board and Old King Cole is that Old King Cole knew how many fiddlers he had!' In May 1949 a Fabian research study of twelve coalfields showed that only three of the eighty-eight respondents thought that miners were adequately consulted, while fifty-nine thought that they were never consulted.[18] Dissatisfaction with the fruits of nationalisation was a contributory factor in a number of unofficial miners' strikes during this period.[19] The *New Statesman*, which took a special interest in the problems of nationalisation, commented on 8 May 1948 that the miners felt no sense of change under public ownership and, on 28 August 1948, that the public boards seemed to many workers to resemble such large firms as Levers or ICI: 'The Boards are remote from the ordinary worker, and the representatives of management with whom he comes into direct contact are nearly all the same persons as before.'[20] The paper's prescription, voiced on 4 March 1950, was by that date a common demand within the labour movement: 'to socialise the nationalised industries'.

The government had maintained the heavy taxes on income imposed during the war, but it was urged by some of its followers to extend its attack on inequality to capital and property as well as income. A perceptive article by Ivor Moresby in *Tribune* on 12 April 1946 pointed out that income distribution remained heavily unequal, and would be blatantly revealed as such when the war-time burden of taxation was reduced. Nationalisation, he continued, should be undertaken not only for reasons of industrial efficiency but in order to reduce 'exploitation and speculation . . . We have now had heavy progressive taxation and death duties for a generation, and yet the distribution of wealth is much the same as before . . . Property begets more property.' At the Labour Party conference of 1950 Roy Jenkins MP, then a contributor to *Tribune*, took a similar line, arguing that 'we have hardly yet scratched the surface of the problem' of inequality of property, which had changed little since 1939. Death duties were too slow and 'a capital levy . . . would be very much quicker'. Like Moresby, Jenkins thought that one of the keys to greater economic and social equality lay in the nationalisation of industry. Theirs were not isolated voices, and a number of MPs and the *New Statesman* joined in the demand for, in particular, a capital levy.[21] But in general the need to bring about equality of property was not pressed as strongly between 1945 and 1950 as were other issues.

A demand frequently heard both in the socialist press and within the party itself was for increased vigour in pursuing socialist goals, for 'more Socialism — not less'.[22] Maurice Webb, chairman of the Parliamentary Labour Party and a widely respected centre figure in the party, wrote in *Tribune* on 23 January 1948: 'The plain truth is we are not yet within miles of Socialism . . . All we have done so far is to make

Socialism *possible*.' Shortly afterwards Ian Mikardo MP wrote in similar vein in a Fabian research pamphlet, asserting that the government's industrial record was no more than 'the very first step in the transition to Socialism'.[23] The case for a faster advance towards socialism was also advocated by Harold Laski, a leading socialist intellectual who was a member of the Labour Party's National Executive Committee. Laski's weekly articles in the Scottish socialist journal *Forward* were concerned above all with foreign affairs, but he wrote occasional articles on domestic policy, including a series at the time of the economic crisis in 1947, when he urged the need for 'a thoroughgoing application of Socialist principles'.[24] A similar line was taken by *Forward*'s editor, Morgan Thomson, who was later, as George Thomson, to move into different fields as minister, Common Market bureaucrat and peer. In an article on 5 February 1949, during the course of a Scottish visit by Herbert Morrison, Thomson attacked as inadequate the policy of 'consolidation' of existing measures of nationalisation which Morrison had been urging since the Labour Party conference of 1948, rather than undertaking new measures of public ownership. Thomson wrote aggressively that there was room in the country for only one Conservative Party, and that the Labour Party, 'pledged to create a Socialist society', had still 'a long way to go . . . Any dalliance with the idea of pausing a while and making the best of things as they are will only endanger the Movement as it did in 1931.'

G.D.H. Cole, like Laski one of Labour's leading intellectuals, made a trenchant attack in the *Political Quarterly* for July-September 1949 on the policy statement *Labour Believes in Britain*, which was heavy with consolidationist assumptions. Cole feared that the party leadership had abandoned its belief in socialism and replaced it by belief in the mixed economy. What sort of Britain should Labour believe in? he asked. 'Surely in a socialist Britain.' In a Fabian tract discussing the policy statement he sharply distinguished between real socialism and 'Keynesian Liberalism, sometimes masquerading as Socialism'.[25]

The demands for 'more socialism' were reflected in resolutions placed on the agenda for the party conference, calling for a faster 'passage to full Socialism', 'an economy that is predominantly Socialist' and 'a plan for the complete Socialisation of our Economy during the 1950 Parliament'. After the election reverse in 1950 many more such resolutions were submitted.[26] The nature of the party conference was such that most of the delegates' time was taken up in discussing specific issues rather than socialism as an abstract principle. However, several delegates were able to argue the case for a basic reconstruction of policy.

In 1948 Hugh Lawson, a war-time MP for the independent Common Wealth Party and later Labour candidate for Rushcliffe and King's Lynn, proclaimed his faith in public ownership for reasons of social justice rather than economic efficiency. The government, he said, was moving too slowly, not too fast. In 1950 William Carter, the delegate from Merton and Morden, told the conference that the 'light of a great joy' which shone in 1945 with the election of a socialist government had faded over the past few years. The pugnacious Harry Ratner of Salford East, a shop steward in an engineering works, pointed out to the same conference that 80 per cent of the economy remained in capitalist hands, charged the party leadership with being more concerned with accommodating Labour's enemies than with 'a genuine socialist programme', and demanded nationalisation of all basic industries.

This sketch of the criticisms and demands voiced by the Labour left cannot begin to do justice to the quantity of such demands, nor to the knowledge and passion with which they were made. But it can at least suggest that pride in the government's record and anxiety about its enemies by no means prevented the existence of an articulate left. A primary problem lay in organising the widespread feelings of dissatisfaction which existed within the party. Ian Mikardo pointed out in an article in *Tribune* on 12 September 1947 the dilemma of the left-wing minority in both the Labour Party and the trade unions: 'If they get together and organise they are condemned as sectarian and as a threat to the solidarity of the Movement, and are thereby crushed, and if they remain informal and unorganised they are outmanoeuvred and picked off one at a time.'

It was not until late in 1948 that the Labour left began to organise itself. In December there appeared the first number of *Socialist Outlook*, a monthly journal which aimed to mobilise the left within the Labour Party, and which from the start was tinged with Trotskyism. Among MPs associated with the paper were Tom Braddock, who wrote a monthly column which was sharply — and sometimes vituperatively — critical of the party leaders, Ronald Chamberlain, who also wrote regularly, Harold Davies, H.L. Austin, Stephen Swingler and Bessie Braddock (unrelated to Tom). Among the rank and file both Bob Shaw and Harry Ratner were frequent contributors.

The movement for an organised left was signally strengthened by an article by Ellis Smith in the co-operative/socialist weekly paper *Reynolds News* on 22 May 1949. Smith wrote that since 1945 apathy and disillusionment had grown up within the Labour Party. He had decided to form a national organisation of socialists based on local branches, inspired by the spirit of socialist pioneering days and the ILP in the period before it left the Labour Party in 1932. His decision, he added, was the result of requests from all over the country. Smith, a skilled engineer who almost alone among the active left wingers of this Parliament was of working-class background, expressed pride in the achievements of the Labour Government, but urged that it should be doing more to improve working and living standards and to move towards socialism.

His initiative was welcomed in a leading article in *Forward* on 28 May, and followed by a meeting held during the Labour Party conference at Blackpool in early June which attracted an audience of over 150 people. In the summer of 1949 the Socialist Fellowship was formed, and local groups were soon established in three parts of London, Reading, Luton, Nottingham, Manchester, Liverpool and Sheffield. The first annual conference was held in London on 27 November, with one hundred delegates from twenty-nine places. Smith was elected president, Tom Braddock and Ronald Chamberlain vice-presidents, and among the members of the committee was Fenner Brockway, who had recently left the ILP to rejoin the Labour Party. The Fellowship aimed, as Brockway pointed out, to work within the Labour Party rather than outside it, and its programme included increased public ownership, workers' control of industry, heavier taxation of the wealthy and a more equal distribution of income, reduced compensation to the former shareholders of the nationalised industries, greater efficiency in industry and improved social services.[27]

The Socialist Fellowship had a willing mouthpiece though not an official organ in *Socialist Outlook*; the paper gave, for example, its front page in November 1949 to an article by Ellis Smith, who made such characteristic demands as a planned economy and a capital levy. But despite its promising start the Fellowship soon fell apart. Braddock and Chamberlain lost their seats in the election of 1950, and after the outbreak of the Korean War in June, Smith and Brockway resigned when the Fellowship's national committee passed a resolution condemning American and British intervention in Korea as 'imperialist aggression'. When the second national conference of the Fellowship was held in September 1950 no MPs were elected to the committee and only Tom Braddock, the new president, remained as a parliamentary veteran. In 1951 the Labour Party conference proscribed the Socialist Fellowship, thus bringing to an end the one organisation which had attempted in these years to move the party to the left from within its ranks.[28]

II

It is likely that without the consistent pressure of the Labour left the government would have taken even fewer steps towards socialism than it did. The eventual decision to go ahead with the nationalisation of steel is the most obvious example, and the Cabinet minutes for 1947 contain numerous references to backbench opinion on the subject.[29] But there were very few cases in which the government was forced to change its policy because of parliamentary pressure, and these few successes were due to the fact that the left was able to draw support from elsewhere in the party. The only considerable victory was in 1947, when party rebellion led to the reduction of the planned term of conscription from eighteen to twelve months. There was nothing comparable on the home front, although there were small successes with social security and civil aviation bills in 1946.[30] The 170 old age pension rebels of 1945 were met with the firm Cabinet decision that 'the Motion . . . could not be accepted', and Herbert Morrison lectured the party, as one member wrote, like Wackford Squeers reprimanding his pupils.[31]

The behaviour of the socialist press was not subject to the direct control of the party leadership. However, there is no evidence that they were seriously disturbed by press criticism between 1945 and 1950 in the way they were to be after the outbreak of the Bevanite rebellion in 1951.[32] The size of the Labour majority and the fact that the criticism of the socialist press alternated with strong defence of the government against the Conservatives were the principal reasons for this sang-froid, perhaps augmented by the somewhat cynical consideration that journalistic activities kept the left of the party occupied with publications of limited circulation. The socialist press was much more influential than its circulation suggested, but Labour voters as a whole were largely untouched by such journals, which were more than balanced by the mass circulation of the loyal *Daily Herald*.

As for the party conference, the National Executive Committee was defeated on nine occasions between 1946 and 1950. The subjects were in some cases of considerable importance; two dealt with publicity, a third with agriculture, a fourth demanded a socialist education policy, two others urged the abolition of the tied cottage, a seventh called for equal pay for women in national and local government, and the final two related to food and clothing subsidies and distribution.[33] There was no indication, however, that the defeats actually changed government policy. Hugh Dalton recorded after the 1947 defeats (on tied cottages and equal pay): 'Neither of these are to be taken very seriously',[34] and *Tribune* wrote on 6 June that many conference delegates had spoken in similar terms.

In short, the Labour left between 1945 and 1950 was vociferous, but largely unorganised and unsuccessful. The remainder of this paper examines the reasons for its weakness.

III

We may begin again with the parliamentary party, nearly two-thirds of whom were newly elected in July 1945. They were a far more middle-class group than ever before, for less than half of the members now came from manual occupations.[35] It was the journalists, the lawyers, the lecturers and teachers who composed the bulk of the parliamentary rebels, including the signatories of *Keep Left*.[36] Their background and education tended to make them articulate and self-confident, but as middle-class members of a working-class party, new to Parliament and with often shallow roots in the labour movement, they reinforced the image held by many trade unionists, including some MPs, of 'unreliable intellectuals'.[37] The circumstances of the time also militated against successful opposition. Not only did the government have a programme of radical measures, but also it had been elected at a time of virtually unprecedented economic crisis. Its urgent priorities, above all the need for higher production and more exports, seemed to most ministers and to many backbenchers to require close co-operation between the government and private industry, and muddied the left-wing argument for socialist measures. Thus Herbert Morrison could declare to the Labour Party conference in 1947, without a sense of incongruity: 'In Britain today the battle for Socialism is the battle for production'. Moreover, Conservative opposition to the government was intense, both in Parliament and, even more important, in the press. It was natural for backbenchers to rally to the aid of their government when it was under heavy economic and political pressure.[38]

Members of Parliament who followed a left-wing line by no means shared a uniform ideology. Old left-right antagonisms had been largely dissolved in war-time, and a programme which united almost all the party had been provided by the 1945 election manifesto, *Let Us Face the Future*. The ILP critics of the 1920s had disappeared as a significant force. Marxist solutions had been fashionable in the 1930s, but seemed inappropriate in the changed conditions of the later 1940s. The war had changed social attitudes on both right and left. It had been followed by a Labour Government sustained by a large parliamentary majority, peacefully carrying out a programme of social reform and nationalisation. Full employment had been maintained in peace-time. These achievements led to a weakening of belief in class conflict and to the acceptance by the left of a gradualist approach to socialism which differed little in kind from that of most of the rest of the party.[39] The left's main function was now to urge the government to move faster than it was doing, rather than along a different road. This rather unsatisfactory ideological stance contributed to the failure of the left to evolve a formal organisation or a common programme. MPs would join in opposition to the leadership on particular issues on an *ad hoc* basis; with the partial and temporary exception of the Keep Left group, there was no tendency to propose an alternative strategy across the whole range of domestic policy. It was, for example, Stanley Evans, chairman of the PLP iron and steel committee, who in an interview with *Tribune* on 20 September 1946 denounced government vacillation over steel nationalisation, but in other respects Evans was an arch right winger, and under pressure from his local party was to resign his seat in 1956.

The Labour left lacked not only organisation and programme, but also leaders. The *New Statesman*'s parliamentary correspondent noted on 5 January 1946 the presence in the government of virtually every potential leader of rebellion, and Richard Crossman, one of the most important figures of the parliamentary centre left, wrote in the same paper on 15 June 1946 that among reformist ministers were to be found 'all the brilliant prophets of the inevitability of violence, Aneurin Bevan, Stafford Cripps, Ellen Wilkinson, Emanuel Shinwell and John Strachey'. It was not until the Bevanite movement of the early 1950s that a leader was found.[40]

Overshadowing all left-wing activities was the lowering tragedy of the Cold War, which progressively destroyed the ardent hopes of left speaking to left and a socialist Europe, substituting the reality of a foreign policy subordinate to the crusading anti-communism of the United States. In such circumstances it is not surprising that many backbenchers were diverted from the creation of socialist Britain to defence and foreign affairs. Attitudes towards foreign policy divided the parliamentary party far more sharply than domestic politics and also divided the left within itself. Large numbers of backbenchers were able to combine from time to time in opposition to Ernest Bevin's conduct of foreign affairs or the adoption of conscription, especially in the early years of the government, but as the Cold War became more bitter most of the centre left of the party, however reluctantly, chose the American side of the struggle. This acceptance of the American alliance and the stigma of 'fellow travelling' attached to the small far left group inevitably reduced the effectiveness of the campaign for 'more socialism' at home and helped to tilt the party balance to the right, not only because of opposition to Russia *per se*, but because the burden of rearmament and dependence upon economic aid from capitalist America were severe disincentives to further moves by the government to the left.[41] Crossman pointed out in the *New Statesman* on 8 January 1949 that the belief that 'left' meant support for Russia had destroyed effective left-wing criticism of the government and prevented the creation of a 'ginger group' within the party. Crossman himself was overwhelmed by Ernest Bevin's attack on the critics of the government's foreign policy at the Labour Party conference in 1947, an attack which played a major part in the disintegration of the Keep Left group.[42]

The Parliamentary Labour Party had no real power besides its theoretical ability to bring down the government, and its influence was very limited. Herbert Morrison, who was far more concerned with party organisation than any other leader, was largely responsible for the establishment of twenty party subject groups in 1945, and he urged his Cabinet colleagues to distribute and digest backbench opinion. But the Cabinet minutes for 1945, 1946 and 1947, the latest available at the time of writing, suggest that ministers were more concerned to control and restrict the expression of parliamentary opinion than to encourage it. It is not surprising that many backbenchers felt that the subject groups, and the regional groups which followed, were merely devices to keep them quiet. Meetings of the PLP itself could lead to storms, but the prestige of ministers, their unwillingness to accept changes in their policies and their appeals to loyalty were always able to carry the day.[43]

If Labour members did step out of line they found themselves confronted with a silken but highly effective discipline, wielded less in Parliament than outside it. The sanctions of the party's National Executive Committee were numerous and powerful and included expulsion, which was used against four foreign policy rebels in this Parliament and also against one right winger, whose dissent from party policy was concerned above all with the nationalisation of steel. The fact that so drastic a threat was held in reserve meant that discipline in the PLP itself could be deceptively lax, and a number of rebellions in the House of Commons, which only rarely attracted the support of an actual or near majority of backbenchers, could be tolerated.[44]

The party leaders could also afford a lax discipline because there was no group of rebels in the House of Commons which had ties with an outside organisation such as the ILP in the 1920s. Hugh Jenkins, later an MP and a minister, wrote to *Tribune* on 19 November 1948, after the collapse of the Keep Left group, saying: 'The body of opinion to support it was there in the Party, but little or no attempt was made to connect the head to the tail. Such an organism tends to be inherently inviable!'[45] It was not until late in the life of the government that Ellis Smith established the Socialist Fellowship, a body with too few influential figures and too far to the left to attract the support which Keep Left might have done. The constituency parties, in turn, which were frequently well to the left of MPs, had little or no control over parliamentary behaviour. A loyalist MP was usually able to go his own way without reference to the view of his local party.[46] Weaker in organisation than in sentiment, the left was thus unable, inside or outside Parliament, to mount an effective challenge to the party leaders.

Trade union leaders played an important role in the structure of the Labour Party organisation, in 1950 controlling five-sixths of the voting strength at the party conference. They were by no means monolithic in their support for the party leadership, for a number of important unions sat on or leaned to the left. None the less, the party executive could count on the votes of three of the four largest unions, the Transport and General Workers, the Mineworkers and the General and Municipal Workers, who between them controlled nearly two million of the six million conference votes.[47] Arthur Deakin of the transport workers and Will Lawther of the miners were solid and dependable figures, staunch allies of the parliamentary leaders in speech and vote. Trade unionists tended to prize loyalty far more than ideological consistency or fidelity to a particular line of policy. The 'labourist' character of the Labour Party meant that the election and maintenance of a Labour government, the culmination of decades of struggle, was an end in itself. Policy, on this view, should be left to the party leaders.[48] Ernest Bevin was thus able to draw on a powerful tradition when in his speech to the party conference in 1947 he accused the critics of his foreign policy of stabbing him in the back, adding that as a product of the trade union movement he was accustomed to the mutual loyalty of both leaders and rank and file.

But trade union solidarity could not have delivered an unwilling Labour Party membership into the hands of the party leadership. Most members of the party, it seems clear, were quite willing to be led. Year after year the party conference was a personal triumph for members of

the platform, as Hugh Dalton noted with satisfaction in his diary.[49]
To some extent harmony at the conferences was due to external
factors, Bournemouth in 1946 being commonly termed a victory
parade, while Scarborough in 1948 and Blackpool in 1949 were influenced by the approach of the next General Election. But left wingers
realised that there were more deep-rooted reasons for the party's docil-
ity. Harold Laski asserted in his *Forward* column of 31 May 1947 from
the Margate conference that delegates looked to the left more for inspiration than for a new policy, seeing in the Labour Government itself the
only alternative to the Conservatives. Writing in *Tribune* on 28 May
1948, after the Scarborough conference, Ian Mikardo reflected that the
failure of the conference to mount an effective challenge to the government arose both from the approach of the election and from a general
movement in the party to the right. Perhaps the most perceptive explanation was offered by Tom Gittins, chairman of the Spelthorne
(Middlesex) constituency Labour Party. Gittins, who was to be expelled
in 1950 for his hostility to the party's foreign policy, wrote in the
Communist *Labour Monthly* for July 1948 that the 'submissive' nature
of the Scarborough conference was due to the support of the unions
for measures of nationalisation and social reform, and also to the forthcoming election (which cast a long shadow). But the heart of his analysis lay in three succinct sentences: 'The British working-class movement
as yet lacks a sound scientific basis for its socialist thinking. It is more
liberal than Marxist. Its loyalty is in terms of persons rather than of
principles.'

The control of the party by its leaders owed much to its National
Executive Committee. Before 1948, only two of the twenty-seven-man
executive consistently took a left-wing line. These were Aneurin Bevan
and, until his retirement in 1949, Harold Laski. A shift in constituency
sentiment to the left is suggested by the election of Michael Foot in
1948, followed by Tom Driberg in 1949 and Ian Mikardo in 1950, but
the constituencies also repeatedly elected such orthodox leaders as
Hugh Dalton, James Griffiths and Herbert Morrison. Bevan, whose
freedom was limited by his membership of the government and Laski,
whose attendance at the policy subcommittee in particular was sporadic,
were useful to the right-wing NEC as left wingers who could wind up
debates by persuading reluctant delegates to give their backing to the
platform. Laski defended conscription in 1947 and persuaded delegates
to remit to the executive in 1948 a motion dealing with the revival of
fascist activities, while Bevan repeatedly appealed to the conference to
support the government, notably in an eloquent speech in 1949 in

which he defended the mixed economy and attacked critics of the administration of the nationalised industries.[50]

Between 1945 and 1950 there was a good deal of adverse comment about the NEC's domination of the party conference through composited resolutions, a tight control of proceedings which severely discriminated against speeches from the floor, and biased chairmanship. Even more attention was given to the government's control of the NEC. Much concern was expressed, notably in the pages of *Tribune*, about the failure of the party conference to play the primary role in determining policy.[51] Seven resolutions and amendments were placed on the conference agenda in 1948, urging that the NEC should carry out resolutions passed by the conference and deploring the fact that much of the conference time was taken up by speeches by party and government leaders. A motion from Herbert Morrison's East Lewisham constituency that conference resolutions should bind the government would have been added to the other demands had Morrison not descended upon the party and strangled the infant resolution before it could survive to the final conference agenda.[52] The most determined effort to shift the balance of power within the party was made by Nat Whine, chairman of the St Marylebone Labour Party and candidate for East Surrey in 1950 and 1951, who sought to reduce ministerial membership of the NEC and concentrate power in the conference. Whine's campaign culminated in a detailed memorandum dated November 1947 which the NEC discussed at length before rejecting it at their meeting on 25 February 1948.[53]

It has already been suggested that an important factor inhibiting rebellion in Parliament and criticism in the constituencies and at the annual conference was loyalty to the government and the party leadership, always a powerful influence in the Labour Party and especially strong between 1945 and 1950. One reason for this loyalty lay in the successes of the government, especially in its early years. Attlee told the Bournemouth 'victory' conference in 1946 that seventy-three bills had been introduced in less than a year, fifty-five of which had been passed.[54] Frank Allaun, then a socialist journalist and later a leader of the parliamentary left, asked in *Labour's Northern Voice* in July 1946 if any British government had achieved so much in one year, and *Tribune* wrote on 8 November that the government in its first session had done 'more revolutionary things to this country than the first three years after the 1917 Revolution did for Russia'. Even Willie Gallacher, one of the two Communist MPs, admitted in the *Labour Monthly* for August 1946 that the first year of the government had 'much to its credit'.

There is no doubt that, if viewed as an instrument of social reform rather than socialism, the Labour government had much to be proud of. Labour was, it rightly claimed in 1950, the party which kept its promises. Twenty per cent of industry was transferred to public ownership. The social security system was restructured and expanded, food was heavily subsidised and the National Health Service created. Above all else, peace-time full employment was maintained for the first time in modern history. These were achievements which impressed the whole party, especially its older members. Sam Watson, the Durham miner who was party chairman in 1950, told the conference that poverty had been abolished.[55] Herbert Bullock spoke to the same conference as the fraternal delegate of the TUC, recalling as a man of sixty-five who had started work at eleven that over half the boys at his school in Bristol had had no boots or stockings, and praising the 'revolutionary changes' brought about by the labour movement. The following year Nellie Cressall, a great-grandmother from Poplar and an old comrade-at-arms of Attlee, took the conference by storm, telling delegates:

> Years ago after the First World War many, many people in my constituency sat in the dark because they had not got a penny to put in the gas. Today what do I find? People come to me creating about the heavy electricity bills they have to pay! . . . I have young people coming worrying me for houses . . . We have got some houses where six families lived once upon a time . . . Whereas in the old days people would get married, as I did, and be contented in two nice little rooms, today our young people want a home of their own . . . I get very needled when I hear housewives complaining because they cannot get the best butter. In my day they never knew what it was. And did they get cow's milk? Not on your life! . . . Did they ever grumble about their meat then? No, because they only had meat once a week and that was Sunday dinner.

To such people Labour's claim to be bringing about a social revolution was self-evident truth.

Throughout the life of the government the redistribution of income brought about by the high level of progressive war-time taxation and largely maintained after the war[56] was hailed as a social revolution. Figures published by the government in April 1950 showed that the share of post-tax personal income going to wages had risen between 1938 and 1949 from 39 to 48 per cent, while the share of rent, dividends and interest had fallen from 34 to 25 per cent. Further figures published the following October showed that the number of people who enjoyed a post-tax income of over £6,000 a year had fallen from 6,560 in 1938-9 to 86 in 1948-9. ('The current joke at the time, among the faithless', John Saville has recalled, 'was that they all had lunch together every day at the Savoy.'[57]) During the same period the amount of income tax paid on an earned income of £50,000 increased from nearly £30,000 to nearly £45,000.[58] Roy Jenkins told the party conference in 1950 that the largest income after tax was still twenty-five times as great as the smallest, but the tax figures seemed a convincing reply to those who demanded 'more socialism'. They were used not only by party publicists and friendly journalists, but by such an independent-minded and deeply respected socialist as R.H. Tawney, who wrote in 1952 that changes in income distribution, together with nationalisation and the expansion of the social services, proved the success of gradualist socialism and that a socialist government could increase the power and raise the standard of living of the working class.[59]

IV

It is clear that the structure of the Labour Party inside and outside Parliament and the social reforms of the government gravely weakened the socialist elan of the Labour left between 1945 and 1950. Its weakness was reinforced by other factors which arose from the difficult economic and social conditions which prevailed in post-war Britain and the failure of the party to make socialists in sufficient numbers to attack capitalism at its roots. Hostility to shortages, restrictions and controls led many voters into apathy, cynicism or antagonism towards the Labour Party and its approach to socialism. There was also a widespread disillusionment with the fruits of public ownership and a marked indifference within the working class itself towards the democratic control of industry.

The left-wing demand for a greater sense of socialist urgency confronted the difficulty that the times were inauspicious once the immediate excitement of victories in war and election had worn off. Labour assumed office at a time when the nation was weary of war and the privations which accompanied it.[60] On 15 September 1945 the *New Statesman* remarked that the British people were tired, that they lacked the material possessions which had sustained them at the start of the war, 'and the moral sanctions of total war have gone. In their place the Government has so far produced nothing more compelling than the warning that a painful period of stern austerity lies ahead.' Sydney Silverman told the party conference in 1946 that there was in the country 'a spirit of cynicism, of pessimism, and of apathy', and the social scientist Eva Hubback wrote in 1948 that 'grumbling might almost be said to be one of our national pastimes'.[61] When Ivor Thomas, formerly a junior Labour Minister, resigned from the party late in 1948, he contrasted the slogans of the French Revolution of 1789 with 'the slogans of the Labour revolution', which, he said, 'appear to be utility, priority, austerity'. Thomas was anything but an unbiased observer, but his charges were typical of many attacks on the government and admitted as not unreasonable by at least one shrewd party supporter.[62] Freedom from austerity and controls was eagerly sought, and symbolised by the Conservative demand to 'set the people free'. Hugh Dalton reflected later: 'We proclaimed a just policy of "fair shares", but the complaint was not so much that shares were unfair, but that they were too small.'[63] A considerable part of the Conservative advance in the election of 1950 was due to public response to constant attacks on shortages, including the gross lack of adequate homes, and on rationing and bureaucracy.[64]

Controls were identified not only with shortages and the absence of consumer choice, but also with the unsavoury and unscrupulous black-marketeering and influence peddling which came to a much publicised climax with the revelations made to the Lynskey Tribunal at the end of 1948.[65] The stigma attached to controls was a particularly severe blow to the left. While everyone in the Labour Party believed in planning and controls of some kind, the right was increasingly content to plan through the budget and other fiscal means. Belief in physical controls of men and materials was a distinguishing mark of most of the left, and particularly of the Keep Left group.[66] The onslaught on controls in Press, Parliament and influential business circles led inevitably to government concessions. As early as November 1946 Attlee announced that the government was 'not in favour of controls for their own sake',[67] and by the time of the election in 1950 the 'bonfire' of controls was well under way. It was thus courageous of Richard Crossman but not politically practical to write in the *New Statesman* on 28 May 1949 that controls and rationing must remain as permanent weapons of socialist planning. Physical controls were also difficult to apply in that they involved planning wages as well as other aspects of the economy. This was a course highly unpopular with large numbers of trade unionists. At the Labour Party conference in 1947 Arthur Deakin, general secretary of the Transport and General Workers Union, said flatly of a wages policy: 'We will have none of that.' As *Tribune* noted on 6 June 1947, a rigorous wages policy would be likely to result in 'an unending series of unofficial strikes which might more than undo the good effects of such a policy'. Against the rocks of trade union opposition, socialist discussion of wages policy dashed endlessly but in vain.

A crucial section of the Labour vote in 1945 had come from the middle class. One opinion poll suggested that the proportion of the middle class who voted Labour declined by about a quarter between 1945 and 1950, and small shifts of opinion were of great importance in the 1950 election, in which the swing to the Conservatives was 3.3 per cent, but their gain in seats (greatly assisted by redistribution in 1948) was fully 40 per cent.[68] Morgan Phillips wrote in a confidential party memorandum after the election that one reason for the Labour reverse lay in the burden of taxation on salaried and professional groups, together with the desire for owner occupation in the suburbs, where the Conservative slogan 'let the builders build' found a ready response. Teachers in particular, Phillips noted, were also aggrieved by the level of their salaries.[69] *The Economist* published an influential series of articles during the election campaign of 1950, estimating that between 1938 and 1948 real wages after taxation had risen by 20 per cent, while salaries had declined by 17 per cent.[70] It seems probable that middle-class resentment of their apparently lower standard of living outweighed any element of working-class rallying to Labour in 1950, especially as younger working-class people tended to take full employment and the welfare state for granted.[71] And, as Herbert Morrison remarked in another confidential post-election memorandum, the middle class were not only numerous but influenced the attitudes of manual workers.[72]

For resentment of controls, austerity and taxation, while voiced especially strongly by middle-class voters, was by no means restricted to them. Even more disliked by the working class, despite relatively high post-war wages, were inadequate housing, a monotonous diet and a rising cost of living.[73] High prices were an obvious Conservative target, and many lower-paid workers in particular must have been tempted to abandon Labour by the unauthorised but vigorous campaign waged in the Beaverbrook press during the election for a minimum wage of £6 a week.[74] In the long term Labour supporters were promised the socialist commonwealth, but in the short term they faced constant appeals for higher production and harder work, symbolised in the un-attractive and unpopular government slogan 'work or want', first used early in 1947. Sagittarius pointed out:

> Trade Unionists will not unlease their powers
> When everything is shorter, but the hours.[75]

Her comment was amplified by an article by Henry Williams in the *New Statesman* on 6 September 1947 about workers in a factory making pre-fabricated houses. Williams informed his middle-class audience that factory workers did not read White Papers or, indeed, care about politics beyond casting their vote for Labour candidates. The nature of repetitive factory work was such as to deaden political consciousness in most cases. The motive for work was not the desire to raise production and bring closer a socialist society, but the desire to earn money. Other socialist writers pointed out that high production under capitalism depended upon fear of dismissal and unemployment. This sanction had been largely abolished under Labour without being replaced by a socialist motivation.[76] The problem was easier to diagnose than to solve.

The principal weapon by which the Labour left had hoped to bring about the transition from capitalism to socialism was public ownership, chiefly expressed through nationalising industry. Yet, as seen above, nothing was so clear by 1950 as the failure of nationalisation as an instrument of socialism. The result was a noticeable demoralisation of the whole party, not just the left. During the General Election campaign of 1950 nationalisation was one of the Conservatives' principal targets. Most leading Labour spokesmen seemed reluctant to defend the existing nationalised industries and even less eager to advocate more public ownership. Voters appear to have been more bored by the issue than actively hostile, but the caution displayed by most of the party leadership inevitably placed the left on the defensive.[77] It was difficult to argue a case for socialism without more public ownership, and highly undesirable to demand the creation of more bureaucratic nationalised industries. Thus Frank Allaun wrote in *Socialist Outlook* in March 1949: 'You can't have socialism *without* public ownership', but in March 1950 he argued in *Labour's Northern Voice* against making 'nationalisation of any industry the issue on which we fight the next election'. Opposing both Morrisonian 'consolidation' and nationalisation of industry on existing lines, also associated with Morrison, the left had to think out a new approach to public ownership, a task not easily accomplished.

Industrial democracy was a subject of constant discussion during these years, and steps towards its introduction were demanded in various parts of the labour movement. Yet such demands ran up against the hard fact that there seemed to be little desire on the part of workers themselves to run their industries. Such was the view of G.D.H. Cole, who had been a passionate and influential advocate of industrial democracy since before the First World War, and who remained after 1945 one of the most influential of socialist thinkers. In a Fabian research pamphlet of 1948 on the *National Coal Board* Cole wrote that the rank and file of the miners 'have at present no real wish to control the industry; they are aware that they have as yet neither the knowledge nor the attitude which would make this workable'. The next year, in a postscript to a Fabian tract by J.M. Chalmers of the postal workers (with a 'rejoinder' by Ian Mikardo) entitled *Consultation or Joint Management?*, Cole commented that there remained with the Labour Party and the TUC doubt and distrust about the feasibility of industry run by workers. Cole shared the doubt: 'The main body even of the active workers in the trade unions is not ready for the responsibility which sharing in management involves . . . Even the present opportunities for the development of joint consultation are not being properly used, because so few trade unionists know what they really want to make of them.' If the TUC reflected the views of its membership, Cole was correct in thinking that there was little demand among workers for a trade union share in the control of industry. The General Council insisted in its report for 1948 that trade unionists who served on the boards of nationalised industries would be placed in an embarrassing and unsatisfactory position of dual loyalty if they retained responsibility to their unions. The next year the Council reiterated its support for the public corporation form of administration without trade union participation, although it felt that 'there were problems of structure and administration which had not yet been solved'. This view was not challenged by Congress.[78]

As the government's term of office wore on a new tone became apparent among many socialists. In the dawn of 4 August 1945 the *New Statesman* had written: 'For the first time the popular vote demands Socialism'. By 12 March 1949 it had decided that electoral opinion was 'not yet ripe' for the conversion of Britain into a socialist country. Articulate voices on the left began to sound a retreat from previously accepted socialist principles, a retreat which paralleled the move to the right in the party as a whole.[79] Writers like Laski and Cole commented[80] that their hopes had been too high in 1945, that socialism could not be introduced faster than the electorate would accept and that the march to the socialist commonwealth would take longer than had been expected by the enthusiasts of 1945. What people had voted for in 1945, Cole remarked in the *Political Quarterly* for July-September 1949, was not socialism but better social services, less social inequality and full employment. Socialists argued that these benefits were unattainable under capitalism, but most Labour voters were unconvinced. His disappointment with the failure of nationalisation was accompanied by a reluctance to undertake further measures: 'No sensible Socialist', he wrote in 1948, 'wants to socialise, or to nationalise, industries merely for the sake of a theory, where public ownership is not necessary for the sake of efficiency or in order to secure conformity with the national economic interest.'[81] The *New Statesman*, in a comment on *Labour Believes in Britain* on 16 April 1949, found it 'Fabian, reasonable and seductive', and added: 'The picture presented is that of steady progress towards a Scandinavian type of Social-Democracy; and that is probably what most people in this country want.' Richard Crossman, writing in the *New Statesman* on 25 September 1948, declared that within a framework of planning and a considerable measure of state-owned goods and services, 'free enterprise . . . becomes an essential component of Socialism'. *Keeping Left*, issued as a manifesto for the 1950 election with an authorship of twelve MPs, seven of whom had also signed *Keep Left* nearly three years earlier, accepted the near-permanence of the mixed economy, saying: 'We are now less concerned about who owns a factory, and more about who manages it and how, and whether it is working according to socialist plans.'

The indictment of the Labour left in this period must lie, not with any failure to criticise government policy, but with its inability to formulate socialist proposals in such a way as to seize the intellectual initiative within the party. Instead the initiative passed to the right, appearing as 'consolidation' with Herbert Morrison and, a few years later, as 'revision' with Anthony Crosland.[82] Morrison's appeal to the middle class to support Labour was echoed by Crossman in an article in the *New Statesman* on 30 October 1948,[83] declaring that the class war was obsolete and using the phrase 'the useful people', invented and popularised by Morrison as a means of uniting social classes in support of the Labour Party.[84] No policy of appealing specifically to the working class emerged from the Labour left unless one includes occasional colourful and controversial phrases by such Cabinet Ministers as Aneurin

Bevan and Emanuel Shinwell.[85] There was a discernible air of bewilderment and, in some cases, of discouragement. *Tribune* admitted on 31 December 1948 that there was much to be learned about 'the application of Socialist measures' and the means 'to instill the spirit of Socialism', and the *New Statesman* pointed out on 10 December 1949 that, despite the enactment of most of the legislation long planned by the Labour Party leadership, the government had 'lost its impetus'. The structure of British society and industrial relations were virtually unchanged, and 'no great advance has been made towards social equality'. The paper could only advocate 'a sudden jolt of imaginative leadership'.[86]

Seeking an explanation of the many problems facing them, left-wing publicists acknowledged that there was little interest in socialism in the country at large. İn an article in the party journal *Labour Forum* for January-March 1948, Woodrow Wyatt MP, then a member of the Labour left, wrote that relatively few people understood the meaning or implications of socialism. Most of the people who voted Labour, he added, supported the party not for ideological but for 'human, personal reasons . . . Their understanding is confined by the limits of their personal experience.' His politician's view was elaborated in a more philosophical analysis by Harold Laski, given before a Fabian audience in the autumn of 1947. Laski pointed out that most people were

> less interested in doctrine than in the results of doctrine. We shall be judged, not by the greatness of our purpose, but by the efficiency with which we achieve it. Man is a conservative animal, whose ideas are imprisoned within a framework he is not easily persuaded to abandon . . . We are trying to transform a profoundly bourgeois society . . . a society, moreover, in which all the major criteria of social values have been imposed by a long indoctrination for whose aid all the power of church and school, of press and cinema and radio, have been very skilfully mobilised; we have got to transform this bourgeois society into a socialist society with foundations not less secure than those it seeks to renovate. We have, moreover, to accomplish this in a dramatically revolutionary period, in which quite literally millions, afraid of the responsibilities of freedom, yearn to cling to whatever they have, however fragmentary, of a security with which they are familiar.[87]

A few years later Crossman wrote that ingrained tradition had fostered obsession with social status and the preservation of oligarchies, and that these features remained throughout British society, in the educational system, the political parties and the trade unions. The leaders, he wrote, in the labour movement as elsewhere, 'profoundly distrust active democracy'.[88] It should also be borne in mind that while the power and status of the working class rose sharply in the war and post-war years, the period of the Labour Government was closer in time to the mainly docile and quiescent period of pre-war economic slump than to the flowering of support for workers' control, public participation in decision-making and equality of social status which was so marked a feature of the later 1960s and 1970s. It may have been true, as socialists claimed then and later, that had a policy of socialist egalitarianism been tried, the results would have engendered enthusiastic working-class support. But it would have been very difficult in a parliamentary system to have introduced such a policy without prior evidence of mass support of a kind plainly lacking at the time.

A disparate body like the Labour left could produce no agreed policy for the general election of 1950; even *Keeping Left*, the most prominent publication of the left, committed only its authors. But over the years of Labour Government a consensus had emerged which was accepted by much of the left within the party.[89] First came a belief in socialist planning of the economy, a considerable though unspecified portion of which was to remain in private hands. Second, heavier taxation of the wealthy was advocated, by death duties, higher taxes on profits, a capital gains tax or a capital levy. Third came measures to 'socialise' the nationalised industries, by appointing socialists and trade unionists to the boards and introducing a measure of workers' control. With this extension of grass-roots democracy was sometimes coupled various means to strengthen the power of the citizen against the state. Fourth was an attack on educational privilege, which was identified more with making the public schools democratic than with the introduction of comprehensive education. Fifth came measures to protect the consumer from high prices, by maintaining subsidies and a measure of physical controls. Finally came the need for more urgency and drive. The signatories of *Keep Left*, augmented by four more MPs who included James Callaghan and Jennie Lee, declared in a letter in the *Daily Herald* on 8 August 1947: 'The hour calls for audacity and imagination'. In similar vein, Harold Laski wrote in *Forward* on 21 January 1950 that the Labour election manifesto was in need of 'a bit of fire and inspiration, of guts and glory'.

These points indicated, with a marked lack of precision, important areas in which the Labour Government had acted inadequately or not at all. Most of them were measures which would win general socialist support. Yet even had they all been carried out, a socialist society in the sense of a fundamental shift in power relations between social classes would have been brought little closer, at least in the short term. The programme, if so it may be called, of the left was limited partly by its pessimism about the possibilities of socialist advance in the domestic and foreign conditions which prevailed in the later years of the government's term of office. But it was also limited by the fact that the Labour left saw the advance towards socialism largely in terms of particular measures of parliamentary legislation. There was little attempt to dwell on fundamental questions of power and wealth, or to work out a coherent socialist strategy dependent upon mass support outside Parliament.[90] Desirable reforms tended to be seen as ends in themselves. This was probably inevitable given the trend of modern British history and the nature of the Labour Party itself. Parties based more firmly on socialist doctrine than was the Labour left had failed to achieve wide popular support. But if its programme was understandable, its position was none the less unenviable. As the 1950s began the left, which saw itself as the conscience and inspiration of the Labour Party, was uncertain of its aims, confused about methods and weak in numbers.

The tiny majority won by Labour at the election of February 1950 was a blow to party unity, since parliamentary weakness precluded bold new measures of legislation, the most effective means of containing the left. In June the Korean War began, and with it a further intensification of the Cold War. Foreign and defence policy clashed sharply with domestic social commitments. The party leaders, a number of whom had been in office without a break since 1940, were weary and overworked, and the strain inevitably began to tell. Ill health forced the resignation in October of Sir Stafford Cripps, the inflexible but masterful Chancellor of the Exchequer, and Hugh Gaitskell, his successor, was a much less dominant figure. In April 1951 the death of Ernest Bevin removed an immense influence for party stability and unity. A few days later Aneurin Bevan resigned from the Cabinet. With his resignation the Labour Party's era of domestic peace came to an end and the role of the left was suddenly transformed.

Acknowledgement

Warm thanks are acknowledged to Ian Cunnison, Margaret 'Espinasse, Ian Mikardo MP, and Ralph Miliband, who kindly read and commented on drafts of this article; to Carol Johnson CBE, secretary of the Parliamentary Labour Party, 1943-59, for helpful information; to the staff of *Tribune*, especially Richard Clements, the editor, and Douglas Hill, the literary editor, for hospitality, reading accommodation and a preview of *Tribune 40*; and to librarians in Hull and London, particularly Judith Woods, Archivist of the Labour Party library.

Notes

1. Two instances are a speech by Clement Attlee, the Prime Minister, to the Labour Party conference in 1948 (*Labour Party Annual Report*, 1948, p. 161); and Herbert Morrison, *The Peaceful Revolution* (1949), p. vii.

2. So Hugh Dalton heard and told his diary on 28 July 1945 (Dalton diary, vol. 33, British Library of Political and Economic Science, London School of Economics). See also John Wheeler-Bennett, *King George VI* (1958), pp. 649-50, 654.

3. *Keep Left* (1947), pp. 10, 45.

4. Sagittarius [Olga Katzin], *Let Cowards Flinch* (1947), p. 36.

5. R.H.S. Crossman (ed.), *New Fabian Essays* (1952), pp. 5-6.

6. For description and analysis of the 1945-50 government see Ralph Miliband, *Parliamentary Socialism* (1961), ch. 9; David Coates, *The Labour Party and the Struggle for Socialism* (1975), ch. 3; and David Howell, *British Social Democracy* (1976), ch. 5. My debt to all three books is gratefully acknowledged.

7. House of Commons, *Notices of Motions*, 12 October 1945, pp. 375-7; 15 October, p. 394; 16 October, p. 424; 18 October, p. 480; *The Times*, 13, 16, 18, 19 October 1945; Robert Jackson, *Rebels and Whips* (1968), pp. 49-50.

8. *The Times*, 7 November 1945. The defeat was later partly reversed; see 419 HC Deb. 5s., cols. 849-56 (18 February 1946); and Arthur Marwick, *Britain in the Century of Total War* (1968), p. 348.

9. *Labour Party Annual Report*, 1946, p. 191; 424 HC Deb. 5s., cols. 1833-4 (1 July 1946).

10. Maurice Webb at the Labour Party conference, 1949 (*Annual Report*, p. 142); in the House of Commons, 17 December 1948 (459 HC Deb. 5s., cols. 1598-9); in *Tribune*, 10 December 1948 and 3 June 1949; Barbara Castle in *Tribune*, 26 November 1948; at the Labour Party conference, 1949 (pp. 161-2).

11. See, e.g., speeches by Fred Lee and Tom Driberg on 7 August, Ian Mikardo and Richard Crossman on 8 August, Ellis Smith, Ronald Chamberlain and John Parker on 24 October, Michael Foot on 28 October, Donald Bruce and Barbara Castle on 13 November, William Warbey on 25 November.

12. Trade union pressure caused a number of the signatories to withdraw their names. House of Commons, *Notices of Motions*, 12 February 1948, pp. 1726-7; *The Times*, 12 February 1948; Jackson, *Rebels and Whips*, pp. 53-4.

13. *News Chronicle*, 9 and 12 August 1947; *The Times*, 12 August 1947; *Tribune*, 8 August 1947; Hugh Dalton, *High Tide and After* (1962), pp. 252-3; Michael Foot, *Aneurin Bevan*, vol. 2 (1973; paperback ed., 1975), pp. 221-2.

14. Labour Party, General Secretary's correspondence: GS 16/9, 11 April 1949. A letter from Woking alleged that the budget proposals were typical of Cripps's 'lack of appreciation of the feelings and conditions of the common people' (GS 20/1, 27 May 1949).

15. *Agendas for Labour Party Conferences* (Transport House library): 1948, pp. 18-19; 1949, pp. 15-17. A study undertaken for the Acton Society Trust in October 1950 showed that only nine of the forty-seven full-time and seven of the forty-eight part-time members of the twelve boards studied were trade unionists. The British Electricity Authority, four of whose twelve members were Labour supporters, was 'the Board with the biggest left-wing element' (Acton Society Trust, ed. G.R. Taylor, *Men on the Boards,* 1951, pp. 6, 9, 12).

16. Policy and Publicity Committee minutes (NEC minutes, vol. 96), 17 January 1949; NEC minutes, vol. 96, 26 January 1949, memorandum by Morgan Phillips, 'Report on Special Area Group Meetings of MPs' (p. 3).

17. *Railway Review,* 10 December 1948, 4 and 11 February 1949. I am grateful to Laurie Harries of the National Union of Railwaymen for assistance on this point.

18. Margaret Cole (ed.), *Miners and the Board* (1949), pp. 6-7, 12. See also the similar conclusions of F. Zweig, *Men in the Pits* (1948), esp. chs. 31-2; and Acton Society Trust, ed. G.R. Taylor, *The Worker's Point of View* (1952).

19. See articles in *New Statesman,* 13 September 1947; 2 and 23 April, 21 May, 2 July 1949; also Frank Allaun in *Labour's Northern Voice,* October 1947.

20. 'It was a common saying that the Government had less power over Lord Citrine [head of the nationalised electricity undertaking] than over I.C.I.' (Anthony Crosland, *The Future of Socialism* (1956; paperback ed., 1964), pp. 316-17).

21. In the House of Commons, John Parker on 24 October 1947, Donald Bruce on 13 November 1947, James Hudson on 6 May 1948; in the *New Statesman,* 29 December 1945; 9 August, 4 October and 15 November 1947; 26 March, 23 April, 24 September, 15, 22 and 29 October 1949.

22. The first use of this phrase I have found is in an article by F[rank] A[llaun] in *Labour's Northern Voice,* September 1947. It was used in slightly different form in *Keep Left* in May 1947 and in a resolution proposed at the Labour Party conference held in the same month (*Labour Party Annual Report,* 1947, p. 137).

23. *The Second Five Years* (1948), p. 11. Mikardo went on to propose the public ownership of a long list of industries and services.

24. *Forward,* 9, 16, 23, 30 August, 6 September, 1 November 1947.

25. *Labour's Second Term* (1949), pp. 7-8, 13-15.

26. There were four resolutions or amendments of this type in 1947, six in 1948, three in 1949 and thirteen in 1950, apart from many others calling for nationalisation of particular industries and related demands (*Agendas for Labour Party Conferences*). See also Addendum, p. 257.

27. *Socialist Outlook,* July, August 1949, January 1950; *Labour's Northern Voice,* December 1949.

28. *Socialist Outlook,* September, November, 1950; *Labour Party Annual Report,* 1951, pp. 13-14, 85-6. *Socialist Outlook* was in turn proscribed in 1954 and folded the same year.

29. PRO. Cab. 128/9, Cabinet 37 (47), item 8 (17 April 1947); Cab. 128/10, Cabinet 64(47), item 2 (24 July 1947); Cab. 128/10, Cabinet 66(47), item 4 (31 July 1947); Cab. 128/10, Cabinet 70 (47), item 6 (7 August 1947).

30. 423 HC Deb. 5s., col. 368 (22 May 1946); Jackson, *Rebels and Whips,* pp. 52, 59-60; R.T. McKenzie, *British Political Parties* (1955), pp. 447-51; J.M Burns, 'The Parliamentary Labor Party in Great Britain', *American Political Science Review,* vol. 44 (1950), pp. 860, 865; R.K. Alderman, 'Discipline in the Parliamentary Labour Party 1945-51', *Parliamentary Affairs,* vol. 18 (1965), pp. 294, 300.

31. PRO, Cab. 128/1, Cabinet 42(45), item 5 (16 October 1945); Dalton diary, vol. 33, 17 October 1945; *New Statesman,* 27 October 1945. Morrison's biographers see his role as that of a pacifier; Bernard Donoughue and G.W. Jones, *Herbert Morrison* (1973), pp. 370-1. The raising of pensions in October 1946, nearly two years before the National Insurance Act was brought into operation, was claimed as a victory for backbench pressure (J.P.W. Mallalieu MP, *Tribune,* 3 June 1949; Alderman, loc. cit., p. 300).

32. See Dalton diary, vol. 40, 20 April 1951, Foot, *Aneurin Bevan,* p. 328.

33. McKenzie, *British Political Parties,* p. 513.

34. Dalton diary, vol. 35, entry for 24-29 May 1947. Both subjects were discussed at a meeting of the Parliamentary Labour Party on 11 June (see note 43), but no resolutions were passed or decisions taken.

35. Of the numerous analyses of the social composition of the 1945 parliament the most comprehensive are J.F.S. Ross, *Parliamentary Representation* (1943; 2nd ed., 1948), part 4, and idem, *Elections and Electors* (1955), part 6.

36. Jackson, *Rebels and Whips,* pp. 63, 82-3, 192-3.

37. William Muller, *The Kept Men? The First Century of Trade Union Representation in the British House of Commons, 1874-1975* (Hassocks, 1977), pp. 88, 228. See also the speech by Herbert Bullock, the TUC fraternal delegate, at the Labour Party conference in 1950 (*Labour Party Annual Report,* 1950, p. 136).

38. As Sagittarius observed *(Let Cowards Flinch,* p. 35):

> . . . Faced with crisis of the utmost urgency,
> The Government a marble calm maintains;
> With warnings dire of national emergency,
> Attlee the slipped initiative regains —
> A time-worn but invaluable device
> For keeping insurrection on the ice.

39. See Richard Crossman, *New Statesman,* 15 June 1946 and idem, *New Fabian Essays,* p. 5. See also Kingsley Martin's review of Margaret Cole's autobiography *Growing Up Into Revolution* (1949), which concludes: 'She seems not fully aware that her revealing account is really a discussion of how she — and a whole generation of British Socialists with her — have grown, not into, but away from, revolution' (*New Statesman,* 14 January 1950).

40. Or at least a standard bearer, as Ian Mikardo calls Aneurin Bevan (private communication, August 1977).

41. As the *New Statesman* noted on 13 March 1948, economic independence from the United States would have involved sacrifices unexpected by and unacceptable to the British people.

42. Dalton wrote with satisfied malice of Bevin's sweeping conference triumph: 'Crossman was obliterated, humiliated and deeply offended' (diary, vol. 35, 24-29 May 1947). For a comment by Crossman, see *New Statesman,* 7 June 1947. For the anxiety of the Keep Left group not to be confused with fellow travellers, see T.R. Fyvel in *Tribune,* 6 June 1947.

43. PRO, Cab. 128/1, Cabinet 47(45), item 8 (30 October 1945); Cab. 128/9, Cabinet 44(47), item 5 (6 May 1947); Cab. 128/10, Cabinet 83(47), item 2 (30 October 1947); Cab. 128/10, Cabinet 93(47), item 4 (4 December 1947); Donoughue and Jones, *Herbert Morrison,* pp. 368-9; Burns, 'Parliamentary Labour Party', pp. 858-60; Alderman, 'Discipline in the Parliamentary Labour Party', pp. 300-01; McKenzie, *British Political Parties,* pp. 447-8; Harold Laski, *Reflections on the Constitution* (Manchester, 1951), pp. 77-8. For accounts of party meetings see the sources cited in note 13, and the report of Morrison's virtuoso performance after the 1949 budget in *News Chronicle,* 8 April 1949. A microfilm

of the somewhat unrevealing minutes of PLP meetings from 1946 to 1955 is
kept at the British Library of Political and Economic Science.

44. Alderman, 'Discipline in the Parliamentary Labour Party'; Laski, *Reflections*,
pp. 79-81; Jackson, *Rebels and Whips*, pp. 202-14. For division lists giving details
of parliamentary rebellion, see Philip Norton, *Dissension in the House of
Commons 1945-1974* (1975), pp. 1-81. For expressions of opinion as revealed
in 'early day' motions, see Hugh Berrington, *Backbench Opinion in the House
of Commons 1945-1955* (Oxford, 1973).

45. Jenkins's witty and revealing letter is well worth reading. Crossman replied
a week later, saying: 'Divisions, in a Party facing an all-out Conservative
onslaught, should be avoided unless they are absolutely necessary.' He also
claimed (as did Ian Mikardo, *Tribune*, 17 December 1948) that most of *Keep
Left's* domestic proposals had become government policy, a claim which confuses
a few specific measures with the purpose and practice of economic planning as a
whole. See Samuel Beer, *Modern British Politics* (1965), pp. 196-202, and
Jacques Leruez, *Economic Planning & Politics in Britain* (1975), pp. 48-61.

46. I owe this point to Ian Mikardo. See also Addendum, p. 257.

47. Martin Harrison, *Trade Unions and the Labour Party since 1945* (1960),
ch. 5; McKenzie, *British Political Parties*, pp. 501-02.

48. Muller, *The Kept Men?* p. 90; Jackson, *Rebels and Whips*, pp. 57,
82-3, 192-3; Burns, 'Parliamentary Labor Party', pp. 865-6; Ian Aitken, 'The
Structure of the Labour Party', in Gerald Kaufman (ed.), *The Left* (1966), p. 18;
Robert Dowse, 'The Parliamentary Labour Party in Opposition', *Parliamentary
Affairs*, vol. 13 (1960); pp. 522-5. See also the discussions of labourism in
Coates, *The Labour Party*, pp. 136-44, and Tom Forester, *The Labour Party
and the Working Class* (1976), pp. 31-42.

49. Entries for 27 June 1946, 24-29 May 1947, 17-21 May 1948, 3-10 June
1949, vols 34-7. See also Harrison, *Trade Unions*, pp. 223-4, and the Addendum
to this article p. 257.

50. This paragraph is based on study of the minutes of the NEC and its sub-
committees. See also Howell, *British Social Democracy*, ch. 5. Kingsley Martin,
Harold Laski (1953), pp. 189-90, reveals in a poignant passage Laski's doubt
and hesitations and eventual decision to surrender his place on the NEC. Of
Bevan's speech in 1949 even the far-left critic Tom Braddock wrote: 'the high
spot of eloquence, a genius of a man' (*Socialist Outlook*, July 1949).

51. See articles by Barbara Castle, 21 June 1946; Harold Laski, 28 June
1946; leading article, 6 June 1947; Ian Mikardo, 28 May 1948. Laski attempted
to establish a special committee to consider relations between the NEC and the
government when the party was in power, but was defeated by ten votes to
seven (NEC minutes, vol. 93, 24 July 1946).

52. *The Times*, 9, 17 March, 20 April 1948; *Socialist Outlook*, January 1949.

53. *Labour Party Annual Report*, 1947, p. 174; *Tribune*, 31 October 1947,
20 February 1948; *Fabian Quarterly*, Spring 1948; NEC minutes, vol. 95, 25
February 1948. There are also references to the Whine affair in McKenzie, *British
Political Parties*, pp. 513-15 and Howell, *British Social Democracy*, pp. 142, 177
(where the Laski initiative on the NEC is misdated).

54. The flow of legislation continued. According to Herbert Morrison (*The
Peaceful Revolution*, p. 90) over 200 public acts were passed in the first three
years of Labour government. See also Frank Illingworth (ed.), *British Political
Yearbook 1947* [1947], pp. 21-3.

55. Watson's claim was rebutted the next day by Sydney Silverman MP.

56. 'The great redistribution of incomes . . . was a product of the war;
Labour has taken it over and preserved it rather than initiated it' (*The Economist*,
4 February 1950).   •

57. John Saville, 'Labour and Income Redistribution', in Ralph Miliband and

John Saville (eds.), *The Socialist Register 1965* (1965), p. 153. This article provides an excellent antidote to the exaggerated claims of redistribution under Labour.

58. PP 1950: vol. XII, Cmd. 8052, pp. 83, 86; vol. XV, Cmd. 7933, p. 15. Similar figures were published in earlier years.

59. R.H. Tawney, 'British Socialism Today', in Rita Hinden (ed.), *The Radical Tradition* (1964; paperback ed., Harmondsworth, 1966), pp. 179-80 (reprinted from *Socialist Commentary*, June 1952). Tawney went on to advocate that 'the next Labour Government should . . . go all out' on the question of redistribution of property (p. 181).

60. See, e.g., the alarming account of the state of the nation's health and diet given by Edith Summerskill MP, Parliamentary Secretary of the Ministry of Food (*News Chronicle*, 18 October 1945).

61. *Current Affairs*, 6 March 1948. See also Mass-Observation, *Puzzled People* (1947), pp. 148-55.

62. 457 HC Deb. 5s., col. 117 (27 October 1948); Donald MacRae, 'Domestic Record of the Labour Government', *Political Quarterly*, vol. 20 (1949), pp. 1-11.

63. Dalton, *High Tide and After*, p. 347.

64. A Labour Party inquest carried out regionally after local government election reverses in November 1947 showed that an enduring pattern had been established: 'The people generally have become a little weary of austerity' (Wales); 'the housing difficulties, the intensifying of food restrictions' (Yorkshire); Conservative 'propaganda on shortages' (Eastern); 'We failed to get the electorate to realise the real facts of the Economic Crisis' (Northern); 'Active Party workers were obviously oppressed by the economic situation' (South-Western); 'The middle class polled very heavily indeed' (West Midlands), (Labour Party, General Secretary's Correspondence, GS 14/6, November 1947). For the experience and conclusion of one perceptive backbencher who lost her seat in 1950, see Leah Manning, *A Life for Education* (1970), pp. 178, 195.

65. John Gross, 'The Lynskey Tribunal', in Michael Sissons and Philip French (eds.), *Age of Austerity* (1963), pp. 255-75.

66. Beer, *Modern British Politics*, ch. 7; Leruez, *Economic Planning & Politics*, part 1. There is an interesting contemporary discussion of the 'two schools of economic thought . . . battling for the allegiance of the Labour Party' by Harold Lever MP in *Tribune* in December 1949. See also B.C. Roberts, *National Wages Policy in War and Peace* (1958), ch. 4.

67. Quoted in A.A. Rogow, *The Labour Government and British Industry 1945-1951* (Oxford, 1955), p. 41.

68. H.G. Nicholas, *The British General Election of 1950* (1951), pp. 4, 296, 320. An analysis by the British Institute of Public Opinion suggested that 21 per cent of the middle class supported Labour in 1945, but only 16 per cent in 1950 (ibid., p. 296n.). See also John Bonham, *The Middle Class Vote* (1954), pp. 130, 168.

69. 'General Election Campaign Report: Personal Observations by the General Secretary', p. 7; NEC minutes, vol. 99, 22 March 1950.

70. *The Economist*, 21 January 1950. Other articles followed on 28 January and 4 February. For elaboration and qualification of these statistics, see Dudley Seers, 'The Levelling of Incomes', *Bulletin of the Oxford University Institute of Statistics*, vol. 12 (1950), esp. pp. 275, 278, 279, 283, 291, 293.

71. Nicholas, *British General Election 1950*, pp. 219-21, 296-8; Roy Jenkins, *Pursuit of Progress* (1953), pp. 148-9; Herbert and Nancie Matthews, *The Britain We Saw* (1950), pp. 296-7, 302-3; Carl Brand, 'The British General Election of 1950', *South Atlantic Quarterly*, vol. 50 (1951), pp. 485, 497.

72. 'The Recent General Election and the Next', p. 2; NEC minutes, vol. 99, 22 March 1950. See also Donoughue and Jones, *Herbert Morrison*, pp. 455-6.

73. The area group meetings of MPs reported to the party NEC on 26 January 1949 (minutes, vol. 96) 'unanimously agreed that Housing, Food and the cost of living were the topics causing most concern in all parts of the country' (p. 3).

74. *Daily Express*, 10, 11, 13, 14, 17 February 1950; *New Statesman*, 18 February 1950; Nicholas, *British General Election 1950*, pp. 153, 157, 163, 179, 220.

75. Sagittarius, *Let Cowards Flinch*, p. 25.

76. Morgan Thomson in *Forward*, 5 February 1949; F.A. Cobb MP in *Fabian News*, March 1949.

77. Nicholas, *British General Election 1950*, pp. 81, 97, 116, 118, 129, 220, 298-9; D. Daiches Raphael, 'The Issues', in S.B. Chrimes (ed.), *The General Election in Glasgow February, 1950* (Glasgow, 1950), pp. 46, 57-63; Jenkins, *Pursuit of Progress*, pp. 89-97; Dalton, *High Tide and After*, pp. 339-40.

78. *Report of . . . the . . . Trades Union Congress*, 1948, pp. 238, 371-8; ibid., 1949, pp 211-22, 406-8.

79. Leon Epstein, 'Socialism and the British Labor Party', *Political Science Quarterly*, vol. 66 (1951), pp. 556-75; Gerhard Loewenberg, 'The Transformation of British Labour Party Policy since 1945', *Journal of Politics*, vol. 21 (1959), pp. 234-57.

80. Laski in *Forward*, 18 June 1949; Cole in a Fabian tract, *Labour's Second Term* (1949), and in the *New Statesman*, 23 April 1949.

81. 'The Socialisation Programme for Industry', in Donald Munro (ed.), *Socialism: the British Way* (1948), p. 55.

82. In *The Future of Socialism* (1956).

83. Written under the pseudonym 'a Labour MP'. See note 89.

84. Donoughue and Jones, *Herbert Morrison*, p. 441; Morrison, *The Peaceful Revolution*, p. 142.

85. See Bonham, *Middle Class Vote*, pp. 28-9, 34-5, 85, 127; Foot, *Aneurin Bevan*, ch. 6. Dalton saw Attlee shortly after the election of 1950, and told his diary on 27 February of Attlee's reaction to the election result: 'Nye, he thinks, has lost us more votes than any other Minister, by his vermin speech & by his statement, during the election, that the middle classes don't really need domestic servants, they only want to be able to order someone about' (vol. 38).

86. See also Richard Crossman's Fabian lecture, *Socialist Values in a Changing Civilisation* (1951) p. 11.

87. Fabian Society Lectures, *The Road to Recovery* (1948), pp. 49-50; quoted in part in Rogow, *Labour Government*, p. 6.

88. *New Fabian Essays*, pp. 28-9. See also idem, 'The Lessons of 1945', in Perry Anderson and Robin Blackburn (eds.), *Towards Socialism* (1965), p. 156 (reprinted from the *New Statesman*, 19 April 1963).

89. What follows is based in part on six long articles written by Richard Crossman for the *New Statesman* between 23 October and 27 November 1948 under the pseudonym 'a Labour MP' (identified by the *New Statesman*, private communication, 6 July 1977) and on Crossman's confidential 'Memorandum on Problems Facing the Party' dated 27 March 1950 and received by the NEC on 26 April (NEC minutes, vol. 99). No one figure spoke for the whole of the Labour left, but Crossman wrote more about future Labour policy than any other member of the left and, despite his reputation for volatility, was an influential figure. He was a principal author of *Keep Left* and *Keeping Left*, assistant editor of the *New Statesman*, and according to George Orwell, helped to determine the policy of *Tribune (The Collected Essays, Journalism and Letters of George Orwell*, vol. 4 (1968; paperback ed., Harmondsworth, 1970), p. 448).

90. For an extended discussion of this characteristic of the left over a prolonged period see Coates, *The Labour Party*, ch. 7. See also Tom Nairn's stimulating essay, 'The Nature of the Labour Party', in Anderson and Blackburn (eds.), *Towards Socialism*, pp. 159-217.

Addendum

Jonathan Wood's interesting M.A. thesis, 'The Labour Left in the Constituency Labour Parties 1945-51', University of Warwick, 1977, did not become available until April 1978, after the completion of this article. The study was based on analysis of resolutions on the agenda of the Labour Party annual conferences during the period. Wood identified as left-wing the eighty-eight constituency parties which submitted two or more left-wing resolutions or amendments on either domestic or foreign issues, nine of which restricted their concern to foreign affairs alone. Most of the resolutions were not fundamentally critical of the course of government policy and only two condemned domestic policy as a whole, particularly the espousal of the mixed economy. The membership of the left-wing parties rose between 1945 and 1950 from 6 to over 11 per cent of individual Labour Party membership. The social composition of the relevant constituencies for which census information is available (though not necessarily of their Labour Parties) was more middle class than the national average, and a high proportion were Opposition-held or marginal Labour seats. About half of the Labour-held left-wing constituencies had MPs who supported the left on at least some important issues (ch. 3, passim).

12 THE PRINCIPAL WRITINGS OF JOHN SAVILLE

Joyce M. Bellamy

The following bibliography includes all published historical works known to the compiler, main political works, review articles and long book reviews. Short book reviews and some ephemeral political writings have been omitted.

I. Editorial Works

1. *Democracy and the Labour Movement: Essays in Honour of Dona Torr*, Lawrence and Wishart (1954), 275 pp.
2. (with E.P. Thompson), *The Reasoner: a Journal of Discussion*, nos 1 − [3] (July-November 1956).
3. (with E.P. Thompson), *The New Reasoner: a Quarterly Journal of Socialist Humanism*, nos 1-10 (1957-9).
4. (with Asa Briggs), *Essays in Labour History*, vol. 1, Macmillan (1960), 363 pp.; vol. 2, Macmillan (1971), 360 pp.; vol. 3, Croom Helm (1977), 292 pp.
5. (with R. Miliband), *Socialist Register*, Merlin Press, 1964 annually to date.
6. *Studies in the British Economy, 1870-1914: special number of Yorkshire Bulletin of Economic and Social Research*, vol. 17 (1965), 112 pp.
7. Occasional Papers in Economic and Social History, University of Hull, nos 1-8 (1969-75).
8. (with J.M. Bellamy), *Dictionary of Labour Biography*, Macmillan, vol. 1 (1972), 388 pp.; vol. 2 (1974), 454 pp.; vol. 3 (1976), 236 pp.; vol. 4 (1977), 236 pp.

II. Books, Pamphlets, Essays and Miscellaneous

9. (with R.W. Gray), *A Preliminary Survey of Productivity in House Construction 1924-1937*, Ministry of Works Technical Notes and Papers, Economic Series no. 3 (1947) [mimeograph], 10 pp.
10. 'The Measurement of Real Cost in the London Building Industry, 1923-1939', *Yorkshire Bulletin of Economic and Social Research*, vol. 1 (1949), pp. 67-80.
11. 'A Note on the Present Position of Working Class History', ibid., vol. 4 (1952), pp. 125-32.
12. *Ernest Jones: Chartist. Selections from the Writings and Speeches*

of Ernest Jones with Introduction and Notes, Lawrence and Wishart (1952), 284 pp.

13. 'The Christian Socialists of 1848', in *Democracy and the Labour Movement: Essays in Honour of Dona Torr* (1954), pp. 135-59.

14. 'A Comment on Professor Rostow's *British Economy of the 19th Century'*, *Past and Present*, no. 6 (1954), pp. 66-84.

15. 'Henry Fielding (1707-1754)', *Labour Monthly*, vol. 36 (1954), pp. 516-19.

16. 'Friedrich Engels et le Chartisme', *La Nouvelle Critique*, no. 72 (February 1956), pp. 73-90.

17. 'Czartyzm u voku rewolocki, 1848', *Zagadrienia Nenki Historyeznej*, vol. 2 (1956), pp. 42-53.

18. 'Sleeping Partnership and Limited Liability 1850-1856', *Economic History Review*, 2nd ser., vol. 8 (1956), pp. 418-33.

19. *Rural Depopulation in England and Wales 1851-1951*, Routledge and Kegan Paul (1957), 253 pp.

20. 'The Welfare State: an Historical Approach', *New Reasoner*, vol. 3 (winter 1957-8), pp. 5-25.

21. (with E.P Thompson), 'John Stuart Mill and EOKA', ibid., vol. 7 (winter 1958-9), pp. 1-11.

22. 'Rural Migration in England and Wales', in *Rural Migration: Papers and Discussion*, First Congress of the European Society for Rural Sociology, 22-28 September 1958, published by the Society (Bonn, 1959), pp. 58-63.

23. 'Apathy into Politics', *New Left Review*, no. 4 (1960), pp. 8-9.

24. 'Henry George and the British Labor Movement', *Science and Society*, vol. 24 (1960), pp. 321-33.

25. Review article of E.H. Phelps Brown, *The Growth of British Industrial Relations*, ibid. (1960), pp. 256-64.

26. 'Trade Unions and Free Labour: the Background to the Taff Vale Decision', in *Essays in Labour History*, ed. with A. Briggs (1960), pp. 317-50; reprinted in M.W. Flinn and T.C. Smout (eds.), *Essays in Social History*, Oxford University Press (1974), pp. 251-76.

27. 'Some Retarding Factors in the British Economy before 1914', *Yorkshire Bulletin of Economic and Social Research*, vol. 13 (1961), pp. 51-60.

28. 'The Authorship of *The Bitter Cry of Outcast London'*, *Bulletin of the Society for the Study of Labour History*, no. 2 (1961), p. 15.

29. 'Dictionary of Labour Movement Biography', ibid., pp. 15-17.

30. 'The Chartist Land Plan', ibid., no. 3 (1961), pp. 10-12.

31. 'Henry George and the British Labour Movement: a Select Bibliography with Commentary', ibid., no. 5 (1962), pp. 18-26.
32. 'Mr. Coppock on the Great Depression: a Critical Note', *Manchester School*, vol. 31 (1963), pp. 47-71.
33. 'Internal Migration in England and Wales during the Past Hundred Years', in *Les Déplacements Humains: aspects méthodologiques de leur mesure*, ed. J. Sutter (Paris, 1963), pp. 1-21.
34. 'Research Facilities and the Social Historian', *Library Association Record*, vol. 65 (1963), pp. 319-23.
35. (with R. Miliband), 'Labour Policy and the Labour Left', *Socialist Register* (1964), pp. 149-56.
36. 'The Politics of *Encounter*', ibid., pp. 192-207.
37. 'Le radici storiche del riformismo laburista in Inghilterra', *Rivista Storica del Socialismo*, no. 23 (1964), pp. 571-91.
38. 'Henry Noel Brailsford', *Tribune*, vol. 28 (24 July 1964), p. 10.
39. 'Labour on the Move', *Times Literary Supplement*, 13 May 1965, pp. 361-2.
40. 'Labour and Income Redistribution', *Socialist Register* (1965), pp. 147-62.
41. 'The Background to the Revival of Socialism in England', *Bulletin of the Society for the Study of Labour History*, no. 11 (1965), pp. 13-19.
42. (with J.W.Y. Higgs and G.A. Marshall), *Report of a United Nations European Study Group on Rural Social Development in Southern Italy* (Rome, 1965), pp. 1-23.
43. 'Urbanisation and the Countryside' and 'Development Problems in Rural Areas', in *People in the Countryside: Studies in Rural Social Development*, United Nations Study Group, ed. J. Higgs (1966), pp. 13-34 and 35-51.
44. Review article of A.J.P. Taylor, *English History 1914-1945*, in *Bulletin of the Society for the Study of Labour History*, no. 12 (1966), pp. 49-58.
45. *Pitt Jr.*, Traduzione di Franco Occhetto [published with *Alessandro I* di Giuseppe Berti], Compagnia Edizioni Internazionali (Rome/Milan, 1966), 78 pp. and reprinted in *I Protagonisti della Storia Universale*, 21 February 1967, pp. 309-36.
46. 'The Present Position and Prospects of Labour History', *North East Group for the Study of Labour History, Bulletin*, no. 1 (1967), pp. 4-6.
47. 'Trades Councils and the Labour Movement to 1900', *Bulletin of the Society for the Study of Labour History*, no. 14 (1967),

pp. 29-35.
48. 'Labourism and the Labour Government', *Socialist Register* (1967), pp. 43-71.
49. 'How can the British Working Class Regain its Voice and Power?', *Tribune*, vol. 33 (7 February 1969), p. 5.
50. 'Primitive Accumulation and Early Industrialization in Britain', *Socialist Register* (1969), pp. 247-71.
51. (with K. Coates, N. Harris and M. Johnstone), 'Britain: Prospects for the Seventies', ibid. (1970), pp. 203-15.
52. 'Some Aspects of Chartism in Decline', *Bulletin of the Society for the Study of Labour History*, no. 20 (1970), pp. 16-18.
53. Review article of D.H. Aldcroft (ed.), *The Development of British Industry and Foreign Competition 1875-1914*, in *Business History*, vol. 12 (1970), pp. 59-65.
54. (with J. Griffith and T. Smythe), *The Arblaster Case: the Findings of a Commission of Inquiry Established by the Council for Academic Freedom and Democracy in October 1970* (CAFD, [1970]), 16 pp.
55. (with P. Higgs), *Craigie College of Education: the Findings of a Commission of Inquiry Established by the Council for Academic Freedom and Democracy in February 1971* (CAFD, [1971]), 24 pp.
56. 'Notes on Ideology and the Miners before World War I', *Bulletin of the Society for the Study of Labour History*, no. 23 (1971), pp. 25-7.
57. 'Oral History and the Labour Historians', *Oral History: an Occasional Newsheet*, no. 3 (1972), pp. 60-2.
58. 'Interviews in Labour History', ibid., no. 4 [1972], pp. 93-106.
59. *The Wakstein Case* (CAFD, 1973), 12 pp.
60. 'The Wakstein Case', *Times Higher Education Supplement*, 30 November 1973, p. 14.
61. 'The Ideology of Labourism', in R. Benewick, R.N. Berki and B. Parekh (eds.), *Knowledge and Belief in Politics: the Problem of Ideology*, Allen and Unwin (1973), pp. 213-26.
62. 'Labour Prosopography', *Social Science Research Council Newsletter*, no. 20 (1973), pp. 5-7.
63. Review article of J.D. Foster, *Class Struggle and the Industrial Revolution*, *Socialist Register* (1974), pp. 226-40.
64. *Marxism and History: an Inaugural Lecture*, University of Hull (1974), 19 pp.
65. 'The Dictionary of Labour Biography' [letter], *Bulletin of the*

Society for the Study of Labour History, no. 30 (1975), pp. 14-17.

66. 'The Twentieth Congress and the British Communist Party', *Socialist Register* (1976), pp. 1-23.

67. 'May Day 1937', in *Essays in Labour History*, ed. with A. Briggs (1977), pp. 232-84.

68. 'The Radical Left expects the Past to do its Duty', *Times Higher Educational Supplement*, 13 February 1976, p. 15; reprinted in *Labor History*, vol. 18 (1977), pp. 267-74.

69. 'Il socialismo e il moviemento operaio britannico' in *Reforme e Rivoluzione nella Storia Contemporanea*, Piccola Biblioteca Einaudi, Turin (1977), pp. 255-90.

III. Introductions and Prefaces

70. Introduction to 'Joseph Redman' [*pseud.* Brian Pearce], *The Communist Party and the Labour Left 1925-1929*, Reasoner Pamphlets no. 1, Hull [1957], pp. 2-7.

71. Introduction to a facsimile reprint of the original edition of *The Red Republican* and *The Friend of the People 1850-51*, ed. G.J. Harney, Merlin Press (1966), pp. i-xv.

72. Introduction to reprint of W.E. Adams, *Memoirs of a Social Atom*, Kelley, New York (1968), pp. 5-24.

73. Introduction to reprint of *Industrial Remuneration Conference [1885]: the Report of Proceedings and Papers*, Kelley, New York (1968), pp. 5-44.

74. 'R.G. Gammage and the Chartist Movement', Introduction to reprint of R.G. Gammage, *History of the Chartist Movement 1837-1854*, 2nd ed. 1894, including Gammage's pamphlet *The Social Oppression of the Working Classes: Its Causes and Cure* [1852?], Cass (1969), pp. 5-66.

75. Preface and bibliographical notes to *A Selection of the Political Pamphlets of Charles Bradlaugh*, Kelley, New York (1970), pp. 5-11.

76. Preface and bibliographical notes to *A Selection of the Social and Political Pamphlets of Annie Besant*, Kelley, New York (1970), pp. v-xiii.

77. Introduction to reprint of R. Owen, *A New View of Society* [1816], Kelley, New York (1972), pp. 1-12 and Macmillan (1972), pp. iii-xvii.

78. Introduction to reprint of *The Life of Thomas Cooper Written by Himself* (1872), Leicester University Press (1971), pp. 7-33.

79. Introduction to *Working Conditions in the Victorian Age: Debates*

on the Issue from 19th Century Critical Journals, Gregg (1973), pp. [1-19] .

NOTES ON CONTRIBUTORS

Joyce M. Bellamy is senior research officer in the Department of Economic and Social History at the University of Hull. She is co-editor with John Saville of the *Dictionary of Labour Biography* and has edited *Yorkshire Business Histories: A Bibliography*.

Asa Briggs is Provost of Worcester College, Oxford. His many books include *Victorian Cities, Victorian People*, the official history of the BBC and *Essays in Labour History* (3 vols. ed. with John Saville).

Margaret Cole, author, biographer and journalist, is president of the Fabian Society and its historian. Until recently she was a member of the Inner London Education Authority and, before that, of the London County Council. She is the author of many books on social history and social problems, some in collaboration with her late husband G.D.H. Cole.

Victor Kiernan, who retired from a personal chair of modern history at Edinburgh University in 1977, has published essays in *The Socialist Register* and several books including *The Lords of Human Kind* and *Marxism and Imperialism.*

Alan J. Lee is a lecturer in history at the University of Hull. He is the author of several essays and contributions to the *Dictionary of Labour Biography* and a study of *The Origins of the Popular Press 1855-1914.*

David E. Martin, a graduate of Hull University, is a lecturer in economic and social history at the University of Sheffield and a contributor to the *Dictionary of Labour Biography*.

Frank Matthews is a graduate of Hull University and a lecturer in the Department of History at the University of Stirling. His study of the Building Guilds appeared in *Essays in Labour History*, vol. 2.

Ralph Miliband taught at the LSE for many years and was Professor of Politics at Leeds from 1972 until 1978. He is currently Visiting Professor of Sociology at Brandeis University, Massachusetts. He is co-editor with John Saville of *The Socialist Register* and is the author of *Parliamentary Socialism, The State in Capitalist Society* and *Marxism and Politics.*

Iris Minor is a graduate of Hull University and was a lecturer in the Department of Economic and Social History in the University of Bristol until 1978. She is at present an associate researcher in the Centre of Asian Studies, University of Hong Kong.

Sidney Pollard is professor of economic and social history at the University of Sheffield. His many books and articles include *The Genesis of Modern Management, The Development of the British Economy 1914-1967* and studies of the co-operative movement in volumes one and two of *Essays in Labour History.*

David Rubinstein is senior lecturer in social history at the University of Hull. He has written *School Attendance in London 1870-1904: A Social History* and *The Evolution of the Comprehensive School* (co-author) and compiled *Victorian Homes.*

INDEX